The Arabic Prose Poem

Edinburgh Studies in Modern Arabic Literature
Series Editor: Rasheed El-Enany

Writing Beirut: Mappings of the City in the Modern Arabic Novel
Samira Aghacy

Women, Writing and the Iraqi Ba'thist State: Contending Discourses of Resistance and Collaboration, 1968–2003
Hawraa Al-Hassan

Autobiographical Identities in Contemporary Arab Literature
Valerie Anishchenkova

The Iraqi Novel: Key Writers, Key Texts
Fabio Caiani and Catherine Cobham

Sufism in the Contemporary Arabic Novel
Ziad Elmarsafy

Gender, Nation, and the Arabic Novel: Egypt 1892–2008
Hoda Elsadda

The Arabic Prose Poem: Poetic Theory and Practice
Huda J. Fakhreddine

The Unmaking of the Arab Intellectual: Prophecy, Exile and the Nation
Zeina G. Halabi

Egypt 1919: The Revolution in Literature and Film
Dina Heshmat

Post-War Anglophone Lebanese Fiction: Home Matters in the Diaspora
Syrine Hout

Prophetic Translation: The Making of Modern Egyptian Literature
Maya I. Kesrouany

Nasser in the Egyptian Imaginary
Omar Khalifah

Conspiracy in Modern Egyptian Literature
Benjamin Koerber

War and Occupation in Iraqi Fiction
Ikram Masmoudi

Literary Autobiography and Arab National Struggles
Tahia Abdel Nasser

The Libyan Novel: Humans, Animals and the Poetics of Vulnerability
Charis Olszok

The Arab Nahḍah*: The Making of the Intellectual and Humanist Movement*
Abdulrazzak Patel

Blogging from Egypt: Digital Literature, 2005–2016
Teresa Pepe

Religion in the Egyptian Novel
Christina Phillips

Space in Modern Egyptian Fiction
Yasmine Ramadan

Occidentalism: Literary Representations of the Maghrebi Experience of the East–West Encounter
Zahia Smail Salhi

Sonallah Ibrahim: Rebel with a Pen
Paul Starkey

Minorities in the Contemporary Egyptian Novel
Mary Youssef

edinburghuniversitypress.com/series/smal

The Arabic Prose Poem

Poetic Theory and Practice

Huda J. Fakhreddine

EDINBURGH
University Press

Edinburgh University Press is one of the leading university presses in the UK. We publish academic books and journals in our selected subject areas across the humanities and social sciences, combining cutting-edge scholarship with high editorial and production values to produce academic works of lasting importance. For more information visit our website: edinburghuniversitypress.com

Edinburgh University Press Ltd
The Tun – Holyrood Road
12 (2f) Jackson's Entry
Edinburgh EH8 8PJ

First published in hardback by Edinburgh University Press 2021

Typeset in 11/15 Times New Roman

A CIP record for this book is available from the British Library

ISBN 978 1 4744 7496 2 (hardback)
ISBN 978 1 4744 7497 9 (paperback)
ISBN 978 1 4744 7498 6 (webready PDF)
ISBN 978 1 4744 7499 3 (epub)

Contents

Series Editor's Foreword vi
Note on Transliteration and Translation ix
Acknowledgements x

Introduction: The Arabic Poem that Jumped the Fence 1
1 Precursors, Terms and Manifestos between Theory and Practice 13
2 The Prose Poem and the Arabic Tradition 34
3 Adonis: Writing Where the World Begins and Begins Again 68
4 Muhammad al-Maghut and Poetic Detachment 107
5 Mahmoud Darwish as Middleman 138
6 Salim Barakat: Poetry as Linguistic Conquest 171
7 Wadiʿ Saʿadeh and the Third Generation of Prose Poets 206
Afterword 254

Bibliography 258
Index 269

Series Editor's Foreword

Edinburgh Studies in Modern Arabic Literature is a unique series that aims to fill a glaring gap in scholarship in the field of modern Arabic literature. Its dedication to Arabic literature in the modern period (that is, from the nineteenth century onwards) is what makes it unique among series undertaken by academic publishers in the English-speaking world. Individual books on modern Arabic literature in general or aspects of it have been and continue to be published sporadically. Series on Islamic studies and Arab/ Islamic thought and civilisation are not in short supply either in the academic world, but these are far removed from the study of Arabic literature qua literature, that is, imaginative, creative literature as we understand the term when, for instance, we speak of English literature or French literature. Even series labelled 'Arabic/Middle Eastern Literature' make no period distinction, extending their purview from the sixth century to the present, and often including non-Arabic literatures of the region. This series aims to redress the situation by focusing on the Arabic literature and criticism of today, stretching its interest to the earliest beginnings of Arab modernity in the nineteenth century.

The need for such a dedicated series, and generally for the redoubling of scholarly endeavour in researching and introducing modern Arabic literature to the Western reader, has never been stronger. Among activities and events heightening public, let alone academic, interest in all things Arab, and not least Arabic literature, are the significant growth in the last decades of the translation of contemporary Arab authors from all genres, especially fiction, into English; the higher profile of Arabic literature internationally since the award of the Nobel Prize in Literature to Naguib Mahfouz in 1988; the growing number of Arab authors living in the Western diaspora and writing both in English and Arabic; the adoption of such authors and others by mainstream, high-circulation publishers, as opposed to the academic publishers of the past; and the establishment of prestigious prizes, such as the International Prize for Arabic Fiction, popularly referred to in the Arab world as the Arabic Booker, run by the Man Booker Foundation, which brings huge publicity to the shortlist and winner every year, as well as translation contracts into English and other languages. It is therefore part of the ambition of this series that it will increasingly address a wider reading public beyond its natural territory of students and researchers in Arabic and world literature. Nor indeed is the academic readership of the series expected to be confined to specialists in literature in the light of the growing trend for interdisciplinarity, which increasingly sees scholars crossing field boundaries in their research tools and coming up with findings that equally cross discipline borders in their appeal.

The Edinburgh Studies in Modern Arabic Literature Series has so far published twenty-one monographs, while many more are under contract or in production. This plethora of monographs, has dealt with a myriad of writers, themes, periods and genres of which not one is concerned with Arabic poetry, the oldest literary genre in the language dating back some fifteen centuries, and until not long ago considered the most important of them all. The fact of the matter is that the popularity of poetry in Arabic (and perhaps not just in Arabic) has been in recession since the latter decades of the twentieth century, systematically losing ground in intellectual and social influence as well as readership and critical interest to the unrelenting advance of the novel. Scholarship, that of this series not excluded, has followed the trend and focused critical endeavor where the greatest bulk, quality and range of literary output is, which is perhaps as things should be. But it is also as things should be when scholarship breaks away from the crowd and follows a little-trodden path to look at a forgotten figure, period, genre or sub-genre. And that is exactly why the current volume will be particularly welcome on the lists of this series. It will be the first volume dedicated to the study of poetry, and not just that but specifically a sub-genre of poetry, the prose poem, which has received the least attention within earlier existing studies of modern Arabic poetry. Not only does the volume in hand revive scholarly interest in the study of poetry generally but it is devoted in particular to a sub-genre that the critical establishment has traditionally viewed as subversive and barely meritorious of recognition as poetry or serious critical attention. Both the early and later exponents of the genre are studied with ample illustrations from their verse, e.g. Unsi al-Hajj, Adonis, Muhammad al-Maghut, Mahmoud Darwish, Salim Barakat and Wadiʿ Saʿadeh, while examined too are European connections and the place of these poetic voices in the context of the Arabic poetic tradition.

Professor Rasheed El-Enany,
Series Editor,
Emeritus Professor of Modern Arabic Literature,
University of Exeter

Note on Transliteration and Translation

In transliterating Arabic terms, I have followed the guidelines of the Chicago Manual of Style and the International Journal of Middle Eastern Studies (IJMES). For author names in Arabic, I provided the transliteration on first mention of the name and used the commonly used English spelling, without transliteration, thereafter.

All the translations are mine unless otherwise noted.

Acknowledgements

The erratic flock of birds, flying toward form or out of it, captures the tension and dilemma of the prose poem. I thank the artist Hussein Madi for the permission to use his work on the cover.

I am grateful to many friends and scholars for their feedback, advice and support. I thank Suzanne Stetkevych and Jaroslav Stetkevych for their generous reading of these chapters and their inspiring dedication to Arabic poetry, now and always. I am lucky to have Roger Allen as a mentor and friend. His feedback on the proposal, drafts and translations was invaluable. I am indebted to Shawkat Toorawa and Tarek El-Ariss for their encouragement and support of the project in its early phases. My gratitude to scholar and friends Wen-chin Ouyang, Sayed Elsisi, Clarissa Burt, Ammiel Alcalay, Rebecca Johnson and Robyn Creswell for providing enriching comments and recommendations.

My special thanks to Mahmoud Hosny for his help in accessing difficult to locate material, and his conversations and companionship in poetry during the writing of this book.

I am grateful for Al Filreis's friendship and encouragement. I thank him, Jessica Lowenthal and Kenna O'Rourke for inviting me to write a commentary series for *Jacket 2*. 'Arabic Modernism's Other Tradition' allowed me a creative space to think through some of the issues related to this project and to expand beyond it. I thank them for allowing me to think about this project with an audience of poetry at large.

I thank the Wolf Humanities Forum at the University of Pennsylvania for offering me a fellowship and the convivial atmosphere in which I worked on early drafts of some of the chapters here. I am indebted to all the fellows in the 'Afterlives' seminar 2017–18, the forum director Jim English and the topic director Emily Wilson for their inspiring work and their dedicated engagement with mine.

I am lucky to have had the support and funding of Penn Global and the Global Engagement Fund (GEF) at the University of Pennsylvania for my project 'The Edge of Poetry: The Prose Poem in Arabic, An Interdisciplinary Collaborative Project'. This allowed me to do much of the groundwork and translations for this project. Funding from Penn Global made possible the collaboration with Al-Bustan Seeds of Culture on the multi-disciplinary project '(Dis)Placed: Expressions of Identity in Transition'. My continuous gratitude goes to Al-Bustan and its founder and executive director Hazami Sayed for her partnership, support, and the many opportunities of cultural exchange she makes happen.

My deepest gratitude to the series editor Prof. Rasheed El-Enany for his support of this project and his valuable feedback, especially on the translations of poems. Working with the editorial team at EUP was a pleasure. I thank them all for their professionalism and care in making this book.

Without the support of my partners in poetry Samaa and Ahmad Almallah, nothing comes to light. My work here and elsewhere is inspired by Ahmad's poetry and his thinking about poems. To him and to Samaa, on her journey toward Arabic, I dedicate this book.

Introduction
The Arabic Poem that Jumped the Fence

Because skill at playing the game is no longer enough now; the question that keeps coming up is: can this game be played at all now and what is the right game to play? (Wittgenstein)

The game of poetry is transgressive by nature. Poetry has little patience for rules and prescriptions. It is a game in which guidelines and limits are merely challenges that beg to be overcome in some fruitful, unexpected way. If meter and rhyme are the most easily recognisable skills, they are surely never enough. The great masters of the Arabic *qaṣīda* are the poets who contended with meter and rhyme and not the ones who merely abided by them. And every committed reader of Arabic poetry knows that the time for a new set of challenges was bound to come, no matter how scandalous and unsettling that prospect was.

In 1960, the Syrian Lebanese poet Adonis (Adūnīs, penname for ʿAlī Aḥmad Saʿīd, b. 1930) published his prose poem manifesto, and the Lebanese poet Unsi al-Hajj (Unsī al-Ḥājj, 1937–2014) published his collection *Lan* (*Won't*) with its seminal introduction theorising the possibilities of poetry in prose. These are the two theoretical cornerstones that launched the prose poem in Arabic. They are the first instances of using the Arabic term *qaṣīdat al-nathr* (prose poem) and thereby announcing the entrance of the phrase into Arabic as a 'simple abstraction'.[1] As such, Adonis and al-Hajj proclaimed the conceptualisation of a category, even if the practice of blurring verse and prose had existed in Arabic literature for centuries before that. Thus, the Arabic prose poem was not invented in 1960 but rather became a thing with a name; it was pointed out as a problem or a cause. Writings that could be described as poetry in prose or prose with poetic qualities go back as far as pre-Islamic prose, the Qurʾān and *Ṣūfī* writings. However, once the phrase *qaṣīdat al-nathr* as a simple abstraction was introduced, this rich pre-history was called into being as a history, and the prose poem became a critical lens or an enclosed class of poetic product. Its major claim was that it was poetry, and that its units were poems entirely freed from the restrains of meter and preconceived form.

But poetry cannot be freed up. It is nothing at all if not tension or orchestrating tension that does not tolerate hanging loosely. Once the Arabic prose poem jumped the fence of meter, it exposed itself to pressing and fundamental questions about the very game of poetry, its possibilities and the new parameters of the playing field. Despite its claims of freedom, individuality, subversive-ness and democracy, the motor force of the Arabic prose poem has thus far been its quest for that organising tension that makes the poem; that deliberateness that guides the wandering and the going astray; that design that sharpens the edges of sentences into music and sculpts nothingness into a clearing.

'One function of the poet at any time is to discover by his own thought and feeling what seems to him to be poetry at that time', Wallace Stevens writes in his *The Necessary Angel*.[2] Poets do not define poetry as much as discover it over and over. Poems are not definitions of poetry as much as they are disclosures of poetry, unveilings of its perpetually hidden and elusive faces. And, the prose poem is the most recent disclosure of Arabic poetry. Although it has now existed in Arabic as a term and a distinct poetic 'genre' since the early 1960s, it remains a novelty that is somewhat out of place. The distance between the Arabic prose poem and the Arabic poetic tradition is to a large extent what has kept it alive and controversial, and what has bestowed upon it a profound critical power by which it has placed every other established Arabic poetic form in question. Even in their attempts at forging a link between their project and the Arabic literary tradition, Arab prose poets have continually insisted on the new-ness of *qaṣīdat al-nathr* and its disruptive agenda.

The term 'free verse' (*al-shiʿr al-ḥurr*) in Arabic in its general reference is often used as a synonym for the Arabic modernist movement of the twentieth century, referring to a project that was launched in the late 1940s and is still on-going today. However, the poets and poems included under this heading do not constitute a homogenous group. Aside from the grand gesture of breaking away from the classical ode, the *qaṣīda* (the metrical and mono-rhyme master-Arabic poetic structure which dominated Arabic poetry from pre-Islamic times until the first half of the twentieth century), the proliferations of the Arabic modernist movement were primarily motivated by distinguishing themselves from each other. Hence, it might be more accurate to study the various disclosures of modern Arabic poetry as responding to each other and growing out of each other, than it is merely to view them in contrast with classical Arabic *qaṣīda* or measure them against outside influences.

A distinct notion of the 'modern' Arabic poem begins to emerge when one considers the variances and inter-connections between the modernist trends and movements of the twentieth century.[3] This approach serves to upset the illusion of a monolithic 'Arabic modernism' by breaking it down into modernist positions with multiple visions and proposals for what the modern Arabic poem can be. This approach also puts in perspective the two often exaggerated stimuli of this experiment: the Arabic literary tradition and the western poetic influence.

There is no doubt that the Arabic *qaṣīda* remains present in the background as a point of reference for much of the innovations of the modernist project, especially on a formal and structural level. Nevertheless, as the modernist experimentations developed and moved beyond the early 'pioneer' years of the late 1940 and early 1950s, the poets and theorisers were more concerned with commenting on and responding to each other's work. The same applies to the role of western poetic influences. I would go so far as to say that, beyond the early phases, western models introduced through the translation of poetry and theory into Arabic were relatively marginal participants in developing the poetics of the modern Arabic poem. The main agent in the elucidation of a new poetics was the on-going and self-absorbed revisions, refinements and modifications of the modern poem, in which the various trends and movements were engaged. And, although one can point within this large experiment to several positions and directions, each presenting an agenda and imagined trajectory for modern poetry, the two most visible manifestations of the modern poem in Arabic are the free verse poem (*qaṣīdat al-taf'īla*), which remains within the parameters of meter even if expanded and loosened, and the prose poem (*qaṣīdat al-nathr)*, the rogue form which defies all pre-existing prescriptions.[4] Many qualities of each are elucidated by the on-going dialogue between the two forms.

The Arabic free verse poem, *qaṣīdat al-taf'īla*, is the antecedent of the two. It dates back to 1949 with the publication of two poems by Nazik al-Mala'ika (Nāzik al-Malā'ika, 1923–2007) and Badr Shakir al-Sayyab (Badr Shākir al-Sayyāb, 1926–64).[5] The poet-critics of the movement, primarily al-Mala'ika, theorised this poem and delineated its parameters to the minutest of details. *Qaṣīdat al-taf'īla* is a variation on the classical meters of Arabic poetry, not an abandoning of them. In fact, al-Mala'ika insisted that the term *al-shi'r al-ḥurr* (free verse) should only be used to refer to this form which employs the rhymes and meters of classical poetry in a 'relatively' free manner but still has clear parameters distinguishing it from prose.[6]

The Arabic prose poem, *qaṣīdat al-nathr,* which later became the rallying point for the *Shi'r* group and their journal founded in 1957, is primarily a response to *qaṣīdat al-taf'īla* and the relatively fixed definition of poetry endorsed by the 1949 modernist pioneers (especially the Iraqi poet Nazik al-Mala'ika).[7] The Arabic prose poem made its biggest statement by claiming to be poetry without any metrical consideration whatsoever. It is more comparable to the French and English free verse than it is to the prose poem in these languages. Prose poets in Arabic often write lineated, lyrical, short or long pieces which are similar in mood, tone and themes to what was written under the aegis of *qaṣīdat al-taf'īla*. It is the absence of meter coupled with the claim of being poetry that made these writings scandalous. It is, thus, necessary to study the Arabic prose poem in its conversation with *qaṣīdat al-taf'īla.*

The English terms 'verse', 'prose' and 'poetry' vary, in their history and associations, from the Arabic term '*naẓm*', '*nathr*' and '*shi'r*'. The free verse poem, in its narrow reference to the verse-poem (*qaṣīdat al-taf'īla*) launched in the early 1950s, is a point of crisis, both in a positive and a negative sense. It represents the limits of loosening Arabic prosody without abandoning it altogether. Of course, this loosening is not the work of the twentieth-century Arabic modernists alone. It is the product of a long conversation with al-Khalil's (al-Khalīl b. Aḥmad al-Farāhīdī, d. 791) formulation beginning with the emergence of the *qaṣīda*'s satellite compositions (the *qiṭaʿ / maqṭūʿāt*) such as the ghazal, the *ṭarḍiyya* and the *khamriyya* to the prosodic re-arrangement of the *muwashshaḥ* and then the daring experimentation of the early twentieth century spearheaded by Lewis ʿAwad (Lūwīs ʿAwaḍ, 1915–90) and his seminal yet often overlooked avant-garde project in *Plutoland and Other Poems for the Elite*.[8] *Qaṣīdat al-tafʿīla* garnered its driving force from all of these previous dances with Arabic prosody and presented itself in the late 1940s as a reconciliation with, a resolution of and freeing up of Arabic poetry, all within the limit of poetry as necessarily, even if not fundamentally, in meter.

However, as long as the verse-poem set limits for itself (and its limits and boundaries are delineated in the works of Nazik al-Malaʾika), there was still room for transgression. In fact, it set the stage for a more radical conversation with poetic form in Arabic, and the prose poem, which appeared on the scene in 1960, did not disappoint.

The Arabic prose poem announced and flaunted the crossing of limits in Arabic poetry; limits that had been blurred and crossed before without being pointed out or signalled as the systematic launching of a new poetic kind. *Qaṣīdat al-nathr* thus presented itself not only as poetry or as writing or as text, but more problematically as an alternate Arabic poem.

The detractors of the prose poem in Arabic as well as its supporters have described it with a host of labels and adjectives that only prove the near impossibility of defining it. It is an 'anti-genre', an 'alternate genre', 'a bastard form', a 'hybrid', a 'lack', a 'gap', a 'deformation', 'a free form',[9] among many other descriptions. The suspicion it raises is caused by the fact that, in most cases, it is written, not with the intention of writing poetry and surely not with the intention of writing prose, but rather with the intention of disrupting our expectations of both. Consider the following examples from Unsi al-Hajj's *Al- Raʾs al-maqṭūʿ* (The Severed Head):

for this reason,
the orchard-keeper said: stand on edge and smell the rage.
The vine has died after that.

لهذا السبب
قال الناطور قف على الشوار وتنشق الغيظ.
ماتت الدالية بعد هذا.[10]

Surely, this poem is not representative of all Arabic prose poems. In fact, it is difficult to find qualities that all Arabic prose poems share. Aside from the lack of meter and the assertion on the part of poets that their texts are poems, the texts produced under the banner of the Arabic prose poem have little in common. Unsi al-Hajj's aesthetic is very distinct from that of other prose poets of his generation, such as Adonis or Fuʾad Rifqa (Fuʾād Rifqa, 1930–2011) or Salim Barakat (Salīm Barakāt, b. 1951). The later generations of prose poets such as Bassam Hajjar (Bassām Ḥajjār, 1955–2009), Abdo Wazen (ʿAbdū Wāzin, b. 1957), Abbas Baydoun (ʿAbbās Bayḍūn, b. 1945), as well as the younger Iman Mersal (Imān Mirsāl, b. 1966), Samer Abu Hawwash (Sāmir Abū Hawwāsh, b. 1972) and Nazem El-Sayed (Nāẓim al-Sayyid, b. 1975) are just as varied and dissimilar. Their texts are heterogeneous. Some are block texts, some are lineated, some are short and contained, while others are long, sometimes divided into sections or sub-poems. Some are narrative, some are not. Hence, when critics write about the prose poem, they tend to reimagine or redraw the subject anew every time rather than engage with it. The prose poem thus turns into a posture or an attitude. Moreover, it transforms in the writings about it into an approach to a thing and not a thing in itself. And for this reason, critical writings about the prose poem are often just as puzzling and diverse as it is itself.

It seems to me that writing, reading and theorising the prose poem are interrelated; one cannot be done without the other. Not only does it put the practice of reading poetry to the test, but the prose poem also implicates the reader and places her in the position of writer and critic as she attempts to navigate the text and understand its claim as a poem.

More than any other poetic form, the prose poem imposes on its reader, as much as its writer, the need to define boundaries. And these boundaries are urgent, both the boundaries on the page, the blank margins that frame a prose poem, which connect it to other pieces in a collection or separate it from them, and the theoretical boundaries which set it apart from prose and poetry while involving them both in its proposition. In fact, the prose poem's ceremonials of entrance and exit are crucial. Reading a prose poem often begins by deciding how and why it begins and ends the way it does. Otherwise the poem risks disintegrating into something else, precisely what it claims not to be – flowing formless prose, as Unsi al-Hajj puts it.[11] Just as urgent to the prose poem is context. Always an important consideration for defining genres, context acquires an added significance in the case of the prose poem and becomes a crucial stipulation for its very existence. Intended readership, the layout on the page and circumstances of publication become all the more important and may perhaps compensate for the lack of generic markers on which readers rely to make sense of a text. In other words, the prose poem with its reliance on context and on contrasting itself against that context, thus highlighting the points of contact and diversion, as M. A. Caws puts it, is a 'frame of privileged space'.[12]

Thinking of boundaries and context together, one can say that the prose poem is a text that can only exist on the edges of genres, at that front line or interface where boundary and context meet. It is that space or moment in which we begin to recognise something that stands out in an otherwise consistent background: a still shot in a streaming video, a person standing still amid a moving crowd, a cloud in a clear sky.[13]

By proposing to redefine the very notion of Arabic poetry and to open it up, the prose poem becomes a space where poetic and extra-poetic imperatives intersect. Furthermore, the prose poem places the relationship with the (non-Arab) other, the connection to the poetic past and attitudes towards the Arabic language in question. Some go so far as seeing the prose poem's proposal as a break and a destruction of the continuity that makes Arabs who they are. It is the history of this movement, its aesthetic values, and the anxiety and scandal it generated that my project seeks to investigate.

The practice of the prose poem is as varied as its practitioners, their backgrounds, their affiliations and their literary/political agendas. Every single prose poem sets or resets the parameters of the form. With that in mind, my study will pose the following fundamental questions: With a poetic practice so varied and diverse, what is the common 'dominant' (Jakobson's term)[14] of the Arabic prose poem? What is its major intervention in the course of Arabic poetry? In what distinct ways does it differ from other aesthetics, and how does it comment on and co-opt earlier aesthetics? And finally, what makes individual prose poems poetry, and how do single prose poems contribute to the validation of the general theoretic framework of the prose poem in Arabic?

Chapter 1 traces the transformation of verse and prose into mediums of poetry. If the free verse Arabic poem remains within the purview delineated for poetry in Arabic by its rearrangement but not abandonment of meter, the prose poem is the first poetic form to jump the fence of the meter and to make a claim of being poetry in uncharted territory. It established itself as a perpetuation of an 'other' tradition, alternate and dissenting in its relationship to the established poetic aesthetic. It became a subversive space from which literary, critical, ideological and social institutions are challenged. This chapter launches from the two prose poem manifestos by Adonis and Unsi al-Hajj and then zooms in on al-Hajj's collection *Lan* as theory and practice.

Chapter 2 turns to the role of the prose poem as a critical framework or lens. The poets/theorists of the Arabic prose poem engaged in a 'motivated' reading of the Arabic prose tradition. They turned to the rich tradition of Arabic prose, singling out texts that helped validate the modern prose poem and offer it Arabic legitimacy. In particular, I examine the ways in which prose poets appropriated the works of mystics such as al-Niffari (Muḥammad Ibn ʿAbd al-Jabbār al-Niffarī, d. 965)[15] and prose stylists such as al-Tawhidi (Abū Ḥayyān al-Tawḥīdī, d. 1023), writings which share the prose poem's generic evasiveness, its linguistic ambiguity and shock effect. I seek to understand how the first generation of prose poets implicated the Arabic tradition in their project and how this critical exercise transforms our understanding of the 'poetic' in Arabic, beyond the limits of meter and prescribed form.

Chapter 3 traces Adonis's ventures in the prose poem from his early experimentations in the collection *Awrāq fī al-rīḥ* (Leaves in the Wind, 1958) to his seminal contribution, his book-long poem *Mufrad bi ṣīghat al-jamʿ* (Singular in Plural Form, 1977) passing through the major poetic stations in his career, including *Aghānī Mihyār al-Dimashqī* (The Songs of Mihyar the Damascene, 1961). This chapter also traces a parallel thread of discovery through translation and anthologising which informed and expanded Adonis's vision of the prose poem as a framework for re-reading and creating. From *Aghānī* to *Mufrad*, Adonis gradually traces, not the disintegration of poetic form from verse into prose, but rather charts the emergence of poetic composition (*kitāba*) and arrives at form as a consequence of language, away from the binary of verse and prose.

Although many scholars and critics today refer to the Syrian poet Muhammad al-Maghut's (Muḥammad al-Māghūt, 1934–2006) foundational role, the relationship between his poetic project and the prose poem as a poetic and critical movement is not a direct one. I argue in Chapter 4 that al-Maghut's intervention was instrumental in paving the way for the subsequent prose poem, although he himself was not an invested prose poet. Without engaging directly in the polemics of form in Arabic poetry, the Maghutian text, particularly in its attitude towards language and subject matter, was instrumental in opening up the Arabic poetic register. And it is with this taunting of the established poetic aesthetic that al-Maghut contributes, even if unintentionally, to the prose poem as subversive and expansive interrogation of the limits of poetry in Arabic. His legacy translates in the works of younger poets, particularly the Egyptian poets of the nineties such as Imad Abu Salih (ʿImād Abū Ṣāliḥ, b. 1967), Iman Mersal (b. 1966), and Usama al-Danasuri (Usāma al-Danaṣūrī, 1960–2007) and their poetics of detachment.

In Chapter 5, I study Palestinian poet Mahmoud Darwish's (Maḥmūd Darwīsh, 1948–2008) courting of and contribution to the prose poem. He never wrote a prose poem but was closely involved in the critical debates that surrounded it. I examine Darwish's intentionally generically evasive writings which he chose to label '*naṣṣ*' (text) or '*yawmiyyāt*' (diaries), as well as his poetic dialogues with Edward Said and fellow poet Salim Barakat in which he contemplates the meaning of poetry and genre limits.

Chapter 6 explores Kurdish-Syrian poet Salim Barakat's (b. 1951) conflation of poetry and prose, as well as his arrival at a definition of the poetic based on jarring and transgressive interventions in language, from his vantage point as an 'other' writing in Arabic. Barakat's work in poetry and in prose posits a distinct definition of the poetic rooted in the interrogation of and close attentiveness to the meaning of grammar and syntax.

In contrast with Barakat's obsessive language work, Chapter 7 turns to poetry that attempts to escape the hold of language in the works of Wadi' Sa'adeh (Wadīʿ Saʿādah, b. 1948), a Lebanese émigré poet who has lived in Australia since 1988. I argue that Sa'adeh represents a stage in which the prose poem becomes less an oppositional poetic practice accompanied by a simultaneous theorising effort and more of a space for free writing. This chapter traces a thread from Sa'adeh to a host of young contemporary prose poets whose poetic investments increasingly exceed the bounds of one language; such as the Lebanese Joumana Haddad (Jumāna Ḥaddād, b. 1970) and Nazem al-Sayyed (b. 1975), the Palestinian Samer Abu Hawwash (b. 1972) and the Kurdish-Syrian Golan Haji (Jūlān Ḥājī, b. 1977).

I describe this later generation's posture towards the poetic engagement as exophonic, using the term metaphorically to signal a degree of divestment from Arabic as a singular linguistic stratum. This is poetry written in the Arabic of the information age, of texting and chatting, of emails, of bilingual and multilingual speakers of the twenty-first century.

Notes

1. Here, I am borrowing from Steven Monte's work on the American prose poem and his use of Michael McKeon's phrase simple abstraction. See Steven Monte, *Invisible Fences: Prose Poetry as a Genre in French and American Literature* (Lincoln: University of Nebraska Press, 2000), p. 22.
2. Wallace Stevens, *The Necessary Angel: Essays on Reality and the Imagination* (New York: Vintage Books, 1951), p. vii.
3. Salma Khadra Jayyusi's *Trends and Movements in Modern Arabic Poetry* (Leiden: Brill, 1977) remains an important survey in English of the modernist project's many manifestations in Arabic.
4. The term 'free verse' is broader than and subsumes *qaṣīdat al-tafʿīla* and *qaṣīdat al-nathr.* Nevertheless, the English term of the free verse Arabic poem is often used to refer primarily to *qaṣīdat al-tafʿīla* written by poets

such as Badr Shakir al-Sayyab, ʿAbd al-Wahhab al-Bayati (ʿAbd al-Wahhāb al-Bayātī, 1926–99), Yusuf al-Khal (Yūsuf al-Khāl, 1917–87), Adonis, Mahmoud Darwish and others. Few scholars, writing in English or in Arabic, pay much attention to the distinction between *qaṣīdat al-tafʿīla* and *qaṣīdat al-nathr* on a structural/formal level. The two terms are often engaged as indicators of ideological and political postures in the poem.

5. The first two free verse poems in Arabic are supposedly Badr Shakir al-Sayyab's '*Hal Kāna Ḥubban?*' (Was it Love?) which appeared in 1947 and Nazik al-Malaʾika's poem '*al-Kūlirā*' (Cholera) which appeared the same year.
6. Nazik al-Malaʾika, 'Introduction', *Qaḍāyā al-shiʿr al-muʿāṣir*, 1st edition (Beirut: Dār al-Ādāb, 1962), p. 219.
7. Ibid.
8. Lewis ʿAwad, *Plutoland wa qaṣāʾid min shiʿr al-khāṣṣa*, 1st edition (Cairo: Maṭbaʿat al-Karnak, 1947). For more on Lewis ʿAwad, see Mounah A. Khouri, 'Lewis ʿAwaḍ: A Forgotten Pioneer of the Arabic Free Verse Movement', *Journal of Arabic Literature* 1 (1970), pp. 137–44.
9. See Adonis, 'Fī qaṣīdat al-nathr (On the Prose Poem)', *Shiʿr* 14 (1960), pp. 75–83; Unsi al-Hajj, 'Introduction', *Lan* (Beirut: Dār Majallat Shiʿr, 1960); Ahmad ʿAbd al-Muʿṭi Hijazi, *Qaṣīdat al-nathr aw al-aaṣīda al-kharsāʾ (The Prose Poem or the Mute Poem)* (Dubai: Majallat Dubai al-Thaqāfiyyah, 2008); ʿAbd al-Qādir al-Janābī, *Dīwān ilā-l-abad: qaṣīdat al-nathr/anṭulujyā ʿālamiyyah (A Diwan Forever: The Prose Poem/An International Anthology)* (Beirut: Dār al-Tanwīr, 2015).
10. Unsi al-Hajj, *al-Raʾs al-maqṭūʿ (The Severed Head)* (Beirut: Dār Majallat Shiʿr, 1963), p. 88.
11. Al-Hajj, 'Introduction', *Lan*, 18. Not that prose is necessarily 'formless'; yet, this is the dichotomy al-Hajj erects between prose as form-less and the poem as form. Other more recent scholars have argued against this prejudiced view of prose and have pointed to a *prosaics* as a field of study congruent to *poetics* in which attention is directed to the formal processes of prose.
12. M. A. Caws, 'Prose Poem', *The Princeton Encyclopedia of Poetry and Poetics*, 4th edition, ed. Roland Greene (Princeton: Princeton University Press, 2012), pp. 1112–13.
13. This relates to a quality that Suzanne Bernard describes as 'coagulation of a moving process'. Todorov translates the relevant section as follows: 'The poem presents itself as a whole, an indivisible synthesis [. . .] We are thus

reaching a basic essential requirement of the poem: it can only exist as a poem on condition that it [. . .] coagulate a moving process in atemporal forms – thereby converging with the requirement of musical form'. See: Tzvetan Todorov, 'Poetry without Verse', *American Poetry Review* 34.6 (2005), p. 9, and Suzanne Bernard, *Le Poème en prose de Baudelaire jusqu'à nos jours* (Paris: Librairie Nizet, 1959), p. 442.

14. 'The dominant may be defined as the focusing component of a work of art: it rules, determines, and transforms the remaining components. It is the dominant which guarantees the integrity of the structure'. Roman Jakobson, 'The Dominant', *Language in Literature*, trans. Krystyna Pomorska, ed. Krystyna Pomorska and Stephen Rudy (Cambridge, MA: Belknap Press, 1990), p. 41.
15. Muhammad b. ʿAbd al-Jabbar al-Niffari is an obscure *Ṣūfī* mystic, a successor of al-Hallaj (al-Ḥusayn b. Manṣūr al-Ḥallāj, d. 922) His surviving oeuvre consists of two books, the *Mawāqif* and the *Mukhāṭabāt*, often printed together. The work has been translated and edited by A. J. Arberry (London, 1935). See A. J. Arberry, 'al-Niffarī', *Encyclopaedia of Islam*, Second Edition.

1

Precursors, Terms and Manifestos between Theory and Practice

The prose poem's existence in Arabic has thus far been a contentious one. This poetic form and the term 'prose poem' used to denote it have existed on the Arabic poetic scene only since the late 1950s. Two seminal declarations introduced the prose poem in Arabic: Adonis's '*Fī qaṣīdat al-nathr*', published in *Majallat Shiʿr*, and Unsi al-Hajj's introduction to his poetry collection *Lan*. Both declarations were published in 1960 and written in light of Suzanne Bernard's 1959 book *Le Poème en Prose de Baudelaire jusqu'à nos jours* (The Prose Poem from Baudelaire until the Present).[1] According to Adonis, the prose poem is 'a distinctive artistic construction by itself'. The form may employ elements such as narrative, but it should do so for 'purely poetic purposes'.[2] In his introduction, al-Hajj declares the prose poem an 'independent genre' (*nawʿ mustaqill*) but notes its ephemeral and unstable nature. Specifically, al-Hajj cautions, because the prose poem is meter-less, it is at risk of disintegrating into prose. This is why, he emphasises, it has to be 'short, condensed, glowing, shocking, and sufficient unto itself'.[3]

Since the appearance of these initial prose poem manifestos, theorists and poets have continued to describe and define the form. But even with a wealth of definitions attempting to limn it, the prose poem has remained elusive, much easier to talk about than to find. Perhaps this is because, as Steven Monte noted, definitions can be misleading, especially when they 'ascend to the level of abstraction where they describe everything but explain nothing'.[4] The elusive and abstract nature of these definitions is perhaps why the debates that have accompanied the prose poem and the positions that have risen around it, whether approving or disapproving, have combined to form one of the most persistent and contentious critical inquiries into Arabic poetry. At the centre of this inquiry is the fundamental question: What is poetry?

At the risk of presenting yet another abstract definition, I sum up what seem to me to be the points that most definitions and statements on the prose poem have established.[5] First, the prose poem is a new genre, a new literary kind. This is specifically related to the post-1960 prose poem and distinguishes it from previously existing poetic prose forms of the early twentieth century. Second, the purpose of the prose poem is poetry, but not all its elements are necessarily those we have thus far associated with poetry. In writing the prose poem, prose moves away from itself toward the poem but does not arrive at it,[6] or at least not at the poem as we know it, and this is where the movement, the dynamism (*ḥarakiyya*), of the genre lies. Third, in the trajectory of the prose poem, both prose and the poem are transformed into something other than what we know them to be, and probably here, in this transformation, is where we expect to find poetry, new, revealed and naked.

The Poetic Line of Tension and Modern Precursors of the Arabic Prose Poem

The prose poem that Adonis and Unsi al-Hajj refer to as a 'new genre' was inspired by Baudelaire's *poème-en-prose*, a term translated by Adonis into Arabic as *qaṣīdat al-nathr*.[7] I return to Baudelaire's influence below, but it is important to note at the outset that 'poetic' prose without meter has long existed in the Arabic tradition. *Saj*ʿ (rhymed prose) initially comes to mind. It is a form of rhymed, rhythmic and stylised prose, the earliest examples of which are the oracular utterances of the pre-Islamic *kuhhān* (diviners). We see more mature examples of *saj*ʿ in the Qurʾān and the later Islamic periods. Some of the prime examples of *saj*ʿ appear in Abbasid prose such as the epistles of ʿAbd al- Ḥamīd al-Kātib (d. 750), Ibn al-Muqaffaʿ's (d. 757) *Kalīla wa-Dimna*, and later the *maqāma*, especially in the works of Badīʿ al-Zamān al-Hamadhānī (968–1008) and his successor al-Ḥarīrī (1054–1112).[8]

In modern times, the literary forms *al-shiʿr al-manthūr* or *al-nathr al-shiʿrī* or *al-fannī* proliferated at the hands of writers such as Jubran (Jubrān Khalīl Jubrān,1883–1931) and Amin al-Rayhani (Amīn al-Rīḥānī, 1876–1940) at the turn of the twentieth century. But these forms, while 'poetic', are not necessarily, insistently poetry. And they are altogether different from *qaṣīdat al-nathr*. S. Moreh distinguished between two groups of writers. The first group wrote *al-nathr al-shiʿrī* or *al-fannī* (poetic prose) and rejected the term *al-shiʿr al-manthūr* (poetry in prose or prose poetry). Among this first group are Muṣṭafā Luṭfī al-Manfalūṭī (1876–1924) and Muṣṭafā Ṣādiq al-Rāfiʿī (1880–1937), who were not poets but prose writers interested in reviving Arabic rhetorical virtuosity and creating a spontaneous artistic Arabic prose inspired by their Romantic or philosophical tendencies. The second group, which is more relevant to us here, includes writers of *al-shiʿr al-manthūr*, including Jubran, Amin al-Rayhani and Muhammād Luṭfī Jumʿa (d. 1953). Moreh describes those in this second group as 'writers who studied Western Literatures at the expense of Classical Arabic rhetoric and who did not master the Arabic meters'.[9] Their works were often short pieces characterised by the unity of subject matter and arranged in stanzas of separate independent lines. Moreover, these pieces of poetry in prose (*al-shiʿr al-manthūr*) often appeared in longer narrative works.

From its very label, *al-shiʿr al-manthūr* already announces a relaxing of tensions. It is safe to say that the works of the writers of *al-shiʿr al-manthūr* do not reflect a preoccupation with form as much as with content. Even when their texts are arranged and broken up on the page into what looks like poetry, they still lack the 'emotional tension typical of poetry',[10] therefore not challenging or speaking to or placing themselves in a tradition of poetic practice in Arabic. It is a different writing practice with different motivations and inspirations.[11]

There is no doubt, however, that these experiments in prose and poetry in the first half of the twentieth century are an important phase in the history of the Arabic prose poem. According to Adonis, the Jubranic style, more so than al-Rayhani's experiments, was influential in blurring the divisions between poetry and prose and possibly paving the way for the Arabic prose poem.[12] However, the tension of form which is posed by texts written under the label of *qaṣīdat al-nathr* was not evident yet. There is a line of tension that extends from the *qaṣīda* to *qaṣīdat al-taf ʿīla* (the Arabic free verse poem) to *qaṣīdat al-nathr* (the prose poem), precisely the post-1960 prose poem of *Sh ʿir* Magazine. What connects these three poetic forms is their claim to be not merely poetic or poetry-like but solely and uncompromisingly poems. The prose poem I am concerned with here, unlike *al-nathr al-shi ʿrī* or *al-shi ʿr al-manthūr*, has to be a poem, as Unsi al-Hajj insists. It cannot risk being a piece of prose that is poetic or merely laden (*muḥammala*) with poetry.[13] And here, in the term 'poem' is the crux of the issue.

George Baker, in his article 'The Jubjub Bird or Some Remarks on the Prose Poem', makes a relevant point when explaining the elusiveness of the prose poem. Baker notes that 'the term "prose" is technical; the term "verse" is technical; but the term "poem" is critical'. He resolves that the term 'poem' when used in 'prose poem' is metaphorical. It is a way of describing 'prose that we happen to like or admire very much'.[14] Baker does not solve the dilemma as much as evade it. His handling of the problematic terminology, however, hints at the challenge that the term 'poem' creates for poets, critics and readers of the prose poem. In the Arabic context, we see Unsi al-Hajj addressing this challenge when he states: 'The poem (*al-qaṣīda*) is more demanding of itself than poetry is of itself. The poem, not poetry, is the world a poet strives to construct [. . .] It is not poetry but the poem, that complete, self-sufficient, and independent world, which is the difficult one to construct in the open, extending, and flowing soil of prose'.[15] Al-Hajj insists that the 'poem', regardless of formal and lexical requirements, is 'the poet's quintessential quarry'.[16]

Thus, the term 'prose poem' is a leap. It is a shift in itself, from definitiveness and technicality to taste and opinion. Nevertheless, al-Hajj insists on the poem as a deliberate construction (*binā ʾ*) which is possible, even if more challenging, 'in the soil of prose'. The prose al-Hajj refers to here is not contrasted with 'poetry' but rather with 'verse'. Here I find it useful to remember Eliot's remark that English has three words: poetry, prose and verse; however, we are actually in need of four.[17] There is a 'prose' that is contrasted with 'poetry' and there is a 'different prose' that is contrasted with 'verse'. We are, therefore, missing a term that indicates this 'other prose' which is the counter of 'verse' and with which poems can be built.

In that sense, when Baudelaire dreams of 'the miracle of poetic prose', he is not dreaming of *al-nathr al-fannī* but rather of *qaṣīdat al-nathr*, of *poème-en-prose* as opposed to the *poème-en-verse*. In his insistence on the term '*binā*'', Unsi al-Hajj, like Baudelaire, is dreaming of the miraculous, of freedom with exactitude, of subjectivity with a plan. He too seems to believe that without precision and predetermination, the prose poem becomes a contradiction instead of a balance and simply disintegrates.

It is worth mentioning here that the dilemma of terms is slightly different in Arabic. Arabic has the term '*shiʿr*' (poetry) which is not the same as '*naẓm*' (verse or versification). The term '*nathr*' (prose) is properly the antonym of '*naẓm*' (verse) and not of '*shiʿr*', although, as in English, it is used as the opposite of both. If, in Arabic, '*naẓm*' and '*nathr*' counter each other, what is the counter of '*shiʿr*' (poetry) and where does one place *sajʿ* (rhymed prose)? *Sajʿ* is often described as poetic but not as poetry. *Sajʿ* also brings into focus rhyme and its role in creating the poetic. The development of Arabic poetry has thus far been a variation on and an expansion of the pre-modern definition of poetry 'as metered and rhymed speech'.[18] The prose poem's proposition further challenges all previous definitions of poetry and challenges us as readers to re-examine and expand what we mean by poetry in Arabic. All the available terms are scrutinised, broken down and reconfigured through the lens of the prose poem as a theorising framework. Whether the theory holds up and stands the poetic executions is another matter.

The Free Verse Poem and the Prose Poem: Problems and Potentials of Terminology

Of all the forms produced in the period of extensive experimentation in the early twentieth century, such as *al-shiʿr al-manthūr* (prose poetry), *al-nathr al-shiʿrī* (poetic prose), *al-shiʿr al-mursal* (blank verse), *al-shiʿr al-maqṭūʿī* (strophic verse), it is *al-shiʿr al-ḥurr* (that is, *qaṣīdat al-tafʿīla*) and *qaṣīdat al-nathr* (the prose poem) that have emerged as central poetic forms with potential lives beyond the experimentation phase. In this context it is important to clarify the differences between the two, especially in light of the chaos of terminology, which is partly due to translation. The adjective '*al-ḥurr*' (free) in the Arabic term *al-shiʿr al-ḥurr* (free verse) is not a technical term but rather a critical term that refers to the relative freedom of *qaṣīdat al-taf'īla* compared to the classical *qaṣīda.*

In other words, Arabic free verse is not free; it by no means corresponds to the English term free verse, or the French *vers libre*. Arabic free verse, which was first theorised by Nazik al-Mala'ika, is poetry written on a variation of al-Khalil's prosodic system. It is a system which adopts the foot (*al-taf'īla*) instead of the two-hemistich verse (*al-bayt*) as its metric unit, allowing the poet relatively more freedom. The mono-rhyme is abandoned in favour of rhyme or rhymes that are more organically called for by content, rhythm and the overall mood of the poem. It is, therefore, less confusing and more accurate to use the term *qaṣīdat al-taf'īla* to refer to the work of these poets than to use the term free verse,[19] especially when it is later compared to or contrasted with the prose poem (*qaṣīdat al-nathr*), which emerged as its competitor. Most of the major modernist Arab poets of the twentieth century wrote *qaṣīdat al-taf'īla*, some adopting it exclusively.

I find it interesting that some free verse poets are among the prose poem's fiercest opponents. Nazik al-Mala'ika absolutely rejected the possibility of unmetered poetry,[20] a position that the Egyptian poet Ahmad 'Abd al-Mu'ti Hijazi (Aḥmad 'Abd al-Mu'ṭī Ḥijāzī, b. 1935) would echo many years later.[21] In the views of its detractors, the prose poem is at best a misnomer and at worst a sorry excuse for the unskilled and untalented. The reason for such vehement positions is that it is the first poetic form to threaten the established understanding of poetry in Arabic thus far, an understanding shared by both poets of the *qaṣīda* and their modernist successors, the poets of the free verse poem; it is an understanding that involved meter regardless of the value or importance allotted to it. The prose poem is the first proposal that insists on declaring itself poetry without meter in Arabic. Although this might seem like a superficial and minor deviation to us today, it, in fact, defies a long and established distinction between poetry and prose in the Arabic tradition.

The *qaṣīda*, the major Arabic poetic form, has always been accompanied by a critical apparatus founded on a sharp and final separation between poetry and prose, whereby poetry was understood as 'metered and rhymed speech'. This definition has been modified in Nazik al-Mala'ika

’s theorisation of the *qaṣīdat al-taf‘īla* (the Arabic free verse poem) but never really abandoned, as is the case in the prose poem. The confrontation between the *qaṣīda* and the Arabic free verse poem took place in the familiar shadow of meter and rhyme. Although for centuries poets and critics would emphasise that it alone did not make poetry, meter remained the safeguard or the symbolic fence. The Arabic free verse poem did not threaten to take it down, to do away with the distinction between poetry and everything else that is not poetry. Other forms of writing could be poetic or even poetry, but none claimed to be poems without meter. The prose poem does just that, more so than any other poetic or prose form before it. This it does primarily through the insistence on the term ‘poem’. Both *qaṣīdat al-taf‘īla* and *qaṣīdat al-nathr* as poems announce a formal engagement. This is where the potential of terminology lies. If we insist on the term ‘poem’ (*qaṣīda*) and assume it possible in prose (*qaṣīdat al-nathr*), just as it is possible in verse (*qaṣīdat al-taf‘īla*), the focus then shifts from the verse/prose dichotomy toward the quest for an ultimate poem and ‘moves on from there to a definition of the poetic’.[22] We can then explore what makes a poem in prose, just as we do when thinking of a poem in verse. Both prose and verse can lead to what Todorov calls ‘the poetic’ and what Jaroslav Stetkevych calls ‘ultimate poetry’[23] in the context of his study of Muḥammad ‘Afīfī Maṭar (1935–2010).

It is much easier for the free verse poem in Arabic to be convincing as a poem. The modified metric system and its use of rhyme, no matter how varied, keep it within the parameters of meter and rhyme. Setting words to meter and rhyme is a familiar tool for building poems, and thus the form of *qaṣīdat al-taf‘īla* (the poem in verse) has a familiar meaning which we understand and accept as poetry. This is probably why the poets of Arabic free verse ultimately focused their work primarily on content;[24] their modified *taf‘īla* system resolved the issue of form by providing a formula, no matter how flexible, which is still related to some of the edicts of the classical *‘amūd al-shi‘r* (the essentials of poetry, literally the tent pole of poetry) in its keeping of the *taf‘īla* and its variation on rhyme. This offered the free verse poets the comfort of a relatively predetermined form.

The work of the prose poem, on the other hand, is much more challenging as a poem. Its medium, that ‘other prose’, is still unfamiliar as a tool for building poems. If the Arabic free verse poem resolved its formal concerns, is the prose poem despite, or precisely because of its seeming formless-ness shifting our attention back to form? Or is it, better yet, a challenge to the very way we have thus far thought of form and content?

Consider the following poem by Wadiʿ Saʿadeh (b. 1948), the Lebanese prose poet of the *Shiʿr* generation:

ماذا على الذين مثلي أن يفعلوا
وأصغر فراشة
هي الأكثر دهشة؟
الدائرة نفسها
المشهد، النافذة، الوجه
أعشاب تأخذها الحوافر.
سأترك الوجوه وأخرج
بلا محفظة ولا زاد ولا عصا
فارغاً
حتى من قميص قلبي
وبرصاصة واحدة أطل على الصمت
هذا الهدف المتراقص أبداً.[25]

What should people like me do
when the smallest butterfly
is the most amazing thing?
The same circle,
the view, the window, the face,
the grass trodden by hooves.
I will leave the faces and go out
without a wallet, provisions, or a cane,
empty,
even my heart
is without its shirt.
And with one bullet I will take on silence
that ever-dancing target.

Upon first impression, this poem is laid out on the page with line breaks, the way a reader of French and English would expect to see an

English or French free verse poem. But to a reader familiar with the prosodic qualities of the Arabic free verse poem, this text is readily perceived as a prose text. It is a typical Arabic prose poem. The question is: How and why is it a poem? It is untitled, and I think it is difficult to talk about *what* it means without considering *how* it means. Two places in the poem stand out to me in particular. The lines: '*wa-aṣgharu farāshatin hiya al-aktharu dahshatan*' (The smallest butterfly is the most amazing) and the lines '*wa-akhruju* [. . .] *fārighan ḥattā min qamīṣi qalbī*' (I will go out [. . .] empty even of the shirt of my heart). I would describe them as tense, unexpected, alluring, mysterious and, perhaps because of all that, poetry. I am not certain of their meaning and suspect that they probably are not expressing meaning as much as they *are* what they mean – that is, they elude comprehension and direct our attention to something else. This reminds me of a statement by the painter Ben Shahn whose insights as a visual artist on form and content seem very relevant in this context. Shahn states:

> Form is formulation – the turning of content into a material entity, rendering it accessible to others, giving it permanence, willing it to the race. Form is as varied as are the accidental meetings of nature. Form in art is as varied as the idea itself [. . .] Form is the very shape of meaning.[26]

Does the prose poem expose the one-ness of form and content in poetry to the extent that it invalidates predetermined relationships between meaning and forms or structures? Is every thought a form and has every meaning a shape? Another example that lends itself to a similar reading is Unsi al-Hajj's poem entitled '*al-Qafaṣ*' (The Cage):

القفص
توقفت وبي رائحة العوسج وفارت الأنوار.
وقعت النساء من النوافذ!
أما بقي طاووس أصيل؟
توقفت وبي رائحة الخبل. سريعا تقصفت أنواري.
فاح حناني المربع.[27]

The Cage

I stopped, afflicted by the scent of boxthorn,
    the lights boiled over.

Women fell out of windows!
No thoroughbred peacock remains
I stopped, afflicted by the scent of stupidity.
Quickly my lights became brittle.
My squared tenderness diffused.

The obtuseness of this text is frustrating. It leaves the reader at a loss as to what it means, but perhaps when meaning is opaque and impenetrable, it has the potential to direct attention towards something else. And since form in this case is yet undiscovered, are we as readers of the Arabic prose poem being directed towards something beyond form and content, something that in Shahn's words we can call the 'the shape of meaning', the formulation of poetry? This has the potential of liberating the reader of poetry from the concern with grasping the 'sense' of the poem and directing him or her towards what Balso calls 'a non-interpretive grasp of the poem'. Balso emphasises, 'one must grasp the "indirect" of the poem as the organizer in the poem of some figures of thought specific to it'.[28]

The prose poem as a proposition promises the reader access to the 'indirect of the poem'; that which lies beyond meaning and form, a mysterious dimension that brings us closer to understanding the essence of the poetic. Nevertheless, this promise is not easily realised. The reader of the prose poem must be armed with patience, tolerance and above all the belief in the proposition of the prose poem in theory, even though that belief is bound to be challenged by individual prose poems in practice.

The Clear-Headed Theorist, the Baffling Poet: Unsi al-Hajj's *Lan*

Unsi al-Hajj's first collection *Lan* (Won't), published in 1960 when the poet was only twenty-three years old, was received as a prose poem manifesto in its introduction and a prose poem practicum in the poems which followed. However, al-Hajj's intervention most pressingly invites us to consider just that: the gap between the prose poem as theory and the prose poem as practice.

Scholars have pointed out that the introduction to *Lan* is a recycling of ideas already put forth by others, namely Suzanne Bernard in her book, reproducing parts of it verbatim.[29] Nevertheless, his introduction is still significant in its own right. It allows us to witness this poet reformulating ideas that matter to him in his own words. This further highlights the extent to which he himself diverges from these stipulations and veers away from them in his own writing. It is as if the act of theorising is a necessary exercise, yet separate and without binding consequences. In the introduction, he fully embraces the theorising mode, presenting a lucid coherent case for the prose poem as a 'new genre', in a vein similar to that which Adonis presents in his own prose poem manifesto 'Fī qaṣīdat al-nathr'.

However, a significant distinction exists between Adonis and Unsi al-Hajj as theorisers of the Arabic prose poem. In his writings and developing ideas on the prose poem, Adonis proceeds to complicate the notion of 'new genre', directing attention to the discursive power of the prose poem as a new framework through which Arabic poetic and prosaic traditions can still be engaged, as we shall see in Chapter 3. Conversely, al-Hajj adamantly insists on the 'newness' of the prose poem as a genre in Arabic. He fiercely guards the break with the Arabic tradition, by erecting a clear-cut dichotomy between the modernist poet and modern times on one hand and the classical Arabic poetic tradition, especially in what he sees as its limited understanding of aesthetics,[30] on the other. This is probably why the implications and consequences of al-Hajj's theoretical work are limited. And more importantly, his poetic practice is insular; it is singular and difficult to imitate or expand on or regenerate.

'Is a poem (*qaṣīda*) possible in prose?' This is the question with which al-Hajj opens his introduction to *Lan.* From the outset, he invites us to confront the contradictory nature of the prose poem and its perceived impossibility. He goes on to sketch the dichotomy that exists in our minds governing the relationship of the two terms 'poem' and 'prose'. He puts forth a succession of statements on prose, poetry and the poem, as if brainstorming on the spot, sorting out his ideas about this issue and these entangled terms as he writes. We witness him, even here in the introduction, contending with the sentences as they are still in the making.

> Prose is unravelled and relaxed (*maḥlūl*, *markhī*); its palms open and its limbs are only tightened up with mastery and artifice within it. The

> nature of prose is flowing, and its purposes are informative and argumentative. It is of a temporal aim whereas the poem is something contrary to all that. The poem is a closed world, self-sufficient and without a temporal purpose. Prose is narrative, and poetry is a tension. The poem is economy in all means of expression. Prose directs itself to something outside of it, it addresses it and lends itself to all oratorical tools [. . .] Poetry turns away from all these preoccupations: preaching, informing, arguing and proving, and builds its connections with the other through deeper means.[31]

Al-Hajj juxtaposes prose with its opposite. However, he wavers here in referring to that opposite sometimes as 'the poem' and sometimes as 'poetry'. By the end of the first paragraph, he makes up his mind. The issue at hand here is not poetry. If it were a question of poetry, then the prose poem would not have been as difficult as it is to imagine. For poetry is a quality, a judgment of taste, an attitude, an effect. The poem, however, is the challenge. The poem is a structure, a thing with edges. It begins and ends and stands starkly against a background, aware of itself and the world within the world it holds. And here, in that distinction between poetry (*shiʿr*) and the poem (*qaṣīda*), perhaps lies al-Hajj's contribution to the theory of the Arabic prose poem, a lucid, resonant formulation of the distinction between poetry and the poem:

> As for the poem, it is the more difficult with itself than poetry. For the poem to be a poem as such, it must make use of the elements of poetry but not be content with them. It should reimagine them and tighten them further in brevity and repetition. The poem, not poetry, is the poet. The poem, not poetry, is the world the poet strives, in his poetry, to create. A poetry collection may include brilliant poetry but not two poems, or it could all be one poem. For the poem (*qaṣīda*), that independent self-sufficient complete world, is what is difficult to build in the soil of prose, which is spread out, open, and loose. Poetry (*shiʿr*) is not difficult for prose (*nathr*) to present, and prose, from earliest of times and in different languages, abounds with poetry and exceeds in its poetic quality that of poetry in verse (*naẓm*).[32]

This is how al-Hajj arranges the puzzle of terms that the prose poem conjures up in any language. He maintains that poetry is the broadest, all-encompassing category. It can exist everywhere in prose and verse. It lives in poems and outside of them. It does not need proof or rules or an effort to exist. Once it is there, we know/feel it there. It is its own proof. The issue at hand is not poetry but the poem. The poem is the more deliberate entity. It is the structure that can be traced, detected and measured. Prose and verse are means by which poems can be built. We, in the Arabic tradition, are more accustomed to identifying poems built in verse; we are attuned to building structures with the ready-made easily identifiable building blocks of verse. However, not every structure built in verse is a poem. The poem then, as al-Hajj is inviting us to understand it, is a deliberate design which at the same time captures poetry: that most elusive and wilful quality. Against what we have been accustomed to in Arabic poetry, against the habits of the tradition, he invites us to allow, in our imagination, for poems built with other means, with new building material which might need some forming and shaping on the spot. Making use of the tools of poetry as well as the tools of prose, the prose poem is a prism that lifts these tools out of their original context and dissociates them from their old purposes in the new 'atemporal block'.

In the introduction to *Lan*, the prose poem is still an abstraction yet to be tested in practice. Al-Hajj appears fully cognisant of the dangers of that and proceeds cautiously. Our knowledge of the prose poem is not 'yet two years old', he states in 1960. 'We haven't seen enough of it to say for sure that it is faulty or will not survive'.[33] Al-Hajj is thus aware that he is speculating on something still taking form in Arabic; a new poem for a new world as he calls it. He invites us to stand with him on the edge of the old world and look to the horizon to see the Arabic prose poem taking form. The poets of the new world are those willing to look over the edge into the unknown. They are madmen, al-Hajj tells us, who know that suffocation and stagnation can only be fended off by crazy acts; by 'destruction, destruction, destruction!'[34] And in the process, many flaws and missteps will be committed. An important take away from al-Hajj's seminal introduction is that the prose poem is a thing in the making and making is messy and difficult. He is reconciled with the fact that, along the way toward achieving the theoretical promises of the prose poem, much flawed poetry ought to be written and many failed attempts at poems ought to be penned; most importantly, the idealised and perhaps romantic ideal of the poetry and poetry making, which has persisted over the ages, will necessarily have to be adulterated and distorted:

> The first obligation is destruction. Pure poetic creation will be suspended in this tempestuous atmosphere, but that is unavoidable. For the rebel to be happy with creation he cannot settle on a volcano. He will waste much time, but destruction is dynamic and sacred.

Al-Hajj warns the reader of his introduction that prose poems require an entirely different taste and palate. Approaching a prose poem with the same set of reading tools used by the reader of Arabic poetry thus far will only lead to frustration. The prose poem is thus a new framework for writing poems as well as reading them. First and foremost, the reader of Arabic poetry ought to prepare him or herself for a blow. The effect of the prose poem is not gradual, not reliant on feet or lines or parts that can be selected or sectioned out.[35] The prose poem has an effect in its totality. It is a radiating block which befalls the reader as an affliction. And its effect is, therefore, a consequence of its content as much as it is a product of its form.

The prose poem, al-Hajj insists, is a world without equivalent *('ālam bilā muqābil*),[36] it is closed off, outside time (*lā zamaniyya*), and without purpose (*majjāniyya*). And, despite his insistence on chaotic destruction and dynamic creation, al-Hajj still traces parameters for the prose poem. He cited the examples of poets Saint-John Perse, Henri Michaux, Antonin Artaud and Suzanne Bernard's work on Baudelaire, as well Edgar Allen Poe's[37] view on the notion of the poem in general to deduce a set of guidelines or requirements for the prose poem. Variations on these guidelines will continue to appear in the writings of all those who theorised the Arabic prose poem after al-Hajj:

> For the prose poem to be a prose poem and not a piece of artistic prose or prose laden with poetic effect, three requirements are to be met: brevity (*ījāz*), intensity (*tawahhuj*), and gratuity (*majjaniyya*).[38]

Some have pointed to al-Hajj's contradicting himself when it comes to implementing these three tenants in his own writing.[39] Intensity and gratuity are debatable and abstract, but it is easy to find evidence of his disregard of the stipulation of brevity. In *Lan* itself, although the majority of the poems tend to be rather short, the last poem is over twenty-six pages long. Nevertheless, al-Hajj defends himself against the accusation of contradiction in his introduction when he back-tracks and comments on his three stipulations by noting that . . .

> These are not negative rules whose purpose is to hinder the poet nor are they ready-made vessels into which any nonsense can be poured to make a prose poem. No. They are a framework, general features for what is deeper and more fundamental: the poet's talent, his internal experience, and his attitude towards the world and humanity.[40]

These rules, he goes on, are features of successful prose poems that have already been written. They are not necessary features that will ensure the success of prose poems that have not been written yet.[41] By that, al-Hajj undermines the very act of theorising something that resists finality, and he reveals the embedded yet fruitful contradiction of such an endeavour. For the prose poem, he reminds us again, is built on the duality of chaotic destruction and geometric organisation.[42]

While it is comfortable and tempting to settle into poetic practices that derive authority from long-standing traditions (*sulṭan al-turāth al-ṭawīl*),[43] the time for discomfort and agitation is upon us. Not only in theory but also practice, the old is to be purged and expunged by extreme measures, by mad and crazed poetic acts. The prose poem is the poem of poets who do not 'sleep on their language' but perpetually reinvent it. In heralding 'modern times', everything, especially language, will be destroyed and built again.

If al-Hajj's introduction is theoretically derivative and constitutes an echoing of the ideas he encountered in the work of Suzanne Bernard and others on the prose poem in French, its emotion and drive in the closing remarks redeem it and perhaps justify some of its failings. Clearly marking his stance on the Arabic poetic tradition as an obstacle and deadweight, al-Hajj announces the practice of the Arabic prose poem as a phase that ought to be crossed with all its dangers and drawbacks. It is an illness or an infection which will purge the body of Arabic poetry from its latent and deep-set habits. This is purgatory. We shall ruin poetry in search of it, he announces. What will be written now is most probably flawed, but what has not been written yet is what will ultimately matter.[44]

In other words, the theoretical framework of the prose poem sanctions a kind of writing which might be wanting yet necessary. It is truly experimental, difficult, distorting, yet with the ultimate purpose of delivering Arabic poetry into a new phase, into a new world. And passages or crossings such as these are often traumatic. This acknowledgment on al-Hajj's part perhaps prepares the reader for the poems that follow in *Lan*. They undeniably upset expectations, both the poetic expectations in Arabic and the theoretical expectation which al-Hajj himself sets up in his introduction.

As *Lan* appeared in the first edition published by *Shiʿr* Journal's publishing house and in most subsequent editions I have seen, there is a blank page that separates the introduction from the collection of poems. On that transitional page, white and tempting, empty yet loaded, a transformation occurs. It is not sudden or unexpected. Al-Hajj tells at the end of his introduction that the situation calls for extreme measures. And extreme measures are what he indeed goes on to illustrate. The lucidity and the logic of his language and voice in the introduction disperse once we transition to his poems. The talk of measured chaos, the pontification on intensity and compactness, even the call for destruction, all that is muddled once we arrive at the poems in *Lan*.

The first poem in the collection is titled 'Identity', alerting us from the very beginning not to expect any sense of direction or guidance from the titles in this work. Very rarely do titles aid in manoeuvring the corresponding texts. Following the introduction, this opening poem is significant in the statement it makes about al-Hajj's idea of the new destructive poem. It opens with the following stanzas:

الهوية

أخاف.

الصخر لا يضغط صندوقي وتنتشر نظّارتاي. أتبسّم، أركع، لكنْ مواعيد السرّ تلتقي

والخطوات تُشعّ،
ويدخل معطف! كلها في العنق. في العنق آذان وسرقة.

أبحث عنكِ، أنتِ أين يا لذة اللعنة! نسلك ساقط، بصماتك حفارة!
يسلّمني النوم ليس للنوم حافّة، فأرسم على الفراش طريقة: أفتح نافذة وأطير، أختبئ تحت امرأتي،
أنفعل!
وأشتعل!...
تعال أصيح. تعال أصيح. إنني أهتف: النصر للعِلم! سوف يتكسّر العقرب، وأتذكر هذا كي أنجب بلا يأس.
تمطر فوق البحر[45]

Identity

I am afraid.

Stone does not pressure my box and my glasses scatter. I smile, I kneel, but the secret appointments converge, the footsteps radiate, and a coat enters! They are all in the neck. In the neck are ears and theft.

I search for you, where are you, pleasure of curse! Your breed is fallen, and your fingerprints dig in.

Sleep surrenders me, there is no edge to sleep, so I trace a method on the mattress: I open a window and I fly, I hide under my woman,

I become agitated!
I burn! . . .

Come, I scream. Come, I scream. I am calling out: Victory to science! The scorpion will break down and I will remember this, so I may procreate without despair.

It rains over the sea

The poem is approximately four pages long, divided into short blocks or paragraphs separated by blank spaces that vary in length. Some single words and sentences stand alone, giving the impression of design or deliberate structuring. One sentence (It rains over the sea) appears twice, as if in a refrain. But making sense of it is torturous and futile. On the level of form, it is unknown territory, which the reader has to learn to navigate as she goes along. On the level of meaning, the text resists the making of meaning and is intentionally jarring. What Unsi al-Hajj achieves here is a poem in Arabic that does not want to be an Arabic poem. It deliberately destroys recognisable semiotic paradigms for poetic composition in Arabic. As he warns us in the introduction, this is the cursed and cancerous poem,[46] and whether we shall survive it is yet to be seen.[47]

The Prose Poem as 'Other'

The prose poem is where the abstract notion of poetry is shattered and built again. Once established formal prescriptions are abandoned, the secret of the poetic remains to be rediscovered. Are they linguistic or sonic or even thematic qualities that make a prose piece a poem? Can any text, if viewed in a particular way, be called poetry?

Once freed from the restrictions of pre-determined form, the prose poem embraces its 'indeterminacy' which appears to be its dominant quality. I borrow the term 'indeterminacy' here from the work of Marjorie Perloff. In her mapping the development of modernism in Anglo-American poetry, she identifies two discrete yet interwoven stands: the symbolist following in the steps of Baudelaire and Eliot and the anti-symbolist mode whose first exemplar is Arthur Rimbaud. The anti-symbolism is characterised by a heightened indeterminacy, 'literalness and free play'.[48] The latter developed into what Perloff labels as the 'other tradition', a lineage that extends from Rimbaud to Pound and Stein to Williams – poets who were experimentalist, deliberate and committed to 'making it new'. If the Arab free verse poets who 'made it new' by loosening the formal strictures of the Arabic poem to the very limit without abandoning them are one strand, the Arab prose poets are the other. Subversive, irreverent and confrontational, these are the poets of destruction and abandon. They plan 'to make it' something entirely different.

The prose poem is the first poetic form to jump the fence of meter and make the claim of poetry, and more problematically of poem-building, in uncharted territory. It has established itself as a perpetuation of an 'other' tradition, alternate and dissenting in its relationship to the established poetic aesthetic, and became a subversive space in which literary, critical, ideological and social institutions are challenged.

Notes

1. Suzanne Bernard, *Le Poème en Prose de Baudelaire jusqu'à nos jours* (Paris: Librarie Lizette, 1959). This book is based on Bernard's doctoral dissertation. Parts of it were translated into Arabic and published in *Shiʿr* Magazine soon after the publication of the book in French. Bernard's work has been credited for the launching of the Arabic prose poem via *Shiʿr* Magazine in the 1950s and 1960s. For more on the relationship between *Shiʿr* group and *Shiʿr* magazine and the rise of the prose poem, see Otared Haidar, *The Prose Poem and the Journal Shiʿr: A Comparative Study of Literature, Literary Study, and Journalism* (Reading: Ithaca Press, 2008).
2. Adonis, 'Fī qaṣīdat al-nathr', p. 81.
3. Al-Hajj, 'Introduction', *Lan*, p. 18.
4. Monte, *Invisible Fences,* 4.
5. See Adonis. 'Fī qaṣīdat al-nathr', pp. 75–83; al-Hajj, 'Introduction', *Lan*, 1960; Ahmad Bazzun (Aḥmad Bazzūn), *Qaṣīdat al-nathr al-ʿarabiyya*, 1996; al-Janabi, 'Introduction', *Dīwān ilā-l-abad.*
6. Adonis, 'Fī qaṣīdat al-nathr', p. 81
7. Ibid. p. 75.
8. For more on *sajʿ*, see Fahd, Heinrichs, and Ben Abdesselem, 'Sad̲j̲ʿ', *Encyclopaedia of Islam*, Second Edition; for more on the *maqāma*, see Brockelmann and Pellat, 'Maḳāma', *Encyclopaedia of Islam*, Second Edition.
9. S. Moreh, 'Five Writers of Shiʿr Manthūr in Modern Arabic Literature', *Middle Eastern Studies* 10.2 (1974), p. 229.
10. Jayyusi, *Trends and Movements*, vol. 2, p. 630.
11. Even when presented in the form of 'poems', as is the case in al-Rayhani's work, particularly his collection *Hutāf al-awdiya* (The Calling of the Valleys, 1910), it is not accurate to describe it as a collection of prose poems. It seems that his purpose was to free his texts from meter and rhyme, or at least to challenge the established metric system. He sometimes employs a variety of different meters in the same text or abandons meter altogether. He inconsistently employs rhyme. It seems therefore that what he intended to write was 'free verse' in the English and French sense of the term. He sometimes calls his work 'free verse poem' (*shiʿr ḥurr ṭalīq*) or poetry in prose (*shiʿr manthūr*). Al-Rayhani does not use the term prose poem (*qaṣīdat al-nathr*) in the same sense as the *Shiʿr* magazine poets in the 1960s did. For more on

the distinction between *al-shiʿr al-manthūr* and *qaṣīdat al-nathr*, see Jayyusi, *Trends and Movements*, vol. 2, pp. 626–49.

12. Adonis, *al-Thābit wa-l-mutaḥawwil: baḥth fī-l-ittibāʿ wa-l-ibdāʿ ʿinda al-'Arab* (Bayrūt: Dār al-ʿAwda, 1974–78), vol. 4, pp. 188–91.
13. Al-Hajj, *Lan*, p. 18.
14. George Baker, 'The Jubjub Bird or Some Remarks on the Prose Poem', *Listener* 85 (1971), p. 748.
15. Al-Hajj, *Lan*, p. 10.
16. Jaroslav Stetkevych, *The Hunt in Arabic Poetry* (Notre Dame: Notre Dame University Press, 2015), p. 244.
17. T. S. Eliot quoted in Keith Waldrop, 'Introduction', to Charles Baudelaire, *Paris Spleen: Little Poems in Prose*, trans. Keith Waldrop (Midtown: Wesleyan University Press, 2009), p. vii.
18. This is Qudama b. Jaʿfar's often cited definition of poetry. See Qudama b. Jaʿfar, *Naqd al-shiʿr*, ed. Muḥammad ʿAbd al-Munʿim Khafājī (Cairo: Maktabat al-Kulliyāt al-Azhariyya, 1979), p. 64.
19. For more on the term *al-shiʿr al-ḥurr*, its various indications, its problems and objections to it, see Ahmed al-Tami, 'Arabic Free Verse: The Problems of Terminology', *Journal of Arabic Literature* 24.2 (1993), pp. 185–98.
20. Nazik al-Malaʾika, *Qaḍāyā al-shiʿr al-muʿāṣir*, p. 219.
21. Ahmad ʿAbd al-Muʿṭi Hijazi, *Qaṣīdat al-nathr aw al-qaṣīda al-kharsāʾ* (The Prose Poem, or the Dumb Poem).
22. Todorov, 'Poetry without Verse', p. 9.
23. Stetkevych, p. 247.
24. Khouri, p. 137.
25. Wadiʿ Saʿadeh, *Laysa lil-masāʾ ikhwa* (Beirut: al-Muʿassasa al-Jāmʿīya lil-Dirāsāt wa-al-Nashr, 1981), p. 33.
26. Ben Shahn, *The Shape of Content* (Cambridge, MA: Harvard University Press, 1957), p. 53.
27. Al-Hajj, *al-Raʾs al-maqṭūʿ*, p. 66.
28. Judith Balso, *The Affirmation of Poetry*, trans. Drew Burk (Minneapolis: Univocal Press, 2014), p. 101.
29. M. A. Deeb, 'The Concept of the poème en prose in Modern Arabic Poetry: Native Tradition and French Influence', *Canadian Review of Comparative Literature* March–June (2010), p. 176.
30. Al-Hajj, *Lan*, p. 22.
31. Ibid. p. 9.

32. Ibid. p. 10.
33. Ibid. p. 12.
34. Ibid. p. 14.
35. Ibid. p. 16.
36. Al-Hajj, *Lan*, p. 19.
37. Ibid. p. 16.
38. Ibid. p. 18.
39. Deeb, p. 177.
40. Al-Hajj, *Lan*, p. 21.
41. Ibid.
42. Ibid. p. 19.
43. Ibid. p. 22.
44. Ibid. pp. 23–24.
45. Ibid. pp. 27–28.
46. Ibid. pp. 23–24.
47. Ibid. p. 12.
48. Marjorie Perloff, *The Poetics of Indeterminacy: Rimbaud to Cage* (Evanston, IL: Northwestern University Press, 1983, p. vii.

2

The Prose Poem and the Arabic Tradition

As a hybrid, suspect and contradictory proposition, the prose poem provides the springboard into a debate in Arabic poetry that touches on issues deeper and more far-reaching than the prose poem itself. In search for poetry, this debate gives rise to questions that call for a more engaged scrutiny of every other established poetic form in Arabic, but especially the *qaṣīda* and the Arabic free verse poem. 'Can the prose poem exist in Arabic or not?' becomes an inquiry that requires an in-depth search for that secret ingredient – that magical recipe – that, aside from meter or rhyme or line breaks or layout on the page, creates poetry. The question 'Can there be an Arabic prose poem?' is a specific instantiation of the more universal 'Can there be a prose poem?' Both sentences pose the same question. However, in the case of Arabic, the question takes on a specific character and added urgency because it threatens to transform a long-standing definition of Arabic poetry in a way that none of the other poetic forms have done, no matter how radical they were thought to be when first introduced. The prose poem, thus, becomes the site where the poetic is interrogated. Is it language or thought that creates the poetic quality of a text? What is it that makes a text a poem?

In addition to posing the question 'What is poetry?' the Arabic prose poem, more subversively, urges us to ask: 'What can be poetry in Arabic?' This is a question not concerned with defining as much as it is concerned with expanding and re-charting. It is a question that threatens what we think we know; it opens it up, blurs it and reinvents it. In a tradition that has long accepted very clear-cut distinctions between poetry and prose, such a prospect is both exciting and unsettling.

There is no history for the prose poem in the Arabic tradition. Much of the force and the provocation of this relatively new poetic form is precisely that: its unprecedented-ness. Placing it in the Arabic tradition is a theoretical exercise whose purpose is to primarily highlight the prose poem's critically charged nature, its fundamental function as an agitator of genre boundaries and a prompt for the ubiquitous and unresolvable questions: What is poetry? And more specifically, how and why is a poem a poem?

Poetry and Prose in the Arabic Critical Tradition

We cannot really speak of a prose poem in the Arabic tradition, but we can speak of poetry and prose as two very separate categories; some very illuminating remarks on the interface between the two have been made. All classical Arab critics, without exception, mentioned meter as a condition for or at least an element of poetry. The very clear separation between prose and poetry in the Arabic tradition is the result of a shared understanding among most Arab critics of the poetic process as bringing extant but independent elements into one structure. This view, most importantly, assumes a certain understanding of the relationship between meaning and form. Meaning exists *a priori*, before and outside of language, whether in poetry or prose. Once meaning is available to the poet, he sets out to find an appropriate vessel; that is what has been referred to as form (*shakl* or *ṣiyāgha*). I will not go into the details of the debate on form and content or meaning (*lafẓ* and *maʿnā*) and the different positions critics have taken as to which of them is the determining factor in the creative process. It suffices to say that both sides of that debate not only agree that *lafẓ* and *maʿnā* are two separate elements, but also that meaning precedes *lafẓ*. This is apparent in the different metaphors used to describe the relationship between the two poles of this dichotomy. Examples of such metaphors include: Ibn Tabataba (Muḥammad Aḥmad Ṭabāṭabā, d. 815) sees a beautiful maid (*jāriya ḥasnā'*) as meaning and the setting (*maʿriḍ*) or the makeup that either does her justice or not as form;[1] Qudama ibn Jaʿfar (Qudāma ibn Jaʿfar, d. 948), the historian, philologist, literary critic and author of

Naqd al-shiʿr, likens poetic composition to carpentry (*nijāra*) and forging silver (*ṣiyāghat al-fiḍḍa*);[2] Abu Hilal al-ʿAskari (Abū Hilāl al-ʿAskarī, d. 1005) uses clothing or re-dressing (*maʿriḍ* or *ḥilya*) to explain the relationship between content and form;[3] and al-Marzuqi (Aḥmad ibn al-Ḥasan al-Marzūqī, d. 1030) invokes the metaphor of the vessel and its contents (*ḥattā yattasiʿa l-lafẓu lahu*).[4]

In light of the relationship between meaning and form portrayed as such, meter takes on an important function as the marker of poetry. It is the fence separating poetry from prose. Nevertheless, we often see Arab critics downplay its centrality in creating poetry. Critics such as Ibn Tabataba and Qudma ibn Jaʿfar have maintained that, although necessary, meter alone is not enough to make poetry. They have suggested other necessary requirements. Ibn Tabataba speaks of taste (*dhawq*), and Qudama places emphasis on the poet's ability to harmonise the discrete elements (*muʾālafa*), stressing that he who lacks the ability to do so does not compose poetry, even if what he produces is metered and rhymed.

In other words, despite the unchallenged role of meter in the practice of poetry, we can find many instances in which critics and poets point to the fact that the secret of the poetic lies elsewhere beyond meter. Although al-Tawhidi's often cited comparison between prose and poetry in *al-Imtāʿ wa-l-muʾānasa* remains within the boundaries of the well-known debate, arguing first in favour of prose then poetry, it offers a few interesting moments when the dichotomy is challenged. For instance, al-Tawhidi quotes a certain Abī ʿĀʾidh al-Karkhī Ṣāliḥ b. ʿAlī saying that meter can sometimes be a liability in poetry, if contrived and not a result of real talent. As a consequence of that, poetry falls under the 'siege of prosody' (*ḥiṣār al-ʿarūḍ*).[5] Al-Tawhidi quotes another person, a certain al-Salamī, probably a poet, who makes a distinction between meters (*awzān*) and tunes or melodies (*alḥān*) which are broader and more flexible; then Abū Sulaymān al-Sijistānī, brings up the terms *īqāʿ* (cadence or rhythm) and speaks of a rhythm in poetry and a rhythm in prose. Al-Tawhidi ends his record of this discussion by offering what seems to be his own opinion on the matter stating: 'the best speech is one that combines subtle expression (*lafẓ*), delicate meaning (*maʿnā*), and shining beauty, and whose form (*ṣūra*) takes a middle position between poetry that is like prose and prose that is like poetry'.[6]

It is important to remember that opinions such as those recorded by al-Tawhidi, although hinting at the possibility of poetry without meter, did not lead to such a practice. Even Abu al-ʿAtahiya's (Abū al-ʿAtāhiya, d. 748) famous statement 'I am above prosody' (*anā akbar min al-ʿarūḍ*) was not a call for abandoning meter, but rather a statement always cited in the context of a debate over the soundness of meter in some of his lines.[7] It is a statement in defence of composing poetry in new, previously unknown meters, but meters nevertheless.

The first major critical effort that completely marginalised meter in the understanding of what makes language suddenly unlike itself, be it poetry or even something more magical, is that of ʿAbd al-Qahir al-Jurjani (ʿAbd al-Qāhir al-Jurjani, d. 1078) in his theory of *naẓm* (formulation or sentence construction). It is worth noting here that al-Jurjani, in his *Dalāʾil al-iʿjāz fi al-Qurʾān* (The Signs of the Inimitability of the Qurʾān), was not primarily interested in poetry but rather in the Qurʾānic text. This could probably be the reason for the ease with which he brushes meter aside when he says: 'Meter has nothing to do with eloquence [. . .] It is not by meter that speech becomes superior'.[8]

His revolutionary theory of *naẓm* is one that concerns itself with composition, arrangement or stringing together of words. The focus thus shifts from a process in which separate things are brought together to a process in which the elements of creation are themselves created in the very process itself. Al-Jurjani defines *naẓm* as '*tawakhkhī maʿānī l-naḥw*' (minding the meanings [generated in] syntactic relations or observing the meaning of grammar).[9] Every ordering (of words) creates a form and therefore a new meaning. Neither exists outside of that process. The inherited but misunderstood dichotomy *lafẓ-maʿnā* is thus reinterpreted by al-Jurjani. 'The wording (*lafẓ*) is no longer a "garment" for a "naked" *maʿnā*. The two are inseparable; no "meaning" can be expressed by two "wordings" equally well'.[10] Al-Jurjani is persistent in his quest for precision and clarity in describing the wholeness of poetic creation. As Kamal Abu Deeb explains, meaning according to al-Jurjani ceases to exist as an independent unit when it enters into poetic expression.[11] Meaning in poetic expression is the image of meaning, what al-Jurjani calls *ṣurat al-maʿnā* (the image of meaning),[12] a phrase that has its echoes in Balso's 'figures of thought' and Shahn's 'shape of meaning' mentioned earlier.

Poetry is not a bringing together of disparate elements, nor is it a fitting of meaning into ready-made vessels. At its core it is a linguistic event, a formulation. Modern Arab poets, especially Adonis, drew upon al-Jurjani's work in their attempts at opening up the definition of poetry in Arabic to new possibilities. Adonis states in his *Siyāsat al-shiʿr* (The Politics of Poetry): 'The difference between poetry and prose is not in meter but in the way language is used', echoing al-Jurjani's definition of simile, which al-Jurjani considered central to poetic language, as 'the way in which meaning is expressed or fixed' (*ṭarīq fī ithbāt al-maʿnā*). Al-Jurjani's theory of *naẓm* gives the phrase 'poetic language' much needed focus and pointedness, especially when used in relation to the Arabic prose poem.

It is intriguing that al-Jurjani's exploration of poetic language originated from his inquiry into the mysteries of *iʿjāz* (Qurʾānic inimitability). Viewing the Qurʾān as a miraculous intrusion in Arabic spurred the question regarding the properties which set it apart from all other literature. The term *iʿjāz* in Arabic means 'miraculous-ness', but also carries the connotation of something that cannot be achieved by a human being, something that cannot be accounted for, and something that renders one powerless as well as challenged.[13] The Qurʾān, in both its content and form, is assumed to be all of that. It is in the way language is ordered and employed (*naẓm*) that al-Jurjani discovers the secret of Qurʾānic language, its inimitability (*iʿjāz*). There is much room for further exploration of the subtleties of al-Jurjani's theory of *naẓm* and the insight it offers into definitions of the poetic, which I will not go into here.

I will only note that the debates on the inimitability of the Qurʾān contribute to and complicate the delineation of the terms prose and poetry in Arabic, as well as their relationship to each other. Although in a category of its own, the discourse on the status of the Qurʾān in Arabic is connected, if not subsumed, into debates about poetry, the old and the new, and the dividing line between poetry and prose.[14] The *sui generis* status of the Qurʾān is established at the interface of poetry and prose as discrete categories. It exists outside both, but in a generic tension with both. What further establishes its uniqueness is the notion of the 'miraculous'.[15] It is the differentiating feature that dispels any similarities between the Qur'ān and the two genres against which it is defined: prose and poetry.

Thinking about these dichotomies and the debates around them simultaneously – *ṭab*ʿ and *ṣanʿa*, *lafẓ* and *maʿnā*, *qadīm* and *muḥdath* in relation to poetry, and *qadīm* and *makhlūq* in relation to the Qur'ān – reveals a double standard applied to the notion of new and new-ness. The new carries a connotation of derivativeness, excess and incomprehensibility when applied to poetry by the critics of the Abbasid *muḥdathūn*. The same critics understand new-ness in relation to the Qur'ān to mean unprecedented, one of a kind, miraculous and inimitable.

This is why poetically charged prose such as *Ṣūfī* prose, which Adonis labels as 'other prose' (*nathr ākhar*)[16] to hint at its potentially subversive nature, was often marginalised. It ran the risk of unsettling a clear and final distinction between poetry and prose which needed to stand in order to preserve the *sui generis* status of the Qur'ān. And it is to this wealth of unexpected, baffling and 'miraculous' prose that Arab prose poets and theorisers returned in their search of a history or pre-history for the prose poem.

The Prose Poem in Arabic Literature: A Lineage in Retrospect

The Arabic tradition abounds with works that are exemplary instances of a poetic 'use of language', although not poetry themselves; they are a kind of 'miraculous' that defy categorisation and are almost incapacitating in their impact on the reader. These are the texts which modern practitioners and theorisers of the prose poem in Arabic have gone back to rediscover and appropriate. It goes without saying that the Qur'ān as a category or genre is the most obvious of these texts. In fact, modern scholars have pointed to a host of ancient texts in addition to the Qur'ān as possible archetypes of prose poem texts, including Gilgamesh, the Psalms and the Songs of Solomon. We also know that the poets themselves engaged with these texts and drew upon them in their meditations on the nature and limits of poetry.[17] Some of the texts have actually only come to the attention of the modern reader in the context of the revived debate around poetry and prose invoked by the prose poem. One such work is al-Niffari's (d. 976) *Al-Mawāqif wa l-mukhāṭabāt*. This work is in a way an Adonisian discovery. Al-Niffari is a *Ṣūfī* whose language is a language of mystery and tension, a language that intentionally obscures and revolves around itself. For example:

> وقال لي: اقعد في ثقب الإبرة ولا تبرح، وإذا دخل الخيط في الإبرة فلا تمسكه، وإذا خرج فلا تمده، وافرح فإني لا أحب إلا الفرحان، وقل لهم قبلني وحدي وردكم كلكم، فإذا جاؤوا معك قبلتهم ورددتك وإذا تخلفوا عذرتهم ولمتك.[18]

> He said to me: Sit in the eye of the needle and stay put. When the thread enters the needle do not grab it, and when it comes out do not stretch it. And be happy: for I love only the happy. Tell them, he received me alone and rejected you all. And when they come to me with you, I will receive them and reject you. And if they were late, I will excuse them and blame you.[19]

The poetic quality of this text lies in the stringing together, the arrangement, the materialisation of meaning, which has a mesmerising, trance-like effect. The challenge that it poses for the reader lies in the turns it takes, in its unexpectedness. Here is another equally fascinating example from al-Niffari. Similarly cryptic, like the previous example, this keeps us wondering not only about what it means but how and why:

> الحروف كلها مرضى إلا الألف، أما ترى كل حرف مائلا، أما ترى الألف قائمًا غير مائل، المرض الميل للسقام فلا تمل.[20]

> The letters of the alphabet are all sickly except the *alif*. Don't you see how every letter slants, but the *alif* stands straight and does not lean? Illness is the leaning towards illness, so do not lean.[21]

But are these excerpts poems? Of course, they are not – that is, if we are to consider the context in which they were initially written. And, of course, they are, if we consider the contexts in which they have later been presented. And 'context', an important consideration for genre, is especially important for the prose poem. Here, publication, layout and readership may signal genre just as much as a work's formal features. Reading such excerpts as poetic is nothing new, but reading them as poetry or rather as poems is the contribution of the prose poem as a theoretical and interpretive framework. This is the contribution of prose poem poets and theorists in their retrospective discovery of the Arabic prose tradition and their reinvention of it as poetic.

An illuminating example of this manipulated or motivated reading of prose works in the tradition is most obvious in Adonis's *Dīwān al-nathr al-ʿarabī*.[22] His selections from al-Tawhidi's *al-Ishārāt al-ilāhiyya* are especially telling. Of course, aside from his seeking out especially 'poetic' lines, he makes the conscious decision to lay them out on the page with line breaks, signals that guide the reader towards reading them as poems. It should also be noted that in the original the passages are taken somewhat at random from much longer passages. For example:

الهوى مركبي،
والهدى مطلبي،
فلا أنا أنزل عن مركبي،
ولا أنا أصل إلى مطلبي...[23]

Passion is my mount,
The guided path is my destination,
Never will I dismount,
Never will I reach my quest …

ذهبت والله قبل أن جئت
وهلكت قبل أن سلمت
وبَطُلْتُ قبل أن حُققت
وبدت قبل أن كنت
وفقدت قبل أن وجدت
واعوججت قبل أن استقمت...[24]

By God, I left before I arrived
I perished before I was saved
Annulled before I was realised
Extinct before I came into being
Lost before I was found
I was bent before I became straight …

Adonis credits writings like the ones cited above for making the prose poem an Arabic form when he states:

> Although originally a Western concept, today the prose poem is an Arabic poem in every sense of the word. It has acquired its Arab-ness especially after its writers have acquainted themselves with *Ṣūfī* writings. They have discovered in the works of writers such as al-Niffari, al-Tawhidi and al-Bisṭāmī, and others, that poetry is not only in meter. The means of expression (*ṭuruq al-taʿbīr*) and the way that language is used (*ṭuruq istikhdām al-lugha*) in these writings is essentially poetic although not metered.[25]

Here, Adonis takes us back to al-Jurjani's 'way in which language is used' to explain the poetic quality of certain writings. This serves to marginalise meter in the search for the poetic, pointing to roots of poetic-ness in the means and ways in which language is manipulated. Adonis and other prose poets admit their indebtedness to al-Jurjani in this respect. This is where the Arabic critical tradition can help create a more focused critical language and provide critical tools for reflecting upon the Arabic prose poem, aside from the circular and dead-end conversations revolving around meter.

Nevertheless, the Arabic literary tradition does not offer textual precedents for the prose poem. Contrary to Adonis's statement above, I believe that the writings of al-Tawhidi and al-Niffari do not make the prose poem more Arabic; rather, it is the prose poem as a theoretical framework that makes these Arabic prose works poetry and, more interestingly, poems. The search for the prose poem in the tradition is a critical reading exercise. What it achieves is not to provide the form with authenticity or Arab-ness. Far from it. It actually imposes the prose poem as a critical framework for reading selections from the tradition as prose poems. We find ourselves reading selections from al-Tawhidi and al-Niffari with an agenda, looking for things that we did not look for before. We do not set out to review the tradition in search of the prose poem; instead, we take the prose poem with us as a critical lens as we go back to reimagine the tradition.

The *Qiṭʿa* and the Prose Poem: A Critical Reading Exercise

Challenging the finality of literary categories is the Arabic prose poem's most significant achievement thus far, or at least the one upon which most critics would agree. When the launching point of reading a text is the assumption that it is a poem, one necessarily interrogates the text and actively searches to justify the assumption upon which the reading is based. This is true for the reading of any text. Genre specification thus serves as a reading signpost. However, when the genre specification is itself at risk of failure, the reading process becomes more critically charged. I will not rehearse the definitions and theories of the prose poem here, nor will I summarise its polemics. My intention here is to demonstrate how the prose poem can serve as a reading lens which zooms in on the elements that justify claiming a composition, whether prose or verse, a poem.

Short poetic compositions (*qiṭʿa/maqṭūʿa*, pl. *qiṭaʿ/maqṭūʿāt*) have existed alongside the longer and more established poem (*qaṣīda*) in the Arabic tradition. Regardless of which one preceded the other, it is the relationship between the two and the mechanics of reading them and juxtaposing them which interest me here. The manner in which *qiṭʿa*s have been recorded, read and connected to each other, in addition to the very label (*qiṭʿa* means fragment) – these all assume that the shorter form is a cut-off from the longer one. Reading short compositions with the idea of the fragment in mind conjures up notions of context and boundaries that become instrumental in the reading process, in a manner similar to what we experience when reading prose poems. Independent prose poems urge the reader to wonder whether they ought to be read alone or whether they signal an 'absent context'. Prose poem collections beg the question of whether they are continuous texts or separate fragments. Short compositions in the works of prominent pre-modern poets have irked critics and redactors in a similar way.[26]

I am particularly interested here in the short composition of the later Islamic period, especially the Abbasid age. These are characterised by a deliberateness we cannot assert about earlier short compositions. They are intentionally composed to be short, and they reveal to us the *qaṣīda* in a consciously transitional moment in its history, looking inward as it prepares to transform into something else: the independent free-standing poetic form (the *qiṭʿa*), which in turn ultimately produced a set of discrete genres: the wine poem, the hunt poem and the *ghazal*.

I suspect a similarity between the way in which the short compositions relate to the longer poem, on one hand, and the way in which the advent Arabic prose poem relates to the established Arabic poem(s) that preceded it (be that the classical poem or the free verse poem, the *qaṣīdat tafʿīla* poem), on the other. There is something about their engagement of boundary and context that invites further investigation. This is true for both these poetic forms, in as much as they stand alone sufficient, unto themselves, in as much as they invite us to read them against a background, against something else. They give the impression of framing something in (or out), of isolating a moment that would have otherwise blended into the background. They can both be described as 'privileged frames of attention'.[27]

For this reason, the classical short composition and the prose poem in Arabic poetry can probably benefit from being read against each other. I am not claiming any direct connection or influence of one on the other, but rather proposing a reading exercise that might help illuminate some of the dominant features of these two poetic forms and the ways in which they operate within the system of Arabic poetry in general. The facts that the former is a short verse composition and that the latter is a poem in prose side-line form as a launching point and invites us to examine other elements which contribute to the poetic charge of the pieces. Structure (*bināʾ*), on the level of both the parts (the phrase or the sentence) and the whole, takes precedence over form as meter and rhyme.

The matter here is a matter of familiarity. As readers of Arabic poetry, we are more familiar with the classical short pieces such as the wine poem or the hunt poem, or at least we have more of a context to draw upon when reading them than we do when reading the Arabic prose poem. Even if one might argue that our ideas about the *qaṣīda*, its parts and motifs (the assumed backdrop for classical short composition), are nothing but a set of after-the-fact imposed critical assumptions about an abstracted idealised generic model, these assumptions still have created a tradition of reading which in itself has resulted in a tradition of writing.

In the context of his work on the hunt poem (*ṭardiyya*), Jaroslav Stetkevych captures the excitement engendered by extracting the new from the familiar. The poet arrives at jarring deviations from what is expected, and 'in doing so, almost shouts out to us: Look at what I have done, wonder, and draw your conclusion'.[28] Nevertheless, the new short composition, so Stetkevych tells us, 'still look[s] back over its shoulder at the genre-time, when it was or could have been part of the *qaṣīda* as master form'.[29] It is this signalling that I am concerned with here. No matter how far off a fragment strays, it is this gesturing towards a familiar poetic world that guides its reader and defines much of what it does. In other words, *qiṭ'a*s of later Islamic periods are intentionally written or composed against a deliberately conjured up absent context. Along the same lines, I claim that the Arabic prose poem, composed beyond the limits of Arabic poetry as we know them and yet insisting on being a poem, looks over its shoulder to signal or measure the extent of this transgression which defines it.

The prose poem, Santilli states, is an 'inevitably elliptical text and always stands in relation to a larger absent whole'.[30] If the classical fragment's absent whole is the *qaṣīda*, determining the prose poem's absent whole is more complicated. We can probably assume that the prose poem on some level evokes its closest contender, the modern free verse poem (*qaṣīdat al-taf'īla*), but it also contends on a more general level, with the sum of our expectations as readers of Arabic poetry. The fragment to the *qaṣīda* is a part transforming into something independent and different. The prose poem to Arabic poetry is an expansion beyond the accepted parameters, proposing poetry in a territory previously not of poetry and, thus, threatening to transform the whole system.

We have not yet developed a tradition or backdrop for reading the Arabic prose poem. This is why it still appears to be out of place or alien in the landscape of Arabic poetry. Reading a prose poem in Arabic is almost always an exercise in negotiation and compromise. In order to sustain the reading of a prose poem, we are forced to reassess our expectations and keep adjusting them. Perhaps, examining the strategies of reading short *qiṭ'a* might shed light on the Arabic prose poem and offer helpful strategies for reading it. Poets, especially when they claim to be revolutionary or avant-garde, exploit our accepted and shared assumptions about poetry.

If poets do that when steering readers towards something 'new', readers too can follow suit. Readers also can depend on strategies of reading the familiar when confronted with the unfamiliar.

In order to anchor this reading exercise, I will look at the prose poem and the classical short composition under three sub-headings, each pertaining to what I see as a shared feature of the two poetic genres/forms: abruptness, creation of new meanings, deliberateness.

Abruptness and its Consequences

The *qiṭʿa* is short and compact, yet it gives the impression of doing all that a longer poem does. This especially applies to the *qiṭʿa* in later Islamic periods, when we can be certain that the short compositions were deliberately composed to be short and did not constitute remnants of a lost whole. In the section of *al-ʿUmda* on short and long compositions (*Bāb fī al-qaṭʿ wa al-taṭwīl*), Ibn Rashiq (Ibn Rashīq al-Qayrawānī, d. 1063) demonstrates that, despite the ceremonial weight of longer poems, the short compositions are a poetic challenge not all poets are up to. A successful short composition is one that can assert itself as a poem. He cites the poet al-Jammāz, who was famous for almost exclusively composing short compositions and who was known to boast: 'I say one verse and it suffices and stands in for many'.[31]

Similarly, the prose poem has been defined by many of its theorists on the basis of its compressed-ness which challenges readers to unpack or decipher it. Although not all Arabic prose poems are short, still almost all critical treatises, introductions and manifestos written to define the Arabic prose poem open with the stipulation of brevity. The abstracted model of the Arabic prose poem is short and, in fact, most long prose poems – such as those that Unsi al-Hajj and Salim Barakat are fond of writing – are made up of separate short subsections in often numbered, titled or untitled parts. These long poems can, therefore, be viewed as collections of short pieces as opposed to a long fluid whole. Thus, it is abruptness perhaps that is more crucial than brevity as a characterising feature of the prose poem.

In defining the prose poem, Caws describes it as a 'field of vision, only to be, on occasion, cut off abruptly'.[32] The abruptness of the prose poem, often coupled with its short length, is meaningful and allows it to stand alone, yet dependent on the ability of the reader to compensate for the absence and to provide the lacking context. Santilli claims that the absence present in the prose poem is what allows it to communicate so much in so little: 'The way the prose poem achieves a high level of intelligibility within a minimal number of sentences is', she states, 'made possible by the absence that it accommodates'.[33] The blank spaces, the silences or absences that surround a prose poem are 'inherent to the experience of reading a prose poem collection'.[34] Consider the following poem titled 'Memory' from Unsi al-Hajj's *al-Raʾs al-maqṭūʿ*:

ذكرى
كمْ
هذا
الليل!
كل نعامة تدفنني[35]

A Memory

How
much
this night!
Every ostrich buries me

Or the following free-standing section from a longer poem by Salim Barakat:

أفق هذا
أفق ذاك:
كلاهما عانة الريح.[36]

A horizon here;
A horizon there;
Both, the crotch of the wind.

The short length, in this case, has meaning or consequences. It allows the composition to exist almost from beginning to end on the cusp of silence. The shorter the composition, the more intense we assume it to be and the more depth we take it to have. Aware of it as part of a larger context, we are also inclined to read it inwardly, searching in it for meaning that is purely a product of its coagulation or crystallisation. Thinking of the network of connections we are used to identifying in a longer poem, we expect to find a similarly complex network in the restricted space of the short composition.

Under the heading of fragments (*maqṭūʿāt*), we fall upon single lines or pairs of lines in the poetry collections of Abbasid poets. Ibn al-Rumi (ʿAlī b. al-ʿAbbās Ibn al-Rūmī, d. 896) and Ibn al-Muʿtazz (ʿAbdallāh b. al-Muʿtazz, d. 869) were especially fond of these one- or two-liners. The examples I will discuss here are both descriptions (*wasf*), but there is something revelatory about them that materialises in the short piece and is a product of the network of connections between the few lines. Very imagist in a way, the description uncovers a meaning or a dimension of meaning impossible before it. Here is Ibn al-Muʿtazz describing a star in the night sky:

والنجم في الليل البهيم تخاله عيناً تخالس غفلةَ الرقباء
والصبح من تحت الظلام كأنه شيب بدا في لمة سوداء[37]

A star appears in the black night, like an eye
dodging watchers' drowsiness,
and morning underneath the darkness like grey
looming in a black lock of hair.

This piece is neither about a star at night nor about grey in black hair nor about morning. This is a piece about stealth. The surreptitiousness of a twinkle in the night sky, of the beginnings of morning, of an eye dodging sleep and of grey invading hair, these all taken together is what Ibn al-Muʿtazz is surprising us with here. All four images are stacked on top of each other, and what holds the piece together as one moment or event is the connection between the word 'dodging' (*tukhālis*) and the preposition 'underneath' (*taḥt*). The power of the realisation or revelation here is compounded by the abruptness of this free-standing couplet. Much of the effect of these two lines would have been diluted had they been included in a longer poem. Similarly, in the following three-line *qiṭʿa*, Ibn al-Rumi describes the colours of a garden:

بنفسجٌ جمعت أوراقه فحكى كحلاً تشرَّب دمعاً يومَ تشتيتِ
واللازوردية تزهو بزرقتها وسط الرياض على حمر اليواقيتِ
كأنها وضعاف القضب تحملها أوائل النار في أطراف كبريتِ[38]

The violet with leaves gathered unto each other, resembled
tear-drenched kohl on the day of parting.
The lapis lazuli one flaunting its blue
amid the garden, against the ruby red,
They are, upon weakened stalks that carry them,
like the beginnings of fire in the tip of a match.

Ibn al-Rumi here blends different colours and strikes a match alight! The excess of colour he provides in the first part of the piece is stacked up on weakening flower stalks that bend under the weight of the imagery and resemble a match beginning to burn. How the piece is closed off is gratifying; it speaks to what Caws identifies as a short poem's 'willful self-sufficiency'.[39] This also speaks to the short compositions' epigrammatic quality which Van Gelder discusses at length in his article titled 'Pointed and Well-Rounded'.[40] I take 'epigrammatic' as also referring to an effect that the short composition possesses. It confronts us with something we already know, as if for the first time. All poetry does that to some extent; however, in the samples that Van Gelder studies and the ones that I am interested in here, this effect is acutely accentuated. What happens in Ibn al-Rumi's piece above is similar to what happens in Barakat's piece cited earlier: the assembling of a shocking image out of unsuspected parts. The shapes revealed in the pieces above (the crotch of the wind, the eye winking in the night sky, the violet-ruby match) are creations of the precise world closed unto itself that is the poem.

Ideas 'Churned' into New Meanings

Critics both classical and modern note the abruptness and compactness of the Abbasid *qiṭʿa* and connect it to creativity or experimentation on the level of meanings or themes.[41] Once untangled from the larger matrix, the short composition often becomes a space for experimenting with themes in a manner unsustainable in longer compositions. In fact, it is in short compositions that we fall upon pithy sayings which are more meaning-oriented and resonate in a manner more direct than that in longer compositions. The poet Ibn al-Zuʿburī defends shorts over longs by stating that short compositions are more penetrating and memorable. Al-Jammāz reveals that all his poetry consists of short composition because he trims it of excesses.[42] One surmises that short compositions, favoured especially by Abbasid modern poets, are poetry bared to its essence; they are flashes or poetic bolts, which rely primarily on producing poetic meaning or ideas, as the poet Muḥammad b. Hāzim al-Bāhilī tells us in the line below:

أبى لي أن أطيل المدح قصدي إلى المعنى وعلمي بالصواب[43]

What keeps me from long praises is my intent for meaning
and my knowing what is exactly right.

The Abbasid short composition achieves its effect primarily by innovating, manipulating, or transforming the listener/reader's expectations of meaning. The Abbasid modernists took advantage of the liberating space in the short pieces to probe and transform themes and motifs in a manner best described by Ibn Tabataba's phrase: 'the churning of meaning' (*makhkhaḍa al-maʿnā*).[44] Ibn Tabataba uses this phrase to describe the poetic process, the making of poetry (*ṣināʿat al-shiʿr*). According to him, the poetic process is launched by the readying of meaning in prose.[45] The poet then finds fitting rhymes and meters and arrives at an 'organising pattern' or thread (*nasaq*)[46] to hold together what he has churned up. Prose poets and theorists would probably find Ibn Tabataba's two-step process flawed and might argue that the 'churned' meaning in prose is already poetry, even before it is placed into meters and rhymes. Nevertheless, his emphasis on a transformed meaning or theme as the basis for the poem is something that applies to what the prose poem in many of its iterations strives to achieve. Ibn Ṭabaṭaba himself goes on to say that some poetry of 'tight precise diction' and 'marvellous composition' sustains its poetic quality even if it were broken back down into prose.[47] Van Gelder notes that Ibn Tabataba here must have had shorter rather than longer poems in mind, such as those by Ibn al-Muʿtazz, the master of the short composition.[48]

Regardless of what Ibn Tabataba would have thought had he been confronted with a modern prose poem, his use of churning as a process for making poetry emphasises the metamorphic quality of poetic language and its ability to generate meaning that did not exist before it. In short compositions, the discovery of meaning as if for the first time is a dominant feature or driving force. Let us consider the following short ghazal by the Abbasid poet Abu Tammam (Ḥabīb b. Aws Abū Tammām, d. 845):

بيّتُ قلبي من هواك على الطوى ورحلت من بلد الصبابة والجوى
لو لم يجرني الهجر منك بلطفه والله لاستأمنت منك إلى النوى
لم ترع لي حرقاً بقلبي قد مضت لو لم يذدها الدمع عنه لاشتوى
هيات كنتُ من الحداثة والصبا في غفلة إنّ الهوى يُنسي الهوى[49]

I stayed my heart in the night, although it hungered for you.
I travelled away from the land of passion and longing.
Had your abandon not been kind, shielding me **from** you,
by God, I would have taken refuge **from** you in distance!
You took no heed of the blisters in my heart.
It would have roasted, had it not been for the cover of tears.
Oh! too young and green I was to realise
that one in love forgets love.

This love poem is about longing to the extent of self-sufficiency or negation of love. Abu Tammam here transforms the motifs of longing, separation and distance into something unexpected: into its opposite. The lover's infatuation is brought to a boil in this line:

Had your abandon not been kind to me, shielding me from you,
by God, I would have taken refuge in distance!

This is where the short composition reaches its utmost intensity and inwardness. And this intensity is achieved through minute details and precise decisions that have a revelatory effect. This intensity, I think, mostly lies in the use of the prepositions 'from' (*min*) and 'to' (*ilā,* translated above as 'taking refuge in'). A lover is expected to desire 'to(ward)' the beloved, whereas here, Abu Tammam's lover is grateful for being shielded 'from' the beloved by abandon; he longs away from the beloved.

The lover is expected to shun distance, but the lover here directs himself to(ward) distance, taking refuge in it.

Although the commentary frames this as a poem about rebounding and moving on from one love to another,[50] I find it much more fitting to read the last line as referring to the same love; more of it extinguishes it. Once love is in full motion, it is no longer in need of its object. Love, like poetry, is closed unto itself and becomes the end in itself. It does not express or describe or plead or argue. It has the effect but not the resolution of a punch line. On the contrary, the meaning is brought to its very limit and left there in the last line (one in love forgets love), further closing the poem unto itself. Certainly, not all short compositions achieve the effect of discovery or invention in this self-sufficient manner. However, when they do, they assert themselves as poems, stand-alone compositions and not merely fragments. Let us consider the following poem about patience by Ibn al-Muʿtazz:

يا من به قد خسرت آخرتي لا تفسدن بالصدود دنيائي
أهمُّ بالصبر، حين يسرف في هجري والصبر نازح نائي
حتى إذا ما رأيت طلعته غيّرني ما رأيت عن راءِ[51]

Oh, you for whom I have lost my hereafter,
do not ruin my world now with your aloofness.
I start towards patience when he exceeds in abandon
while patience is distant and elusive,
but once I see his face,
it turns me away from what I had set out for.

This piece captures the pull of love. The lover is redirected from patience towards his aloof beloved in spite of himself. The tension of the piece lies in the sentence that begins with 'I start towards patience' (*ahummu bi-ṣ-ṣabr*), and it further intensifies by the interjecting sentences, leading up to the turn back to the beloved in 'but once I see his face'. This short poem is a poem about being torn apart in love. The speaker is pulled in opposing directions, and he is in the middle suspended between patience and endurance on one hand and passion and indulgence on the other. All this is set up in the first line by the pull or tension between 'hereafter' and the 'world now'. It is a meaning achieved through the opening juxtaposition and the structure of the sentence that follows; the long and interrupted sentence: 'I start towards patience . . . but once I see . . .'

The modern prose poem depends on a similar process of churning meaning, taking it to its limit and leaving it there. In its avoidance of music, overt rhythm and familiar rhetorical devices, meaning or ideas become the prose poem's medium. The majority of Arabic prose poems can be described as thought-poems,[52] in that they rely primarily on manipulation of themes, an opening up or shaking down of themes in a transformative way. And often this exploration of theme ends with heightened tension and a lack of resolution; a quality Caws describes as the prose poem's 'strangely reticent irresolution'.[53] The prose poem thus often directs itself at our comprehension to challenge or disrupt it in some way. The effect of this can be revelatory, even if that which is revealed is all too familiar, as is the case in this piece by Nazem El-Sayed:

استعملتُ وعودي كلها
وها أنا
أجلس مع حاضري
ملتصقاً به مرتجفاً
كسابح نادم بين ضفتين
يقيس أمامه بخلفه.[54]

> I have used up all my promises
> and here I am
> sitting with my present
> clinging to it, shivering
> like a swimmer, regretful between two riverbanks
> measuring what lies ahead with what lies behind.

El-Sayed's poem contemplates the present moment. As it progresses, the speaker is stripped of all before him and ahead of him. The poem gathers itself inward, 'clinging' to a point mid-way between two banks, between past and future. The state of suspension is achieved through the build-up towards the image of the swimmer. The line breaks here further intensify it by emphasising 'my present', 'shivering' and the two 'riverbanks'. The piece fulfils itself with the word 'regretful'. Not hesitant or undecided, the swimmer is regretful as he contemplates the two opposite riverbanks and measures the possibilities that could be against each other. The poem ends with this closing off or collapsing of directions, in a moment suspended in mid-stream.

Another example of this revelatory approach to meaning is the following poem by Bassam Hajjar titled 'Wall':

جدار
شخص
من الحجارة والكلس
تفضحه الرطوبة
والشقوق
كمن يتكلم في نومه.[55]

A wall
A person
of stone and plaster
exposed by moisture
and cracks
like one speaking in his sleep.

Much more is achieved here than an anthropomorphising of the wall. The juxtaposition of wall and person on one hand and exposure through moisture or involuntary speech on the other makes this poem. The poem defines the wall against or rather through its very opposite in our minds which is exposure (*faḍḥ*). By the end of the poem, we are left thinking not about the wall but about the 'person' and the cracks and exposures that define him or her.

Hajjar is a prose poet and a translator fond of exploring themes to their very limits. A great example of 'churning meaning' comes from his collection *Mihan al-qaswa* (The Vocations of Cruelty). In a cycle of poems titled 'Pain' (*alam*), he opens with an epigraph from Anna Akhmatova's 'Requiem':

لا ليس أنا، إنه غيري من يتألم.
مثل هذا الألم ما كان في طاقتي واحتمالي[56]

No, it is not I; it is someone else that hurts
Such pain is beyond my ability and endurance

Hajjar takes the idea of a pain so intense that it feels like another's and runs with it. He composes nine subsequent poems, all titled 'Pain'. The poems transform the theme of pain, 'churning' it and finding it in the most unexpected places. Pain is a 'needle pulling thread'; 'a stone or a light or a lonely lily'; 'a mouth dry without thirst'; 'merciless whiteness of empty, smooth sheets'. Pain, Hajjar's poem reveals, is 'not pain but the place of pain after it had ceased'. Here are four poems from this cycle:

الألم

إبرة تسحب الخيط
بين التخاريم
أصابع تومئ
ويد تقلّد ظلها
على الجدار.
لا الرشاقة
بل الألم.[57]

Pain

A needle pulling thread
through holes,
fingers signalling,
and a hand imitating its shadow
on the wall.

Not grace
but pain.

الألم

نحيا
في الغياب الذي هو
مكانك.

الأبناء قساة

والتنفس هو أيضاً
من أشغال القسوة.

نحيا
في المكان الذي هو
غيابك.

حجرٌ
أو ضوء
أو زنبقة
وحيدة
وبيضاء وبيضاء
وبيضاء

وبلا قلب[58]

Pain

We live
in the absence that
was your place.

Sons are cruel
and breathing, it too
is an exercise of cruelty.

We live
in the absence that
was your place.

A stone
or a light
or a lily
alone
white, white
white,

and heartless.

الألم

سرير
ومخدة ريش،
دثار مطرز
وبياض بلا رحمة
لملاءات شاغرة وملساء،

سرير
نظيف ومرتب ومتروك

بجانب سرير.[59]

Pain

A bed
a feather pillow,
an embroidered quilt
and the merciless whiteness
of empty, smoothed-out sheets,
a bed
clean tidy and abandoned

next to a bed.

الألم

ما لا يقال
إلا
همساً،

لا الألم،
بل مكانه بعد أن يزول،
مكانه الذي له
يبقى موجعاً
لشدة ما يزول.[60]

Pain

What is only said
in whispers,

not pain
but its place after it has ceased,
its place that belongs to it,
continues to hurt
in as much as it fades.

Nevertheless, such experimentation with meaning is not always well-guided; the result is sometimes simply enigmatic. This is when the poem becomes a frustrating mind-game as in the case of this poem by Unsi al-Hajj:

الطير الأسود

أصابعي
كي تشرح فمكِ
تجذف في الرصاص
وحين يحين موعدي...
فجأة
برعبه القديم
الطير الأسود يوقظكِ
صمت المجذاف
يسكنكِ
نظر المجذاف.[61]

Black Bird
My fingers
to interpret your mouth
they paddle in lead
and when my time comes . . .
suddenly
with its ancient terror
the black bird will wake you
the oar's silence
inhabits you
the oar's sight.

It is more difficult to identify a process in al-Hajj's poem. Nevertheless, the reader is tempted to follow al-Hajj's thematic play for clues. All the parts of the opening sentence are shocking: 'my fingers interpret your mouth'. Interpreting and 'paddling in lead' in the third line are connected, foreshadowing the 'oar' that appears at the end of the piece, mute and sighted. 'Muteness' and 'sight' are similarly associated with each other, either as equals or opposites. The black bird, the title of the poem, remains an enigma, appearing near the end in relation to an addressed 'you'. It is hard to say what this poem achieves beyond setting us up as readers to search for a process. The poem does not allow us much beyond its play on ideas. It intentionally interrupts its own train of thought, as if purposefully deflecting the possibility of comprehension.

In all the examples above, the prose poem and the classical short composition do not express meaning or explain it, but rather attempt to achieve it or disclose it. It is not accessibility or comprehension that the poem strives for, but rather a presence of meaning that is at once self-evident and entirely new. Meaning is thus invented or transformed when the 'initiative is truly surrendered to the words'.[62] These short compositions lay claim to poetry most when every little word, every minute decision is revelatory – like music,[63] in which the medium and its message are one and the same. It is as if language in these compositions has a mind of its own, revealing in its minute details and subtle shifts nuances or shades of meaning that do not exist outside the poem.

Deliberateness and the Meta-poetic 'Dominant'

If the *qaṣīda* conveys a message outside of itself (*qaṣd*), the *qiṭʿa* does not necessarily. Some *qiṭʿa*s are more reflective or meditative upon a single moment or occasion or experience. They do not make a point as much as create an effect (*athar*). This relates to a quality of the prose poem modern theorists have labelled as gratuity (*majjāniyya*), meaning that the prose poem has no purpose or intention beyond itself. I find that quality rather mindboggling and frustrating to the reader, and I cannot help but associate it with self-consciousness or self-reflexive-ness. In other words, when short pieces are without purpose beyond themselves, they are calling attention to the very process of composition. They and their inner workings become the purpose.

The Abbasid *qiṭʿa* in particular provides a fitting counterpart for the prose poem in this reading exercise because the work of *muḥdath* poets, in general, was informed by preoccupying critical questions[64] and by their eagerness to exploit the expectations of the audience to the full. Thus, self-reflexive deliberateness is a feature that the *qiṭʿa* and the prose poem share, or perhaps it might exceed being merely a shared feature to become the 'dominant' (in the Jakobsonian sense of the term) of both poetic forms. This deliberateness governs and transforms all the other components, and it is what guarantees the integrity of these compositions as poems.[65] Thus, these two poetic forms do not merely share that they are written with a heightened consciousness, but that they depend on this heightened consciousness to be read as well.

Of course, not every short composition is self-reflexive, but the compactness of the form and its self-sufficiency allow for reflections on the poetic process that cannot be accommodated in the outward-oriented longer piece. Consider this enigmatic piece by Abu Tammam, labelled by redactors as a ghazal:

لو تراه يا أبا الحسن   قمراً أوفى على الغُصُن
قمراً ألقت جواهره   في فؤادي جوهر الحزن
كل جزء من محاسنه   فيـه أجـزاء من الفتـن
لي في تركيبه بدع   شغلت قلبي عن السنن[66]

If you would see it, Abū Ḥasan,
a moon rising over the branches,

a moon whose jewels have tossed
in my heart the essence of sorrow.

Every detail of its charm
is an element of enticement.

In composing it I display novelties
that have diverted my mind from law and tradition.

The poet's deliberate incorporation of critical terminology such as *fitan* (enticement), *bidaʿ* (novelties), *tarkīb* (construction, composition) and *sunnan* (rules, tradition) is inspired by the debates on Abbasid badīʿ poetry.

There are similar short meta-poetic pieces in the works of almost all *muḥdath* poets such as Abu Tammam, al-Buhturi and Ibn al-Rumi. However, if the short *qiṭʿa* allowed the Abbasid poets these asides to comment on their poetic processes, habits, achievements and so on, the meta-poetic aside, the poet's soliloquy is the very aesthetic of the prose poem. It is easy to point to thematically meta-poetic prose poems in the works of almost every prose poet, such as this untitled piece by Wadiʿ Saʿadeh:

هناك مشروع قصيدة
ضفة
أفرش عليها السمك الواجف في رأسي.
اذهبي
يا امرأة سوداء على بابي يا مراكب
اذهبي
أحلامي كافية لأغلق هذا الباب
وأنام
مياهي كافية
لأغرق.[67]

There is a project for a poem
a bank
on which I spread the fish writhing in my head.
Go away,
black woman at my door, boats,
go away
my dreams are enough to shut this door
and sleep
my waters are enough
to drown in.

However, more fundamental than such thematic meta-poesis, there is an essential self-reflexive-ness in the prose poem which governs the practices of writing it, reading it, and critiquing it. We read prose poems, regardless of their theme, primarily to answer the question: Are they poems, and how so? The lack of meter and rhyme and other recognisable common poetry markers makes this more of an issue in the modern prose poem than in classical short compositions. The *qiṭʿa* remains within the structural paradigm of the recognisable poem, and thus its meta-poetic questions are more direct and less urgent.

The dominant self-reflexive-ness of the prose poem is not a thematic motif or a secondary referential quality but exists in the very fabric of its poetic discourse. This meta-poetic assumption is almost necessarily a pre-requisite for reading a prose poem, and it becomes especially urgent in un-lineated Arabic prose poems. Consider the following untitled piece from Nazem El-Sayed's collection *Ard maʿzūla bil-nawm* (A Land Isolated by Sleep):

> والزواريب التي تستدرج المارة من أقدامهم. والبنايات التي تكزُّ على أسنانها. والسيارات المركونة قرب الرصيف بانتظام كأنها في زحمة سير. والنفق الذي يقذف السيارات المسرعة إلى الضوء. وأولئك الذين يخترعون أسباباً واهية للمشي. والموهبة التي تتنزّه مع صاحبها. وكلب الرجل الذي ينتبه، يُخفض رأسه ويمضي مغمضَ العينين.[68]

> And the alleys that lure pedestrians away from their feet. And the buildings that clench their teeth. And the cars parked on the sidewalk. In line. As if stuck in traffic. And the tunnel that shoots speeding cars out into the light. And those who invent flimsy excuses for walking. And the talent that strolls with its owner. And the man's dog who becomes alert then lowers its head and walks on with eyes closed.

Although seemingly narrative, this piece does not sustain the narrative thread and resists reaching a resolution. The claim of poetry here is a guiding cue that makes the practice of reading highly deliberate and motivated. It begins with a subscription to the claim of poetry, a suspension of disbelief and then a search for poetry in this unfamiliar territory. The piece depends on the repetition of a sentence structure creating a pattern. The conjunction 'and' weaves the phrases together and produces a certain rhyme, which is both semantic and sonic.

Without the claim of poetry as a frame, reading this piece can be an unguided endeavour. Paradoxically, the persistent examining of poetry and further of the poem is what sustains these pieces' claim as poems. Of course, the prose poem's meta-poetic dominant is much more urgent and fundamental to its existence than that of the classical short *qiṭʿas* in some of its instances.

To assert itself as a viable addition to the realm of poetry in Arabic and if it is to live up to the claims made by its poets and theorists, the prose poem has to do more than say in prose what the Arabic verse poem (the *qaṣīda* or the *qiṭ'a* or *qaṣīdat al-taf'īla*) has already said in verse. It has to demonstrate not prose's ability to be poetry in the general sense of the word, as has already been done by Arab prose writers, from al-Jāḥiẓ (d. 868) to Jubran. It has to prove that prose can build a poem, can be the soil for processes of poetry. The question may be broader than this. What is it that could not have been done in the free verse poem that now can only be done in the prose poem?

In its interrogation of poetry and its limit, the Arabic prose poem allows for a new conception of form that does not exist outside the poem but grows from inside of it. It invites us as critics and readers of Arabic poetry to revisit our understanding of structure in poetry (*binā'*) and to use that to arrive at form. This has the potential of redefining poetic forms that have been cast as rigid and fixed.

This after-the-fact, invented history of the prose poem in Arabic is an exercise in reading the Arabic prose poem against the backdrop of the tradition, as much as it is an exercise in reading selections from that tradition in light of the prose poem. It serves to expand our understanding of what poetry is and what poetry can be in Arabic. It loosens the grip of meter, highlighting poetry as primarily a linguistic event.

However, if the dilemma of poetry is resolved, the dilemma of the poem is not. The prose poem will have to remain at its very core a meeting of odds, a miracle of the most difficult nature. It is more the challenge of constructing the poem than the search for poetry that gives the prose poem its contentiousness and intensity, but also its great potential. Far from being an easier or more forgiving poetic practice, the prose poem, on the contrary, can and should be the more difficult. For it occurs within invisible fences, as Steven Monte puts it; invisible fences, but fences, nevertheless. Writers of the Arabic prose poem have a wealth of examples in their tradition of theoretical and textual sources that help them as they redefine the poetic in Arabic. The tradition abounds with examples that constitute what we might call a pre-history for the prose poem in Arabic, or better yet, a history in retrospect, history in the wake of the prose poems they are writing and are yet to write.

Notes

1. Muhammad Ahmad b. Tabataba, *ʿIyār al-shiʿr*, ed. ʿAbbād ʿAbd al-Sātir (Beirut: Dār al-Kutub al-ʿIlmiyyah, 1982), p. 14.
2. Ibn Jaʿfar, p. 17.
3. Al-ʿAskari, p. 196.
4. Ahmad b. al-Hasan al-Marzuqi, *Sharḥ dīwān al-Ḥamāsah*, ed. Aḥmad Amīn and ʿAbd al-Salām Hārūn, 4 vols. (Cairo: Lajnat al-Taʾlīf wa al-Tarjamah wa al-Nashr, 1968), vol. 1, p. 18.
5. Abu Hayyan al-Tawhidi, *Kitāb al-imtāʿ wa al-muʾānasah*, ed. Aḥmad Amīn and Aḥmad al-Zayn (Beirut: Dār Maktabat al-Ḥayāt, n.d.), vol. 2, p. 133.
6. Ibid. vol. 2, p. 145, translation by Klaus Hachmeier, 'Rating Adab: At-Tawhidi on the Merits of Poetry and Prose', *al-Qantara: Revista de Estudios Arabes*, 25.2 (2004), p. 381.
7. Shukrī Fayṣal, 'Editor's introduction', *Abū al-ʿAtāhiya: akhbāruhu wa-shiʿruhu* (Damascus: Maṭbaʿat Jāmiʿat Dimashq, 1965), p. 34.
8. ʿAbd al-Qāhir al-Jurjani, *Kitāb Dalāʾil al-iʿjāz*, ed. Maḥmūd Shākir (Cairo: Maktabat al-Khānjī, 1984), p. 474.
9. Ibid. p. 55.
10. K. Abu Deeb, 'al-D̲jurd̲jānī', *Encyclopedia of Islam*, Second Edition.
11. K. Abu Deeb, *Al-Jurjānī's Theory of Poetic Imagery* (Warminister: Aris and Phillips, 1979), p. 52.
12. For more on al-Jurjani's use of the terms '*lafẓ*', and '*maʿnā*' and '*ṣurat al-maʿnā*', see Lara Harb, 'Form, Content, and the Inimitability of the Qurʾān in ʿAbd al-Qāhir al-Jurjānī's Works', *Middle Eastern Literatures* 18.3 (2016), pp. 310–12.
13. G. E. Grunebaum, 'Iʿd̲jāz', *Encyclopedia of Islam*, Second Edition.
14. For example, see Abu Bakr Muhammad al-Baqillani, *Iʿjāz al-Qurʾān*, ed. Aḥmad Ṣaqr (Cairo: Dār al-Maʿārif, 1972), pp. 51–56 and pp. 57–65; al-Jurjani, *Dalāʾil al-iʿjāz*, p. 262.
15. Sophia Vasalou, 'The Miraculous Eloquence of the Qurʾān: General Trajectories and Individual Approaches', *Journal of Qurʾānic Studies* 4.2 (2002), pp. 23–53.
16. Adonis, *Dīwān al-nathr al-ʿarabī* (Jablah: Dār Bidāyāt, 2012), p. 9.

17. Adonis's preoccupation with Qurʾānic text and Qurʾānic language is evident in many of his poetic and critical works, most evident among these engagements is his book *al-Naṣṣ al-Qurʾānī wa-āfāq al-kitāba.* Unsi al-Hajj's engagement with biblical language is also clear. His translation of *The Song of Solomon* and his introduction to it are an important contribution to the debate around poetry and prose, the prose poem and its possibilities in Arabic. See Unsi al-Hajj, *Nashīd al-anāshīd* (Beirut: Dār al-Nahār, 1967).
18. Al-Niffari, *Kitāb al-Mawāqif wa-yalīhi Kitāb al-Mukhāṭabāt*, ed. Arthur Arberry (Cairo: Maktabat al-Mutanabbī, 1983), p. 75.
19. Also see Arberry's translation, ibid. pp. 81–82.
20. Ibid. p. 205.
21. Also see Arberry, ibid. p. 174.
22. Adonis, *Dīwān al-nathr al-ʿarabī.*
23. Ibid. vol. 2, p. 278.
24. Ibid. vol. 2, p. 293.
25. Adonis, *Siyāsat al-shiʿr: dirāsa fī al-shiʿriyya al-ʿarabiyya al-muʿāṣira* (Beirut: Dār al-Ādāb, 1985), p. 76.
26. 'Encumbering trifles' is a phrase that Van Gelder uses to describe modern critic's attitude towards al-Mutanabbi's short compositions. They pose a challenge especially in the oeuvre of a master of the *qaṣīda* such as al-Mutanabbi. Thus, they are often overlooked or dismissed. Although classical critics often focus on single lines in the treatise, a practice for which they have been criticised, nevertheless these one or two verses are often selected from the longer poems. In general, the short compositions are not the focus of study. A number of earlier Abbasid poets were fonder of and more skilled in the short composition than al-Mutanabbi. In the *dīwān*s of Ibn al-Rumi or Abu Tammam or al-Buhturi, the short compositions are seen as spaces where the poets step out of the ceremonials of the longer form and experiment. Ibn al-Mu'tazz, especially, is a master of the short composition. Nevertheless, the poems that make a poet's reputation remain are the long *qaṣīdas*. See G. J. H. Van Gelder, 'Al-Mutanabbī's Encumbering Trifles', *Arabic and Middle Eastern Literatures* 2.1 (1999), pp. 5–19.
27. Caws, 'Prose Poem', pp. 1112–13.
28. Jaroslav Stetkevych, *The Hunt in Arabic Poetry*, p. 44.
29. Ibid. p. 144.
30. N. Santilli, *Such Rare Citings: The Prose Poem in English Literature* (Madison: Fairleigh Dickinson University Press, 2002), p. 22.

31. Ibn Rashiq al-Qayrawani, *al-ʿUmda*, ed. Muhammad Muḥyi al-dīn ʻAbd al-Ḥamīd (Beirut: Dār al-Jīl, 1972), vol. 1, p. 187
32. Caws, p. 1112.
33. Santilli, p. 22.
34. Ibid.
35. al-Hajj, *al-Raʾs al-maqṭūʿ*, p. 83.
36. Salim Barakat, *Ṭaysh al-yāqūt* (Beirut: Dar al-Nahar, 1996), p. 93.
37. ʿAbdallah Ibn al-Muʿtazz, *Dīwān* (Beirut: Dār Sādir, 1961), p. 19.
38. Ibn al-Rumi, *Dīwān*, ed. Majīd Trād (Beirut: Dār al-jīl, 1998), vol. 1, p. 615.
39. Caws, p. 1112.
40. G. J. H. Van Gelder, 'Pointed and Well-Rounded: Arabic Encomiastic and Elegiac Epigrams', *Orientalia Lovaniensia Periodica* 26 (1995), pp. 101–40. Also see Adam Talib's study of the development of the Arabic classical short poem genre (*maqṭūʿ*) in the Mamluk era: *How Do You Say 'Epigram' in Arabic? Literary History at the Limits of Comparison* (Leiden: Brill, 2018).
41. Roger Allen, *The Arabic Literary Heritage: The Development of its Genre and Criticism* (London: Cambridge University Press, 1998), p. 123–25; G. J. H. Van Gelder, *Beyond the Line: Classical Arabic Literary Critics on the Coherence and Unity of the Poem* (Leiden: Brill, 1982), p. 66; Ibn Rashiq, vol. 1, pp. 186–89.
42. Ibn Rashiq, vol. 1, p. 187
43. Ibid.
44. Ibn Ṭabaṭaba, *ʿIyār al-shiʿr*, p. 11.
45. Ibid.
46. Ibid.
47. Ibid. p. 13
48. Van Gelder, *Beyond the Line*, p. 66.
49. Habīb b. Aws Abu Tammam, *Dīwān Abī Tammām*, ed. Muḥīyī al-dīn Ṣubḥī (Beirut: Dār Ṣādir, 1997), vol. 2, pp. 401–02.
50. Ibid.
51. Ibn al-Muʿtazz, p. 9.
52. For more on the idea of the thought-poem, see, Judith Balso's discussion of Wallace Stevens in her *The Affirmation of Poetry*, pp. 24–25.
53. Caws, p. 1113.
54. Nazem El-Sayed, *Manzil al-ukht al-ṣughrā (The Youngest Sister's House)* (Beirut: Riad El-Rayyes Books, 2010), p. 27.

55. Bassam Hajjar, *Sawfa taḥyā min ba'dī (You will Survive Me)* (Beirut: Al-Markaz al-'Arabī, 2001), p. 29.
56. Ibid. p. 168.
57. Ibid. p. 170.
58. Ibid. p. 172
59. Ibid. p. 176.
60. Ibid. p. 179.
61. al-Hajj, *al-Ra's al-maqṭū'*, p. 67.
62. Tsvetan Todorov, as quoted in Marjorie Perloff, *The Poetics of Indeterminacy*, p. 3.
63. Marjorie Perloff, *The Dance of the Intellect* (London: Cambridge University Press, 1985), p. 120.
64. Huda Fakhreddine, *Metapoesis in the Arabic Tradition: From Modernists to Muḥdathūn* (Leiden: Brill, 2015).
65. K. M. Newton, 'Roman Jakobson: The Dominant', *Twentieth Century Literary Theory: A Reader* (New York: St. Martin's Press, 1997), pp. 6–10.
66. Abu Tammam, vol. 2, p. 456.
67. Sa'adeh, *Laysa lil-masā' ikhwa*, p. 34.
68. Nazem El-Sayed, *Ard ma'zūla bil-nawm (A Land Isolated by Sleep)* (Beirut: Riad El-Rayyes Book, 2007), p. 69.

3

Adonis: Writing Where the World Begins and Begins Again

Adonis is probably one of the most representative figures of Arab Modernism. He is among the pioneers of the movement and its major theorisers. He is quoted whenever the question of tradition and modernism is posed. It is very easy to see him as an advocator of either side of the dichotomy. He is the avant-garde and the conservative at the same time, the experimentalist and the revisionist. He is one of the first poets to introduce the prose poem in Arabic and one of the first to criticise it as well.[1]

Scholars and critics of the modernist movement in Arabic poetry consider Adonis the representative of the move forward, away from the 'traditional' towards a more 'modern' and in many ways 'westernised' vision of poetry. However, when Adonis speaks of his cultural formation and the influences that shaped him as a poet, he turns back to his upbringing in classical Arabic poetry and the Qurʾān. Although he does mention his exposure to western works of literature, especially French, and western literary theories, these were instances of confusion most of the time. His engagement of western literary works and thought was always working alongside or against his grounded-ness in the Arabic literary and linguistic tradition. In his literary biography *Hā anta ayuhā al-waqt* (There you are, O Time!), he describes his experience at the University of Damascus as the beginning of change. The question which preoccupied him was: 'What do I read now?'[2] 'Al-Mutanabbi (Abū al-Ṭayyib al-Mutanabbī, d. 915), Abu Tammam, al-Sharif al-Radi (Muḥammad b. al-Ḥusayn al-Sharīf al-Raḍi, d. 1016), al-Buhturi (al-Walīd b. ʿUbaydallā al-Buḥturī, d. 897), al-Maʿarri (Abū al-ʿAlāʾ al-Maʿarrī, d. 1057) and tens of other Diwans and poetry collections especially Abu Tammam's *Ḥamāsa . . .*'[3] were the canon that Adonis brought with him to the university where it was to be shaken, altered and revised.

At Damascus University and due to his interaction with translated works and foreign languages, Adonis began to view the Arabic literary tradition from a distance. He states, 'tradition (*turāth*) seemed, through the methods and visions of teaching [at the university], an opposite, not to life alone but to humanity and progress altogether'.[4] By this token, he struggled to read in French, an experience which he describes as strenuous and frustrating,[5] but effective, nevertheless. A gap, or rather a distance was forming between him and the literary tradition that shaped him: a space for vision. However, there was a constant voice in his head that whispered, 'Hold on, resist and beware of falling into anything but yourself . . .'[6] This tension between an advent literary taste and a firmly grounded one is what led Adonis to a daring intervention and a guided shaking up (*khalkhala*) of models and ways of thinking and writing which may have seemed unshakable.

This chapter will trace Adonis's ventures in the prose poem from his early experimentations in *Qaṣā'id 'ūlā* (1957) and *Awrāq fī al-Rīḥ* (1958) to what I see as his seminal contribution, his book-long poem *Mufrad bi ṣīghat al-jam'* (1977) passing through major poetic stations in his career, including *Aghānī Mihyār al-Dimashqī* (1961). Before delving into key poems, I will trace a parallel thread of discovery through translation and anthologising which informed and expanded Adonis's vision of the prose poem as a framework for re-reading and creating. This second thread is represented in Adonis's discovery and translation of Saint-John Perse (1957) and his work as an anthologist in *Dīwān al-shi'r al-'arabī* (1964) and then the later *Dīwan al-nathr al-'arabī* (2012). The introduction to the latter serves as a post-script, as Adonis's final or most recent word on the prose poem debate.

Saint-John Perse: The Foreign Intercedes on Behalf of the Self

Adonis first entered the apprenticeship of the prose poem,[7] when he fell upon Saint-John Perse's *Amers* while visiting the offices of *al-Adīb* magazine in 1957. He recalls the profound and immediate effect Perse's poem had on him. 'I was immediately captivated by the text. I had the impression of reading something that arose from the deepest part of myself'.[8] He would soon after publish his translation of the ninth section of *Amers*, 'Étroits sont les vaisseaux' (*ḍayyiqatun hiya al-marākib*), in the 1957 fall of issue of *Shiʿr*.

This translation is Adonis's very first attempt at a prose poem. And Saint-John Perse's mark will remain visible in Adonis's later prose poem corpus. The Adonisian prose poem borrows the aesthetic of Perse's long meandering text, punctuated by shifts in tone and voice. It is a form gone astray (*shakl ḍillīl*), as Muḥammad Maẓlūm puts it,[9] producing a prose poem that deviates from all of Suzanne Bernard's stipulations, as well as those stipulations that Adonis himself and his contemporaries theorised in their manifestos. The prose poem that Adonis and those who followed in his steps went on to write is deeply marked by Perse's grand indeterminate structure.

Through translating Perse, Adonis found a conduit for instilling something new into the Arabic poem, something new and with authority. The translated French text was thus a site of Arabic self-discovery. The translation was not concerned with the French text, but rather with its effect and the consequences of introducing it in the target language. Thus, when errors in translation are pointed out to him, as often happens, Adonis, the translator, insists that his investment when translating is in 'the genius of the language of arrival rather than the laws of the language of departure'.[10] His proficiency in French (or English for that matter)[11] is thus beside the point. It is still his skill in agitating Arabic that really matters here.

Translation played a mediating role in the overall *Shiʿr* project, not between the self and the other, but rather between the self and the new altered self which was the aspiration of this modernist movement's quest of refusal and re-imagination. The foreign interceded on behalf of the Arab self. Creswell states that the introduction of a large corpus of translated poetry was not the *Shiʿr* poets' signal achievement. The achievement was in suggesting to their local audience through 'editorial and compositional methods' that, by reading certain foreign texts, they can reconnect with the depths of their historic identity and re-emerge different and renewed.[12]

This conception of translation sits at the heart of Creswell's definition of *Shiʿr's* poetic modernism. He sees the Arab (and especially the Beiruti) modernism materialise in translation (*naql*) where translation 'is not understood as a process of passive reception or linguistic transfer but rather as a historical act of preservation, displacement, and transformation'.[13] Displacement is the keyword here. The canon had to be shaken up, prodded so that it may shift and release its dynamic energies. The prose poem in Arabic is thus a genre created through translation, through this act of displacing and disfiguring, by which the modern French interrogates the Arabic canon and furthermore reconnects it with the farthest reaches of its Mediterranean and Near Eastern heritage.[14]

عبثاً ترسم لنا الأرض القريبة حدودها. موجة واحدة
من العالم، الموجة ذاتها منذ طروادة
تدحرج إلينا خاصرتها. بعيدا عنا في المدى الأرحب كان
هذا النفس، من قديم، مطبوعا.[15]

> En vain la terre proche nous trace sa frontière. Une même vague par le monde, une même vague depuis Troie
> Roule sa hanche jusqu'à nous. Au très grand large loin de nous fut imprimé jadis ce souffle …[16]

Adonis thus rides the surge of Saint-John Perse's poem which will connect him to the 'wave of the world, the one wave since Troy'. The displacement which occurs in Adonis's encounter with Perse and in his exercises in translation motivates and informs the altered or translated canon[17] he will create in his anthologies, his projects of 'internal translation'.[18]

A Tradition Framed: Adonis, the Curator

Like every true modernist, Adonis is preoccupied with the past, with the inheritance of the dead. Yet, his reading of that bequest is a transformative one. It is a co-optation and an enlisting of the past into his project for the present and the future. In 1964, Adonis embarked on a project of re-appropriating the Arabic poetic tradition by compiling his selections of poetry from the pre-Islamic era until the end of the nineteenth century in *Dīwān al-shiʿr al-ʿarabī*. This is not merely an anthology or a research project in literary history but a poet's attempt at personalising his tradition.[19] Any selection process, he insists in the introduction, 'no matter how it tries to make use of objective aesthetic values, remains personal and subject to thousands of fancies, conscious or unconscious, fixed or transient'.[20]

However, this revision of the Arabic poetic tradition was only made possible by a prior step away, which Adonis documents in *Hā anta ayuhā al-waqt* when he recounts his struggle to learn French and to read in languages other than Arabic.[21] The purpose of *Dīwān al-shiʿr al-ʿarabī* is thus not a return to the past as much as it is an invitation of the past into the present moment. Adonis's reading of the tradition is in fact a quest for a vision of what poetry should be and where it was heading. He criticises the manner in which the Arabic canon has been refracted in the lenses of mediators such as transmitters, commentators and critics. Without the mediation of secondary 'readings',[22] Adonis forges in *Dīwān al-shiʿr al-ʿarabī* his personal take on the Arabic poetic canon in the hope of revealing its previously silenced dynamic creative forces. In his counter-canon, as Creswell describes it,[23] Adonis selects whole poems or excerpted lines that speak to him personally and respond to what seemed to him pressing questions on poetry and poetics. He reorders lines and chooses the versions of lines he prefers, remaining loyal to nothing but his poetic taste[24] and his agenda to translate this inheritance into his project.

Forever pre-occupied with the potential of margins, Adonis presents in his major critical work *al-Thābit wa-l-mutaḥawwil* (The Fixed and the Dynamic) a vision of the manner in which the centre and margin of the Arabic literary tradition interact and propel each other forward. *Dīwān al-shiʿr al-ʿarabī* is *al-Thābit wa-l-mutaḥawwil* in practicum, a subversive alternate imagination and curation of the Arabic poetic tradition. In the margins towards which he steers us in *al-Thābit wa-l-mutaḥawwil*, many prose writings such as those by al-Kindi (Abū Yūsuf Yaʿqūb b. ʾIsḥāq al-Kindī, d. 873), al-Niffari and al-Tawhidi are signalled as springs of latent energy, as possible sites of eruption. It was therefore a matter of time before Adonis incorporated the eruptive energies of Arabic prose into his grand *Dīwān* project.

In 2012, he turned to the latent potentials of Arabic prose and compiled his *Dīwān al-nathr al-ʿarabī*. It is a reading of the Arabic prose tradition motivated by Adonis's prior poetic excursions into prose and his various critical interventions on behalf of its poetic powers. It is worth noting here that Adonis embarks on this project many years after the emergence of the prose poem as an abstraction in Arabic poetics. Thus, *Dīwān al-nathr al-ʿarabī* is to be received in the light of Adonis's involvement with the prose poem and its theoretical and practical unfolding in Arabic. And, this pre-occupation, the framing of prose into poetry, necessarily informs and shapes this translation of the Arabic prose tradition, as discussed in Chapter 2.

In the introduction to *Dīwān al-nathr al-ʿarabī*, Adonis offers a clear statement on the achievements and possibilities of the Arabic prose poem as a reading lens or framework – a statement possibly more succinct and balanced than his previous manifestos and declarations on the topic. I will pause at some of the major points that he raises in the introduction and use it as an entry point to reading a thread of poems leading up to *Mufrad bi-ṣīghat al-jamʿ*, his major contribution to the prose poem project in Arabic.

In *Dīwān al-nathr al-ʿarabī*, Adonis frames his selections from Arabic prose as poetry, as evident in the examples discussed in Chapter 2. He collects them in a *dīwān*[25] and lays them out on the page, sometimes lineated, sometimes not, thus successfully implanting the notion of 'poem' in the reader's mind. Arabic prose, in its aesthetic possibilities, remains an 'unexplored continent', he announces. For, due to the hegemony of verse in the Arabic tradition, we often fail to recognise some of the most innovative breakthroughs that occurred in prose, poetic innovations sometimes more complex and difficult than the ones in verse.[26] In his argument for the need to rediscover the aesthetics of Arabic prose, and especially *Ṣūfī* prose, Adonis invites us to view the literary tradition as a tradition of 'artistic creativity'. Once creativity is set as standard, tradition is transformed from something established to something in process. And thus, the binary of old and new, past and later, is disrupted, and the tradition ceases to be an anchor and becomes a springboard, a perpetual starting point.[27] The 'creators of the poetic' whom Adonis has in mind here are all prose writers, rebels, who set out in search of the secret recipe of 'the poetic' in the open territory of prose:

> *Ṣūfī* prose is a linguistic explosion in Arabic writing. It has a chemistry that leads to the innovation of forms of expression unavailable in poetry. It is a chemistry that makes prose a space infinitely open unto unknown things and forms.[28]

The 'chemistry of prose' is prose's unruly and unexpected potential for releasing previously unknown forms. In *Dīwān al-nathr al-ʿarabī*, Adonis aims to unlock that chemistry and enlist the Arabic prose tradition as a partner in the realm of the poetic.[29]

Consequently, he sees the emergence of the prose poem, with all of its seeming contradiction and tension, as inevitable. He claims that prosody (*ʿarūḍ*), which had been established as a definer of poetry in Arabic, is only an after-thought, a consequence of the poetic, not an engenderer of it. Metrics, and any set form for that matter, cannot possibly contain poetry, for limits in poetry are but an invitation for transgression. Poetry's temptation to overwhelm its forms is great. Adonis admits that it is only natural for a poetic tradition, especially one that is formally inclined like Arabic, to eventually become frustrated with its established forms.[30] Poetry built with prose, unruly unexpected and flowing prose, is nothing but the expected overflow of poetry outside set boundaries, in search for forms that sprout in its wake.

The prose tradition that Adonis showcases in this project is prose with the potential of expanding the parameters of both poetry and prose together. It invites us to return to the 'purely Arabic' notion of 'composition' (*inshāʾ*), of building and structuring with the Arabic language.[31] The *nathr* (prose) of the *Dīwān al-nathr al-ʿarabī* is the *nathr* with which poetry (*shiʿr*) and the poetic (*al-shiʿrī*) are made. This is not prose, the counter of poetry,[32] but it is an 'other' prose (*nathr ākhar*) whose aesthetic horizons remain unexplored. And 'if some assert that it is not poetry, then we can similarly assert that it is not just prose. It is a new kind or genre of writing/composition (*nawʿ kitābī jadīd*)'.[33]

However, the practitioners of the prose poem in Arabic are not content with merely calling it a new kind. They insist that their texts are not just texts or writings but poems. Their claim to the term poem (*qaṣīda*) is an insistence on belonging, even if forcefully, to a tradition of poetry-making (more specifically *qaṣīda*-making) in Arabic, and at the same time a deliberate expanding and redefining of what a poem (*qaṣīda*) in Arabic is or can be.

'Poetry is form and the poem, no matter how it strives to free itself from restrictions, is ultimately formation and structure. Isn't the prose poem then a call for form-less-ness and hence at odds with the very notion of poem?'[34] Adonis's response to this question which he poses to himself is simple: Language. 'Poetic composition', he states, 'is a perpetual reformulation of what lies within it, not outside it'. By that he suggests that language, whether in form or not, is always formulation and structure in itself. Language always thinks in form. The 'poetic' lies in the 'fissures and explosions' which transform language into a new composition or structuring every time.[35]

New Poetry and the Horizon of Meaning

Modernism, as Adonis understands it, is a drastic reimagining and reordering of the world.[36] Poetry is a continuous violation of rules and a transgression of limits; it is a change in the order of things, in the order of viewing things.[37] As a result, the issue of meter and rhyme which is foregrounded in most of the discussions of modern poetry in the Arab world becomes secondary. Without a revolution in poetry as vision, there is nothing new. Adonis decisively resolves the on-going debate over what is new and what is not in poetry, by strictly reducing the issue of verse and prose to a minor detail. He states:

> To recognize the newness of a poem, it is not enough to examine its structural surface: for example, if it were metered, we'd say it is 'old' and if it were in prose, we'd say it is 'new' or 'modern'. On the contrary, it is inevitable to closely consider the structure of that verse and its poetic language. Similarly, it is necessary to consider the structure of that prose and its poetic language. Only then will we discover that what we had thought of as modern is truly old and what we had thought of as old is truly modern or new.[38]

Adonis continues to explain the change brought about by the modernist project on the level of meter and rhyme, but he eventually admits that poetically speaking these changes are meaningless.[39] Many prose poems, he claims, can be described as old and traditional because they fail to present anything new on the level of the image or the vision, whereas many pre-Islamic poems can prove to be more 'modern' in their vision than poems written in the second half of the twentieth century.

As he makes his way towards legitimising the prose poem as poetry in Arabic, Adonis establishes the superfluous-ness of meter in creating the poetic. He however supports it with the quotation, not from the translated French and English poetry and theory introduced by *Shiʿr*, but by a quotation from 'Abd al-Qāhir al-Jurjani's *Dalāʾil al- iʿjāz*:

> Meter has no role in determining eloquence and rhetoric. If it has, then every two poems written on the same meter should be equally eloquent [. . .] Meter is not what gives speech its artistic value.[40]

The inseparable relationship of form (*lafẓ*) and meaning (*maʿnā*) established by al-Jurjani proves Adonis's point that modernism cannot be achieved through a profound intervention on the level of meter and form without one on the level of meaning and vision. Implicating al-Jurjani as such is a modernist act of displacement and internal translation. Adonis is not merely introducing a 'new' idea that challenges the standard Arabic definition of poetry as 'metered speech', but he is embedding it deep into the tradition. He is allowing the prose poem to become Arabic and the whole of the Arabic tradition to be read through the lens of the prose poem, as he shows us in the *Dīwān al-nathr al-ʿarabī*.

Adonis's first prose poem '*Waḥdahu al-ya's*' (Despair Alone), written on the coattails of his translation of Perse's 'Étroits sont les vaisseaux', appeared in the 1958 fall issue of *Shiʿr*. However, before that, in his first collection *Qaṣāʾid ʿūlā* (1957), Adonis exhibits a preoccupation with creating 'fissures and explosions' in language. Although these explosions remain contained in form (*qaṣīdat al-tafʿīla*), they pave the way for a more dramatic and comprehensive shattering of the ready-made mould, which was to follow. *Qaṣāʾid ʿūlā* contains short rhymed and metered pieces in which he demonstrated his idea of poetic language as the forging of new connections. Most of the pieces aim at innovating new dimensions of thought through imagery. For example, in a poem titled '*al-Thāʾir*' (The Revolutionary), the image of the wound, which is relatively common especially in nationalist poetry that often celebrates heroic sacrifice and martyrdom, is given a new twist:

كل جرحٍ
هو في آفاقنا طلة صبحٍ.[41]

Every wound
Is on our horizon a break of morning.

Similarly, in the same poem, the sunrise is described as sin:

في بلادي تشرق الشمس المضيئة
كالخطيئة.[42]

In my country the glowing sun rises
like sin.

The associations of the wound with the break of morning and the sun with sin invite a shedding of established associations with the sun and sunrise, triggering a reconsideration of all parts of the metaphor. With an unexpected formulation of phrases, a new dimension of meaning is engendered. A representative example of that in *Qaṣā'id 'ūlā* is the following short poem titled 'Mashrūʿ li-taghyīr al-ashyā'' (A Project for Changing Things).

أمسِ، فأره
حفرت في رأسيَ الضائع حفره،

ربما ترغب أن تسكنَ فيهِ
ربما تطمح أن تملك فيهِ
كل تيهِ

ربما ترغب أن تصبح فكره...[43]

Yesterday a mouse
dug in my confused head a hole.

Maybe it wants to settle in it,
maybe it seeks to possess
all deserts in it,

maybe it wants to become a thought.

Here, Adonis does not merely compare a thought to a mouse, but rather shows us the metaphor unfold. The mouse seeks and aspires (*targhab, taṭmaḥ*) to become a thought. By digging, settling and occupying, a thought materialises and becomes aware of itself as a thought. The key-word in this piece is *ḍā'i'* (absent, lost), describing the head, the stage or landscape of the thought's emergence. It resonates with the later *tīh* (desert, wasteland). This burrowing into the scattered and wandering head, settling in it and desiring to orchestrate its unruliness is how a thought takes hold of the mind. This is also how a new thought emerges from a familiar exhausted language and rejuvenates it. Here, in this digging into 'the body of language',[44] its layers, its connections and associations, is the key to the poetic in Adonis's view.

His second collection, *Awrāq fī al-rīḥ*, came out in 1958 and included a slightly revised version of '*Waḥdahu al-ya's*' (Only Despair) which had appeared earlier in *Shi'r*.[45] This same poem will appear in a final, more substantially revised version in *Aghānī Mihyār al-Dimashqī* in 1961, this time titled 'Marthiyyat al-ayyām al-ḥāḍira' (Elegy for the Present Days). Thus, Adonis finds his prose poem through a process of translation, revision, editing and rewriting. 'Only Despair' and the other early experiments become sites of experimentation, re-writing and excavation. They will re-emerge in a new form or rather remain in transformation.

In *Aghānī Mihyār* and *Mufrad bi-ṣīghat al-jam'*, he goes on to show us how language invents the poetic over and over. However, in these two projects, pursuing the 'poetic' in the 'fissures and explosions' of language has dramatic ramifications on form. From *Aghānī* to *Mufrad*, Adonis gradually traces, not the disintegration of poetic form from verse into prose, but rather charts the emergence of poetic composition (*kitāba*) and arrives at form as a consequence of language, away from the binary of verse and prose.[46]

Language New in the Songs of *Mihyār*

Published in 1961, *Aghānī Mihyār al-Dimashqī*[47] consists of seven parts. The first six parts are structured similarly. Each one has a separate title and begins with a prose-passage labelled Psalm (*mazmūr*), which is then followed by a number of short poems, all metered on the *taf'īla* system. Each one of these six parts[48] presents a side or dimension of the persona, Mihyār. The prose psalm presents a general state or characteristic of Mihyār which is then re-presented in the verse passages that follow.

Aghānī Mihyār is not a 'narrative with a central hero' as it might seem, but a series of 'turns and returns',[49] as Creswell describes it while charting ruptures, fissures, binaries in voice, attitude, cadence, language and mood.

Thus, the collection charts the binary of verse and prose, keeping it at the forefront of the reader's consciousness, tauntingly inviting the reader to question limits and dividing lines. What solicits further meditation here is this *other* prose we find ourselves juxtaposing with 'poetry'. This is exacerbated by the fact that the word 'psalm' does not merely indicate prose. It rather conjures up a model of prose which intentionally courts the poetic and the musical and challenges prose out of its association with the straightforward and the functional, bringing it into the realm of the unexpected, the uncharted and the potentially magical.

The psalms, in the first six parts of the book, serve as entries into the subsequent sections which are more decidedly poems. However, the psalms are intense, rhythmic and therefore 'poetically charged' in their language, sometimes more than the subsequent pieces contained in form. For example, the Psalm titled 'The Magician of Dust' opens as follows:

> أحمل هاويتي وأمشي. أطمس الدروب التي تتناهى، أفتح الدروب الطويلة كالهواء والتراب –
> خالقاً من خطواتي أعداءً لي، أعداءً في مستواي، ووسادتي الهاوية والخرائب شفيعتي.
> إنني الموت، حقاً.[50]

> I carry my abyss and I walk. I erase the lapsing paths and I open pathways long like the air and the soil. Of my steps I create enemies of mine enemies that are my equals. My pillow is the abyss, and the ruins are my intercessors. I am death, truly.

This opening paragraph is representative of the movement of the whole piece. It alternates between short compact phrases followed by longer drawn-out sentences which expand on the phrases without diluting their intensity. The psalms thus read as if in ebb and flow, a holding back and packing in then followed by a release and an opening up:

إنني نبي وشكّاك.
أعجن خميرة السقوط، أترك الماضي في سقوطه وأختار نفسي. أفلطح العصر وأصفّحه، أناديه – أيها العملاق المسخ أيها المسخ العملاق وأضحك وأبكي.
إنني حجة ضد العصر.
أمحو الآثار والبقع في داخلي. أغسل داخلي وأبقيه فارغاً ونظيفاً. هكذا تحت نفسي أحيا.[51]

I am a prophet and a cynic.
I knead the yeast of fall. I abandon the past in its fall and choose myself. I flatten the age and layer it. I call it to – You giant troll! You troll giant! and I laugh and cry.
I am proof against the age.
I erase traces and stains inside me. I wash my inside and leave it empty and clean. That is how, underneath myself, I live.

'*Aslamtu ayyāmī*' (I've Surrendered my Days), a poem that follows in this section, elaborates on the notions of the abyss (*hāwiya*) and death (*mawt*) present in the psalm. The poem is meticulously measured, contained in strict form. The meter is *al-kāmil* and Adonis exactly adheres to the metrical pattern of *majzū' al-kāmil* (*mutafā'ilun, mutafā'ilun, fā'ilun*). If we were to rearrange the piece on the page, it would become a classical Arabic poem made up of seven two-hemistich verses. The opening lines of this poem are as follows:

أسلمت أيامي لهاوية
تعلو وتهبط تحت مركبتي
وحفرت في عينيَّ مقبرتي.
أنا سيد الأشباح أمنحها
جنسي وأمس منحتها لغتي
...
الشمس قبرة رميت لها
أنشوطتي والريح قبعتي.[52]

(أسلمت أيامي لهاوية تعلو وتهبط تحت مركبتي
...
أنا سيد الأشباح أمنحها جنسي وأمس منحتها لغتي
...
الشمس قبرة رميت لها أنشوطتي والريح قبعتي)

I have surrendered my days to an abyss
that rises and falls beneath my carriage.
I have dug my grave in my eyes.
I am the lord of ghosts, I bestow my species
upon them and yesterday I gave them my language.
…
The sun is a lark to which I threw
my noose, and the wind is my hat.

Reading these two samples against each other, the measured and anticipated music of the verse piece contrasts the dynamic, playful and unexpected rhythm that emerges in the prose. Adonis here lures his reader into a reconsideration of poetry (*al-shiʿr*) and the poetic (*al-shiʿrī*), and he exposes both form and music as consequences of language and its structures.

The experiment of *Aghānī Mihyār* is a deliberate and motivated exposition of the dichotomy of verse and prose as a set-up against which the poetic is then discovered on both sides of the binary, housed in language and in the manner with which its processes are deliberate (*tawakhkhī*) and formulated (*bināʾ*). For example, the disruption of syntax, whether in the prose or verse pieces, has the same effect and is what makes the language in both cases 'new'. In the Psalm titled 'The Knight of Strange Words', Mihyār is described as follows:

يقبل أعزل كالغابة وكالغيم لا يردُّ، أمس حمل قارة ونقل البحر من مكانه.
يرسم قفا النهار، يصنع من قدميه نهاراً ويستعير حذاء الليل ثم ينتظر ما لا يأتي. إنه فيزياء الأشياء –
يعرفها ويسميها بأسماء لا يبوح بها. إنه الواقع ونقيضه، والحياة وغيرها.[53]

He approaches unarmed like the forest, and like the clouds, he cannot be repelled. Yesterday, he carried a continent and moved the sea. He draws the backside of the day; he creates a day from his feet. He borrows the shoe of the night and waits for that which will not come. He is the physics of things. He knows them and names them with names that he does not reveal. He is reality and its opposite. He is life and its other.

The inverted position of the adjectives with respect to the nouns to which they are related is effective because in both cases it places much more emphasis on the adjectives that Mihyār is being described with. Instead of saying 'he approaches unarmed like the forest and un-repelled like the clouds' or 'he approaches like the forest unarmed and like the cloud un-repelled', he chose to say: 'He approaches unarmed like the forest and like the cloud un-repelled'. The disrupting of the parallelism has a de-familiarising effect which places more emphasis on the adjectives that are the points of disruption. The emphasis placed on the adjectives also directs more attention to the strange metaphors that are being made here.

In the poem 'New Testament', Mihyār is described as a monk 'with stony drowsiness/ burdened by distant languages'.

يجهل أن يتكلم هذا الكلامْ
يجهل صوت البراري،
إنه كاهن حجريٌّ النعاسْ
إنه مثقل باللغات البعيده.[54]

He knows not how to speak such speech,
ignorant of the sound of the wilderness.
He is a soothsayer of stony drowsiness,
burdened by distant languages.

The striking image of stony drowsiness is an example of the new horizon of meaning Adonis forever strives to create. The association of stone with drowsiness is unexpected but very effective. Stone here could be a representative of the state of complete indifference, complete detachment and aloofness. When the adjective stony (*ḥajarī*) is used to describe drowsiness, it adds to the boredom and fatigue, a heaviness that is ultimate and inescapable. Mihyār is a language still becoming, heralding the distant, the strange and disruptive.

إنه لغة تتموج بين الصواري
إنه فارس الكلمات الغريبه.[55]

He is a language quivering among the masts
He is the knight of strange words.

Adonis's theory is most potent when embedded in his poetic praxis. *Aghānī Mihyār* is a resounding poetic statement. Many of the claims and anxieties of Arab modernist thought and experience are woven into the poems of the collection. Creswell finds in the last poem of part six 'Nūḥ al-jadīd' a daring rewriting of the biblical and Qurʾānic myth of Noah, as well as a statement on the modernist poet's role as the preserver and the rejector of the old, the voyager and the shaper of the new world, the translator, the agent of destruction and continuity.[56]

The seventh and final part of the books is structured in a different way. It is titled *al-Mawt al-muʿād* (The Repeated Death), and it consists of nine elegies (*marāthī*). Four of these elegies are dedicated to significant literary and historical figures from tradition. Again, Adonis chooses these figures for a reason which propagates his on-going implication and re-appropriation of tradition.[57] This last part does not begin with a prose psalm; however, in the last two of the elegies, '*Marthiyyat al-ayyām al-ḥāḍira*' (Elegy for the Present Days) and '*Marthiyat al-qarn al-awwal*' (Elegy for the First Century), Adonis breaks the binary of verse and prose with which he had flirted up to that point in the collection. In the last two pieces he shifts from metered verse to prose in the same poem. Thus, he allows the same text to house both the measured and the unruly.

عربات النفيْ
تجتاز الأسوارْ
بين غناء النفيْ
وزفير النارْ
آه الأشعار
رحلتْ مع عربات النفيْ.

الريح ثقيلة علينا ورماد أيامنا على الأرض.
نلمح روحنا في بريق شفرة أو على طرف خوذة، وخريف الممالح يتناثر فوق جراحنا
وما من شجرة أو نبع.[58]

The caravans of exile
cross the walls
through the songs of exile
and the exhale of fire

O poetry
has departed with the caravans of exile.

The wind is heavy upon us and the ashes of our days are on the ground.
We glimpse our soul in the gleam of a blade or on the ridge of a helmet.
The briny autumn gusts over our wounds. There is no tree, no spring.

In *Aghānī Miyhār*, Adonis charts the road to poetic composition and maps it both in form and outside of form. He traces the coming out (*khurūj*) and the sprouting poetry in the soil of this *other* prose; prose with 'chemistry' and 'magic'.[59] This is how *Aghānī Miyhār* guides us towards and prepared us for *Mufrad bi-sīghat al-jam*ʿ, a long prose poem in which Adonis 'explodes' language and orchestrates the resulting chaos into poetry.

Adonis's Prose Poem: Singular in Plural Form

*Mufrad bi-ṣīghat al-jam*ʿ was first published in 1977. Adonis continued to edit it and revised it until 1988, finally publishing a version subtitled *ṣīyāgha nihāʾiyya* (A Final Formulation). The title, the revisions and the subtitle of the final version, all hint at this work's preoccupation with the notion of poetry in its most abstract sense. The finality of the 1988 formulation is tentative; in fact, the claim of it being a final rendition is an emphasis on the impossibility of finality with a text such as this. There could be no *ṣīyāgha nihāʾiyya* (final formulation) for a *Mufrad bi-ṣīghat al-jam*ʿ (Singular in Plural Form). This text and every reading of it is an on-going disclosure (*hatk*), opening (*fatḥ*) and shaking up (*khalkhala*)[60] of our expectations. After having dislodged Arabic poetry from its rootedness in verse (meter and rhyme) in previous experiments, Adonis presents us with a poem, an exposition of poetry in its plurality, in all of its proliferations.

If *Aghānī Mihyār* is the starting point of the journey towards *Mufrad*, *Dīwān al-Shiʿr al-ʿArabī* (1964–68), Adonis's major revision of the Arabic canon, as well as his critical study *al-Thābit wa al-Mutaḥawwil* (1974) are stations on that road. The energies garnered through revising the Arabic poetic canon and personalising it in *Dīwān al-shiʿr* and then theorising the intense relationship between centre and margin, the fixed and the dynamic in *al-Thābit*, manifest themselves in *Mufrad bi-sīghat al-jam*ʿ as a poem of *khurūj,* of transgression, overstepping boundaries and coming out into a space open unto all possibilities.

1. The Body of Language

The poem is comprised of four sections: 'Genesis' (*takwīn*), 'Body' (*jasad*), 'History' (*tārīkh*) and 'Semiology' (*sīmyā'*). The four main sections vary in length and layout. Each is divided into subsections, some titled and some numbered. Genesis begins with a sub-section titled 'mappings' (*takhṭīṭat*) which opens as follows:

لم تكن الأرض جسداً   كانت جرحاً
كيف يمكن السفر بين الجسد والجرح
كيف تمكن الإقامة؟
أخذ الجرح يتحول إلى أبوين والسؤال يصير فضاءً
أخرج إلى الفضاء أيها الطفل
خرج علي
يستصحب
شمس البهلول   دفتر أخبارٍ   تاريخاً سريا: للموت[61]

The earth was not a body   it was a wound
How is it possible to travel between body and wound?
How is it possible to settle?
The wound began to transform into parents and the question turn into a space
Come out into the open, Child.

'Ali went out
accompanied by
The Buhlūl's sun, a notebook of accounts, a secret history of death.

This opening of the poem is expansive in its mood and provocative in its tone, representative of the text in its entirety. From the very first line, the poem announces its landscape as the body of language. The word *jasad* (body) is immediately associated with language in Adonis's discourse and the wound with writing; a specific mode of writing that aims to penetrate, to expose and to re-imagine anew. *Mufrad* opens with a negation of the language as a final body and an opening up, a probing of it as a wound.

The negation of finality very soon transforms into an incitement to wound, disturb and penetrate the surface of things. ‘Come out into space, Child’. The open space (*faḍāʾ*) which the child, ʿAlī, is invited into is a product of questioning, ‘The wound began to turn into parents and the question into a space’. ʿAlī is urged to set out on the journey of this monumental poem, a journey in language from body to wound and back, from the fixed to the dynamic and back. After such a journey, settling is no longer possible, and language is left open unto an infinity of ‘forms and images’. As ʿAlī grows and journeys in this poem, the map of the journey and the form of the poem are revealed in his wake. Earth and body are language. The open landscape which sprawls in all directions and all dimensions,[62] temporal and spatial, is altogether Adonis’s meditation on form (*shakl*) which language begets in its private exultations and its unanticipated thinking processes:

باسم جسدي الميت - الحي   الحي - الميت
ليس لجسدي شكل
لجسدي أشكال بعدد مسامه
وأنا لا أنا
وأنتِ لا أنتِ
نصحح لفظنا ولسنانينا
ونبتكر ألفاظاً لها أحجام اللسان والشفتين،
الحنك
أوائل الحنجرة
ويدخل جسدانا في سديم دَغَلٍ وأعراس
ينهدمان
ينبنيان
في
لجة
احتفال
بلا شكل ←
بطيئاً   سريعاً
نحو ما سميناه الحياة
وكان فاتحة للموت.[63]

In the name of my body the dead- the living   the living-the dead
        My body has no form
        My body has as many forms as pores
And I am not I
And you not you
    We rectify our speech and our tongues
    We innovate utterances in the sizes of the tongue and lips
        the palate
        the beginnings of the throat
and our two bodies enter the haze of a jungle and weddings
    they are destroyed
    they are built
    in the tumult
    of a celebration
    without form →
        slowly   quickly
        towards what we have called life
        and was the beginning of death.

Channelling the Abu Tammamian 'You are not you',[64] Adonis transforms the negation into a proliferation. The 'I' and 'you' are singulars exploded into a plurality of possibilities. Their singular shared speech (*lafdhanā*) by their two tongues (*lisānaynā*) proliferates into plural 'utterances in the sizes of the tongue and lips'. The design of this text is an exponential burgeoning, an organic growth of a body, dead and living, living and dead. It is a body, not formless, but harbouring all forms as it is broken and reformulated. Writing thus becomes a surrender, a rejoicing in language's expansive body, its layered-ness, its contradictions and its elusiveness:

لا أكتب
    أتناسل في غبطة جديدة
    هي غبطة أن أعرف حين لا أعرف
لا أكتب
    أختبرك أيها الجسد
    الاحتمال، الظلّ

الظاهر، ما يلوح، الأرجح
الهيئة
المسطّح عمقياً"[65]

I do not write
I procreate in new felicity
The felicity of knowing when I do not know
I do not write
I experience you, O body
the probability, the shadow
the manifest, what looms, the probable
the shape
the flattened in the depth …

'Flattened deeply' (*musaṭṭaḥ 'umqiyyan*) is an apt way of describing the sprawling form of this text. It is an expansive text with depth; as it spreads out, its surface remains dense. The sections and subsections proliferate and unfold from each other, as if the text perpetually expands and grows out of itself. Connections are made, signalled and intuited, in all directions and on all planes. There are arrows, equations marks, worlds in bold font and a seemingly meticulous layout. All these do not necessarily have a specific meaning which require deciphering as much as they are a representation of the endless possibilities of meaning in this text. The ebb and flow of long and short lines we see in the psalms of *Mihyār* is intensified in *Mufrad*'s scrupulous indentations and line arrangements. The edges of the text on both sides are staggered and in motion, adding yet another layer of signs. It is a structure built on beginnings, interruptions and shifts.

2. Beginning and Beginning Again

True to the spirit of opening, rupture and coming out, *Mufrad* is a series of beginnings. The first three sections begin with variation on the three lines cited above.

The earth was not a body   it was a wound
How is it possible to travel between body and wound?
How is it possible to settle?

The wound began to transform into parents and the question turn into a
space
Come out into the open, Child.

'Ali went out
accompanied by
the Buhlūl's sun, a notebook of account, and a secret history of death.[66]

The three lines are repeated with slight but significant variations. They are lineated differently, suggesting a different reading every time and disclosing the potential of latent other formulations. The keying of silence, emphasis, phraseology and line breaks in every rendition is an invitation to consider what makes the poetic in the text, as well as in its reading, performance and impact.

The layout on the page and the lineation of this supposedly 'form-less' text are deliberate, guiding the reader's attention, with indentation, to the beginnings of lines instead of the usual endings, the seats of rhyme. The poem appears to advance and retreat in the right margin of the page, as if in preparation for an imminent clash or an explosion.

Lines 2 and 3 are two questions indented, moved away from the right margin, allowing a visual continuity between lines 1 and 4. The indented lines, thus, function as asides or interjections, signalling a multiplicity of voices and tones from the very threshold of the poem. In addition to line breaks and indentations, Adonis cues our reading of the first three lines by inserting spaces in the middle of the line, an unusual practice in an Arabic text. These blanks are more effective and disruptive than punctuation. They de-familiarise the line as a unit. The first line is thus broken into two utterances which are emphatically juxtaposed and contrasted by the inserted space.

The wound which transforms into a question in 'Genesis' transforms into a homeland in 'History':

لم تكن الأرض جسداً   كانت جرحاً   كيف يمكن السفر
بين الجسد والجرح كيف تمكن الإقامة؟
أخذ الجرح يتحوّل إلى وطن والسؤال يصير تاريخاً
← اخرج أيها الطفل [67]

The earth was not a body   it was a wound   how is travel possible
between the body and the wound how is settling possible?
The wound began to transform into a homeland and the questions
into a history

Come out O child →

In 'Body', the opening is chopped up into shorter lines:

لم تكن الأرض جرحاً
كانت جسداً   كيف يمكن السفر بين الجرح
والجسد
كيف تمكن الإقامة؟

أيها الأطباء العطارون السحرة المنجمون
يا قرّاء الغيب
ها أنا أمتهن أسراركم
أتحول إلى نعامة = أزدرد جمر الفجيعة
وأهضم صوّان القتل 68

The earth was not a wound
It was a body   how is it possible to travel between the wound
and the body
how is settling possible?

You physicians apothecaries magicians astrologers
Readers of the unknown
Here I am exercising your secrets
transforming into an ostrich = swallowing the embers of calamity
and digesting the flint of murder

In this third iteration, the phrase 'between the body and the wound' is reversed into 'between the wound and a body', suggesting a movement in a different direction now, a return. The negation which opens the entire text, 'the earth was not a body', is affirmed here, 'it was a body'. The lineation in the opening's third iteration highlights the word body, lining up the repetitions of the word on the page, stacking them on top of each other. Then 'the readers of the unseen' are introduced (physicians apothecaries magician astrologers). The body and its readers (the physicians) are grouped with the diviners of the unseen (*al-ghayb*). The body is thus revealed yet again as a language, as a surface to be deciphered and excavated.

The unfolding variants of the opening in the first three sections gesture towards a heuristic for reading each section and, ultimately, for navigating *Mufrad bi ṣīghat al-jamʿ*. The fourth section, 'Semiology', breaks the chain of variations and opens with something new:

سيري أيتها الحقول، بخطوات من القشّ
اخلعْ قميصك أيها الجبل
الضوء يعبر وتعبر حشراته
الأدغال تعبر
وتعبر خواصر التلال

وأنا
مكسوّا بالزمن ورماده
يرميني الشجر من نوافذه
يتلقّفني فضاء تسيّجه أفخاذ غير مرئيّة
بين أمواج من الثمر أبحث فيها عن برعم التيه
حيث ترفعني صارية اللّذة وتختلط الصخور بالأشرعة
حيث الجسد سرداب والشهوة قلعة محاصرة
وأقول: سيكون فضاؤنا وحشاً أخضر
لكن،
أيها الحب المقبل – الجسد المقبل
أين أُسكنكَ
وماذا أستطيع أن أمنحك
غير ذاكرة الفراشات؟ [69]

Proceed, O fields, with straw steps
Take off your shirt, O mountain
The light passes and its insects pass
The jungles pass
and the hips of the hills
And I,
cloaked in time and its ashes,
am tossed by trees from their windows
am caught in a space fenced by invisible thighs
in waves of fruit I search for the bud of wilderness

where the mast of pleasure raises me and the rocks mingle with sails
where the body is a tunnel and lust a besieged citadel
I say: our space shall be a green monster
but,
O future love – future body
where should I dwell in you
what can I give you
but the memory of butterflies?

Aptly, 'Semiology' breaks from the repeated paradigm of openings and sets up new signs. The imperative 'proceed' and 'take off' and the repeated verb 'pass' all create a clearing, an arrival of some sorts in a new landscape still taking shape, hinted at by the future tense in 'Our space shall be a green monster' and the future love and body anticipated at the end of this section.

However, in section 5 of 'Semiology' we encounter the opening refrain of the poem once again, this time delayed and adjusted to make a statement about language and language re-imagined:

لم تكن الأرض جرحاً
كانت جسدا
كيف يمكن السفر بين الجرح والجسد،
كيف تمكن الإقامة؟

أخذ الجرح يتحول إلى كلمات
والجسد يصير سؤالا ←
.. وانكسرت عشبة طلعت من ساقها فراشة
طلع من رأسها برعم بلون الشهوة[70]

The earth was not a wound
It was a body
How is it possible to travel between wound and body
How is it possible to settle?

The wound began to transform into words
And the body to become a question →

..and a blade of grass broke, from which a butterfly emerged
from whose head a bud the colour of lust emerged

The wound which morphs into a question, then a homeland, then a probing of the unseen, 'transforms into words' in the final section of the poem.

3. Anchoring the Expanse

As already mentioned above, the poem consists of four sections – Genesis (*takwīn*), Body (*jasad*), History (*tārīkh*) and Semiology (*sīmyā'*) – varying in length and layout and divided into subsections, some titled and some numbered. In the opening section quoted above, Adonis provides a legend for navigating this overwhelmingly expansive text. The two anchoring elements are highlighted in bold type. The first is ʿAlī, and the other is the list of three things that accompany ʿAlī on his journey: the Buhlūl's[71] sun, a notebook of accounts and a secret history of death.

a. ʿAlī

ʿAlī, the child, is a persona fashioned on Adonis's biography. He turns his autobiography into a thread around which he allows the splinters of civilisation, history, language and tradition to hover. Real places and events punctuate the text and ground the poem's voice which alternates, for the most part, between address in the second person and declarations in the first person, garnering the energy of the apostrophe to propel it forward.

Two geographical spots anchor the poem: Qaṣṣābīn, Adonis's village of origin in Syria, and Mount Ṣannīn in Lebanon. From Qaṣṣābīn to Ṣannīn, 'the arc of a lifetime is drawn'[72] from birth, the first wound, to the history of that wound, where it transforms into thought and language. The personal history is scaffolding for a communal, collective and even universal history, as it is etched and carved out in language. Adonis re-imagines important stations in his life using the language of rupture and opening. Here he is remembering his mother and the beginnings of language:

لم تكن أمّه تعرف اللغة، وهي التي علمته الكلام حين جرى الكلام بين شفتيه التهب مكان...
الحنين
وخرجت الشهوة من أصابعه [73]

> . . . His mother did not know the language, but it was she who taught him speech.
> When speech flowed between his lips, the place of longing blazed and lust sprung out of his fingers

And here he portrays his relationship with his wife, the poet and critic Khālida Saʿīd, who also wrote under the penname Khuzāmā Ṣabrī:[74]

جسد يكبر في الخزام والخالدة
ينحدر يعلو يستشرف
يجمع الضفاف ويقرأ هذيان القصب
جَسَسْتكِ بعينيَّ
رقصاً يتقدم في خطوات الفصول...[75]

A body that grows in lavender and the immortal one,
It descends, it rises, and looms.
It gathers the banks and reads the ravings of reeds.
I felt you with my eyes,
a dance proceeding with the steps of the seasons . . .

In 'Semiology', Adonis embeds his personal timeline in the poem, taking us from his birth in 1930 to 1975.[76] Even though the autobiographical is only one thread among the many that run through the poem, it is the most easily recognisable one. The autobiographical thread functions as the spindle around which Adonis wraps or weaves the poem. The metaphor of weaving on a spindle is apt here. Around the backbone, the splinters and patches of the poem's body rotate.

c. Three Axes: The Buhlūl's Sun, a Notebook of Account and a Secret History of Death

The provisions of ʿAlī's journey are the Buhlūl's sun, a notebook of account and a secret history of death. These become the patches with which the poem is woven. They are the *ruqa*ʿ (patches, tatters, shreds) laid out, organised, scattered and spun around. These three categories of patches, the raw material or the building blocks, reveal the poem's sources, its driving forces and the old upon which Adonis will erect a 'dissembling' structure. By 'dissembling' I am referring here to a hidden network that holds the structure together through synecdochic and metonymic associations which otherwise seem entirely illogical and inefficient.[77] On the surface, the poem is a congregating of disparate parts, but below the surface deep currents run, currents that constellate the pieces together without fixing them definitely. *Mufrad bi-ṣīghat al-jam*ʿ is thus a kinetic structure, a dynamic configuration. Its design is not evident or in place but in the process of falling into place. 'Dissembling' is also an appropriate way to refer to the manner in which Adonis camouflages the excerpts he quotes from the sources of this poem. In the parts labelled patches (*ruq*ʿ*a*, pl. *ruqa*ʿ) and pertaining to the three currents, Adonis embeds excerpts from books of history and theology, as well as biographies into his poem.

The three currents which hold the structure together yet keep it mobile are all driven by the tension between latent and manifest. The Buhlūl stands in for madness as cover for wisdom. This figure is a symbol of truth that is excavated from the margins which are dismissed as irrelevant or flawed or illicit. The fact that Adonis chooses to signal the Abbasid madman specifically has connotations relating to madness as it speaks to power and hegemony. The Buhlūl's truth is a 'sun' which reveals, exposes, burns. Hence the threat of this latent truth is emphasised. This sun not only has the power to reveal things as they truly are, but more threateningly as their opposites:

رقعة من شمس البهلول ←
لكي يكون ما هو
خرج من نفسه ← خرج
وبقي فيها شخص لا يعرفه

أتأبط الليل
هديةً لكل جسد   أبلّغ هذه الرسالة:
اتّصل كما يتصل البحر باليابسة ←
يلتصقان لكن لا شراكة بينهما
كلاهما نقيض الآخر

- لكن، لماذا أنا جميلة أيها البهلول؟
- لأن السفينة هي التي تراكِ، لا الموجة.[78]

A patch of the Buhlūl's sun →
  So that he may be what he is,
  he stepped out of his self→he stepped out
    and in there remained someone he doesn't know

I place the night under my shoulder
    A gift for every body   I convey this message:
    Connect as the sea connects to land →
    They touch without a partnership between them
    each is the other's opposite.

-But, why am I beautiful O Buhlūl?
-Because it is the ship that sees you, not the wave.

The notebook of accounts is Adonis's way of signalling the memory of the language he is re-inventing here. In this strain of patches, he co-opts the genre of the *khabar* and *akhbār* writing. He employs the accounts of rebels and outlaws in the tradition as templates for writing an alternate memory and alternate history. His own autobiography sometimes becomes the subject of these accounts.[79] The patches in all three strains are often in quotations, marking them as borrowed or found excerpts summoned into this new structure, keeping us wondering which sections are borrowed and which are newly composed. The notebook of accounts emphasises this tension between old and new, borrowed and invented, inviting us to view *Mufrad* as a framework within which everything can *become* poetry:

رقعة من دفتر أخبار ←
"...هكذا
عرفت الأنثى نفسها   عرف الذكر
يجتمعان   بشهوة اللحم والعظم   لإيداع الماء في
بيته
يندفع الماء ← يكون له
سمع يمتلئ بتعويجات الصوت
أظافر تهدي إلى مواضع الحكّ
رئة   مروحة لحرارة القلب
عظام أوتاد لجر الحركة

رقبة برج من الخرز
ليطول ذكر الحكمة."[80]

A patch from a notebook of accounts →

"... Thus
the female knew herself   and the male knew
they join   in the lust of flesh and bone   to deposit the water
in its house
the water gushes → it acquires
hearing flooded with the twists of sound
and nails that guide to the location of the itch
and a lung   a fan for the heat of the heart
and bones pegs for drawing motion
and a neck a tower of beads
so that the memory of wisdom may persist."

This excerpt describing the joining of female and male in sexual intercourse and the ensuing conception of a foetus is placed in quotation marks. Adonis invited us to consider where it could have possibly come from: a genesis-like story, a medical manual.[81] Whether he is indeed quoting another text or not is irrelevant here. What is most urgent is the layering of possible contexts and reading settings.[82] The excerpt or quotation exists on plural reading planes. One of these many planes is that of *Mufrad* as a poem where the excerpts and quotations are transformed into poetry, or at least into prompts inviting us to consider what poetry can be. The act of reading is therefore unsettled as well. The readers of *Mufrad* are implicated in its processes of wounding, opening up and beginning anew. This is not a text written for us to read, but a space where both reading and writing, writing and reading are on the verge of happening. Everything that is summoned into this space will be written and read for the first time.

And here, as a space or framework which transforms everything inside it, lies the subversive power of *Mufrad.* This is further highlighted in the third axis or strain that runs through the poem: a secret history of death. Again, the phrase 'secret history' hints at the core tension between latent and manifest, between depth and surface, centre and margin. The patches or leaves of the secret history of death hint at the cryptic dimension of this text. The act of writing or patching together is an act of decoding or unlocking encrypted messages with devastating consequences.

رقعة من تاريخ سرّيّ للموت ←
يستعير　　يبتكر حكايات يجرح كواحلها
ويتابع خيط الدم　　ينظر إلى الزمن يتحطم بين يديه
إلى المكان يتوشح بحطامه
يلتفت وراءه
أنصاب وتماثيل تحمل حروفاً
أ و ر ف ي و س
أ د و ن ي س
يتحقّق أنها نظائره وأسماؤه
من
السّيمياء
والشرق.[83]

A patch from a secret history of death →

He borrows　　he invents stories whose ankles he slices
he traces the thread of blood　　and looks at time shattering in his hands
at place cloaking itself in its ruin
he glances behind him
idols and statues carrying letters
O R P H E U S
A D O N I S
He ascertains they are his counterparts and his names
from
the semiology
and the East.

The secret history is a borrowing and an inventing of the borrowed anew. It is a violent rewriting or slicing of old stories and shedding light on them from a different angle. Writing, as is the case in this poem, is a remoulding of time and place and the setting up of new relationships (semiology) and a new language.[84] A poet is he who can see the idols and statues of the past (*al-thābit*) over his shoulder as he moves ahead (*al-mutaḥawwil*).

He recognises himself, his name or names, in that past and moves on. By that not only the present time and place are 'shattered' and 'ruined', but the perspective on the past is also transformed. The secret history of death that Adonis threads into his text is transformative. It is the subversive under-current he is constantly interested in uncovering. He uses it here in *Mufrad* to connect this experiment to the disruptive motor force which propels the Arabic tradition forward by challenging and agitating the status quo. In his critical works, such as *al-Shiʿriyya al-ʿarabiyya* and more centrally *al-Thābit wa al-mutaḥawwil*, he has assigned to this undercurrent the Shiite, the *Ṣūfī*, the heretical, the Zoroastrian, the other non-conforming attitudes and standpoints. He employs this transformative subversive attitude here to announce, among other things, the expanding of Arabic poetry's limits; the reinvention of what has been borrowed. All the shreds and patches which hover and scatter have the potential of gathering, of joining together in a new order, a semiology, a new language. The poem however does not settle or arrive at the new order but rather continues to move towards it. This is a structure 'written on the brink',[85] at the site of the first wound which will either rejuvenate or kill.

The opening (with all its variations) and the ending of this monumental poem echo each other. And central to understanding the connection between opening and ending is the question: What is a wound? And how does it relate to the body? The wound as disruption and disconnection, as well as an opening, an uncovering of plurality in what is seemingly singular are both present. If earth represents the body of language, and if the wound is the beginning, this poem is a perpetual breaking of ground. It is a launching; a poem on the brink of beginning:

أفق على شفا أفق[86]

A horizon on the brink of a horizon

Only when we arrive at the very end of this massive text, does it really begin to begin:

أنت أيها الإشلاء الباقية من أحلامنا
تحوّمي حول صبواتنا
أجسادنا نتوء الطوفان

وليس في أنقاضنا غير المحيطات
والآن أول البحر
أنا الصارية ولا شيء يعلوني
والآن أول الأرض.[87]

And you, the remaining splinters of our dreams,
hover over our passions.
Our bodies are protrusions of the flood.
Nothing in our ruins but oceans
And, now is the beginning of the sea.
I am the mast and nothing rises above me
And, now is the beginning of the earth.

Mufrad bi ṣīghat al-jam`* is the 'open poem' Adonis talks about in his *Muqaddima lil-shi`r al-`arabī (Introduction to Arabic Poetry). It is a text in which the poet replaces the 'single infinite form with the plural infinite forms and proclaims poetry to be a transcending of old generic limits towards a spacious world of postures, spiritual and expressive states that lie beyond all limits and genres, beyond all rules and conventions'.[88]

This poem is a practicum of Adonis's most abstract and theoretical ideas about poetry. 'There is no discrete entity called poetry',[89] he tells us, and *Mufrad* is the performance of that statement. What truly exists is the poet and the poem. In the succession of poems and their building on each other, the notion of poetry reveals itself and continues to transform. Poetry is the succession of poems, of structures built one after the other, one on top of the other, completing each other, erasing each other. Poetry is a horizon that perpetually moves farther and farther. And the poem is the longing for poetry. It is the endless building of roads in the direction of that horizon, that unattainable mark in the distance where the old world ends and the new one is forever about to begin.

Notes

1. Adonis believes that Arab poets have failed to understand the true dimensions of the modernist project and have focused on the superficial issues of form and prosody which alone do not make a modern poem. He is always wary of poetic practice settling into prescriptions, and this applies to his view of

the prose poem project in Arabic. See the opening of the 1992 version of his 'Bayān al-ḥadātha' where he warns of the prose poem falling into automation and imitation which plagued the free verse poem before it. Adonis, 'Bayān al-ḥadātha', *al-Bayānāt*, 2nd edition (Tunis: Sarās lil-nashr, 1995), p. 55, and his article 'al-Irtidād', *al-Ḥayāt Newspaper*, 7 April 1994.

2. Adonis, *Hā anta ayuhā al-waqt:sīra shiʿriyya* (Beirut: Dār al-Ādāb, 1993), p. 26.
3. Ibid.
4. Ibid. p. 27.
5. Ibid. p. 28.
6. Ibid. p. 29.
7. Robyn Creswell, *City of Beginnings: Poetic Modernism in Beirut* (Princeton: Princeton University Press, 2019), p. 106. For more on Adonis and Saint-John Perse, see Creswell, pp. 106–12.
8. Quoted in Creswell, p. 109, from 'Conférence d'Adonis donnée à la Fondation Saint-John Perse le 9 octobre 1993', *Souffle de Perse* 4 (1993), trans. Anne Wade-Minkowski, pp. 4–9.
9. Mohamad Mazloum, 'Baḥthan ʿan ẓilāl Saint-John Perse . . . al-ʿarabiyya' (In Search of Saint-John Perse's Arab Shadows), *Al-Ḥayāt Newspaper*, 15 December 2015.
10. Creswell, p. 223, n. 33.
11. His translation with Yusuf al-Khal, of T. S. Eliot's 'The Wasteland' is another often criticised translation. See *Al-Arḍ al-kharāb* (Beirut: Dār Majallat Shiʿr, 1958).
12. Creswell, p. 109.
13. Ibid. p. 14.
14. Ibid. p. 223, n. 35.
15. Saint-John Perse, *Manārāt*, trans. Adonis (Damascus: Dār al-Madā, 1999), p. 104.
16. Saint-John Perse, *Collected Poems*, trans. W. H. Auden, Hugh Grisholm et al. (Princeton: Princeton University Press, 1983), p. 450.
17. Creswell, p. 15
18. Ibid. Creswell borrows the phrase 'internal translation' from Pascal Casanova's *The World Republic of Letters* (Cambridge, MA: Harvard University Press, 2004), p. 238.
19. Adonis, 'Introduction', *Dīwān al-shiʿr al-ʿarabī* (Beirut: Dār al-Fikr, 1986), p. 9.

20. Ibid. p. 13.
21. Adonis, *Hā anta ayuhā al-waqt*, p. 28.
22. Ibid. p. 55.
23. Creswell, p. 153
24. Adonis, 'Introduction', *Dīwān al-shiʿr al-ʿarabī*, p. 32.
25. The Arabic (originally Persian) word for poetry collection. See H. L. Gottschalk, G. S. Colin, A. K. S. Lambton, and A. S. Bazmee Ansari, 'Dīwān', *Encyclopaedia of Islam*, Second Edition.
26. Adonis, 'Introduction', *Dīwān al-nathr al-ʿarabī*, p. 7.
27. Ibid. p. 15.
28. Ibid. p. 8.
29. Ibid. p. 8.
30. Ibid. p. 9.
31. Ibid. p. 10.
32. Adonis, *Kalām al-bidāyāt* (Beirut: Dār al-Ādāb, 1989), pp. 27–30.
33. Ibid. p. 9.
34. Adonis, *Dīwān al-nathr al-ʿarabī*, p. 15
35. Ibid. p. 15.
36. Ibid. p. 68.
37. Adonis, *Zaman al-shiʿr* (Beirut: Dār ʿAwda, 1972), pp. 10–12.
38. Adonis, *Hā anta ayuhā al-waqt*, p. 86.
39. Ibid. p. 76.
40. Ibid. p. 90.
41. Adonis, *Qaṣāʾid ʾūlā* (Beirut: Dār Majjallat Shiʿr, 1957), p. 82.
42. Ibid. p. 84.
43. Ibid. p. 54.
44. 'The body' (al-jasad) is a central concept, trope, metaphor and medium in Adonis's poetic world. It is a recurrent word in many of his titles: *Raʾs al-lugha, Jasad al-ṣaḥrāʾ* (The Head of Language, the Desert's Body), *Awwal al-jasad ʾākhir al-baḥr* (The Beginning of the Body, the End of the Sea), *Tārīkh yatamazzaq fī jasad imraʾa* (A History Shredded in a Woman's Body). In an interview he states: 'Poetry comes from the direction of the body and the dream not the direction of thoughts. There is no poetry without thoughts, but these are thoughts that come through the body, the individual body that's independent of others. Poetry is born singular and then becomes a point of intersection or meeting with others [. . .] If a poet speaks of his body truly, then he is a modernizer'. Interview, Beirut, 11 July 2019.

45. In the first four years of the journal *Shi'r*, Adonis published three daring prose poems: '*Waḥdahu al-ya's* (*Shi'r*, no. 7–8), '*Arwād yā amīrat al-wahm*' (Arwad! Oh Princess of Illusion) (*Shi'r*, no. 10) and '*Marthiyyat al-qarn al-awwal*' (Elegy for the First Century) (*Shi'r*, no. 14).
46. 'A modern poem ought to be studies on the basis of its particular structure, that is the relationships created in the text: constructions, images, symbols. By language here, we are not referring to mere discrete sonic unit but more than that, words are relationships'. Adonis, '*Bayān al-ḥadātha*', pp. 52–53. Also see Adonis, *Muqaddima lil-shi'r al-'arabī*, 3rd edition (Beirut: Dār 'Awda, 1979), pp. 113–14, on the prose poem as a manipulation of language according to new imperatives.
47. The persona Mihyār al-Dimashqī is an adaptation of the fifth-century poet Mihyār al-Daylamī (died 428 H). Adonis's choice of this particular figure is not arbitrary. Al-Daylamī is a poet of Persian origins who converted from Zoroastrianism to Shi'īsm, something that directly speaks to Adonis's main interests: marginality and rebellion. Adonis himself comes from an Alawite background, one of the sects of Shi'ī Islam. See Adonis, *al-Thābit wa-l-mutaḥawwil*. In this book which is based on the doctoral dissertation he presented at Sorbonne University, Adonis claims that marginal suppressed voices (dynamic, *mutaḥawwil*) constantly challenge the establishments of state and religion which are static (fixed, *thābit*).
48. The first six parts are titled as follows: *Fāris al-kalimāt al-gharība* (The Knight of Strange Words), *Sāḥir al-ghubār* (The Magician of Dust), *Al-'ilāh al-mayīt* (The Dead God), *'Iram dhāt al-'imād* (Iram of the Pillars), *Al-zamān al-ṣaghīr* (The Little Time), *Ṭaraf al-'ālam* (The Edge of the World).
49. Creswell, p. 115.
50. Adonis, *Aghānī Mihyār al-Dimashqī*, 2nd edition (Beirut: Manshūrāt Mawāqif, 1970), p. 39.
51. Ibid. pp. 40–1.
52. Ibid. p. 73
53. Ibid. p. 13.
54. Ibid. p. 25.
55. Ibid.
56. Creswell, pp. 11–14.
57. These figures are 'Umar ibn al Khattāb, Abū Nūwās, al-Hallāj and Bashshār ibn Burd. All, except 'Umar ibn al-Khattāb are figures who challenged the established norm and were marginal and defiant in every way. 'Umar ibn

al-Khattāb, the second caliph after the Prophet, has among the Muslim populace a common image as the ideal ruler who was honest and modest and did not abuse the power he had. There are many stories that virtually have become folktales about his modesty and uprightness.

58. Adonis, *Aghānī Mihyār*, p. 211.
59. Adonis, 'Introduction', *Dīwān al-nathr al-ʿarabī*, p. 8. Adonis borrows the words 'chemistry' and 'magic' from Abd al-Qāhir al-Jurjani's discussion of poeticity and metaphor (*majāz*), See al-Jurjani, *Asrār al-balāgha*, ed. Maḥmūd Shākir (Cairo: Maṭbaʿat Madanī, 1991), pp. 343–44. Also see Adonis, *Muqaddima lil-shiʿr al-ʿarabī*, p. 126.
60. The three terms *hatk*, *fath* and *khalkhala* are recurrent in the Adonis's discourse on poetry. In another poem which went through a series of revisions in its formulation and in its political investment, '*Muqaddima li-tārīkh mulūk al-ṭawāʾif*' (An Introduction to the History of Petty Kings), Adonis's poetic voice states:

أنا ساعة الهتك العظيم أتت وخلخلة العقول
هذا أنا - عبرت سحابة
حبلى بزوبعة الجنوْن
...
هذا أنا أصل الغرابة بالغرابة.

I am the hour of dreadful agitation and the shaking loose of minds
This is what I am – A cloud passed by
Pregnant with a hurricane of madness
[. . .]
This is what I am: uniting strangeness with strangeness

Adonis, *A Time Between Ashes and Roses*, trans. Shawkat Toorawa (Syracuse: Syracuse University Press, 2004), pp. 44–45.

61. Adonis, *Mufrad bi-ṣīghat al-jamʿ: ṣīyāgha nihāʾiyya* (Beirut: Dār al-Ādāb, 1988), p. 9.
62. Adonis, *Mufrad bi-ṣīghat al-jamʿ*, p. 146.
63. Ibid. p. 148.
64.

You are not you and the abode is not the abode –
Passion has faded, and desires become weak.

لا أنت أنت والديار ديار   خفّ الهوى وتولت الأوطار

Abu Tammam, vol. 1, p. 321.

65. Adonis, *Mufrad bi-ṣīghat al-jam'*, pp. 231–32.
66. Ibid. p. 9.
67. Ibid. p. 41.
68. Ibid. p. 91.
69. Ibid. p. 169.
70. Ibid. p. 209.
71. Buhlūl is an Abbasid figure referred to as the 'lunatic of al-Kūfa'. Al-Jahiz mentions him in *al-Bayān wa al-tabyyin* as a Shi'ī and a simpleton. Ibn al-Jawzī makes him a contemporary of Hārūn al-Rashīd. He becomes the hero of erotic tales in al-Nafzāwī's *al-Rawḍ al-'āṭir* which places him in the times of al-Ma'mūn. See Editors, 'Buhlūl', *Encyclopaedia of Islam*, Second Edition. Although based on this historical figure, the Buhlūl became the prototype of the 'wise fools' (*al-'uqalā' al-majānīn*). Adonis exploits the layered-ness of this figure, the tension it creates between surface and depth, between overt simplicity and latent plurality, between seeming harmlessness and jest on one hand and hidden ability to expose and subvert, on the other hand. See U. Marzolph, ''Uḳalā' al-Madjānīn', *Encyclopaedia of Islam*, Second Edition.
72. Khalida Sa'id, *Jurḥ al-ma'nā* (Beirut: Dār al-Sāqī, 2018), p. 23.
73. Adonis, *Mufrad bi-ṣīghat al-jam'*, p. 49.
74. *Khuzāmā* or *khuzām* means lavender and the adjective *khālid* means immortal.
75. Adonis, *Mufrad bi-ṣīghat al-jam'*, p. 103
76. Ibid. pp. 176–77.
77. Michael Sells, 'Guises of the Ghūl: Dissembling Simile and Semantic Flow in the Classical Arabic Nasīb', in *Reorientations: Arabic and Persian Poetry*, ed. Suzanne Stetkevych (Bloomington: Indiana University Press, 1994), p. 133.
78. Adonis, *Mufrad bi-ṣīghat al-jam'*, p. 125.
79. Ibid. p. 49.
80. Ibid. p. 21.
81. This quotation does not exist verbatim in any other text I was able to find. Moncef Ouhaibi suggests two possible source texts which Adonis might have had in mind while composing these lines: an Arabic translation of Plato's 'Timaeus' from his *Dialogues* and a section from al-Ghazālī's *Iḥyā' 'ulūm al-dīn* or some other such text commenting on the Qur'ānic verse: 'It is He who has created man from water: then He has established relationships

of lineage and marriage' (25:54). See Moncef Ouhaibi, 'Adūnīs fī ḍiyāfat al-Ghazālī wa Aflāṭūn', *Al-Awān*, 14 February 2008, https://www.alawan.org/2008/02/14/أدونيس-في-ضيافة-أفلاطون-و-الغزالي-2/ (last accessed 20 October 2020).

82. Jacques Derrida, *Monolingualism of the Other or Prosthesis of Origin* (Palo Alto: Stanford University Press, 1998), pp. 81–82.
83. Adonis, *Mufrad bi-ṣīghat al-jamʿ*, p. 25
84. See Adonis, 'Bayān al-ḥadātha', pp. 52–54.
85. Derrida, p. 81.
86. Adonis, *Mufrad bi-ṣīghat al-jamʿ*, p. 136.
87. Adonis, *Mufrad bi-ṣīghat al-jamʿ*, pp. 238–39.
88. Adonis, *Muqaddima lil-shiʿr al-ʿarabī*, p. 107.
89. Ibid.

4

Muhammad al-Maghut and Poetic Detachment

Muhammad al-Maghut (1934–2006) is a Syrian poet credited with being one of the founders of the prose poem (*qaṣīdat al-nathr*). Unlike most other pioneers of the prose poem, al-Maghut kept a distance from theorising efforts. He was not invested in theorising the new form, nor did he insist on or subscribe to the term *qaṣīdat al-nathr*. He preferred to assume the position of the outsider, politically and socially as well as poetically, eventually distancing himself from the *Shiʿr* group.[1]

Despite al-Maghut's reputation as one of the leading prose poets,[2] the relationship between his poetic project and the prose poem as a poetic and critical movement is not a direct one. I argue here that al-Maghut was instrumental in opening up the Arabic poetic register, particularly due to his lack of engagement with the term 'prose poem' and its theoretical implications. He wrote a verse-less text, in stark contrast to the verse poem (*qaṣīdat al-tafʿīla*), the established modern Arabic poem until then. Without engaging in the polemics of form in Arabic poetry, al-Maghut contended with poetry in an abstract sense.

His poems acquire their force from a unique posture towards language and towards the role of the poet. Instead of writing a poem, al-Maghut seems more interested in challenging the accepted conceptions of what a poem is. And it is in this taunting of the established poetic aesthetic that he contributes, even if unintentionally, to the prose poem as subversive and expansive interrogation of the limits of poetry in Arabic.

At one of the journal *Shiʿr*'s regular Thursday gatherings in Beirut, Adonis read to the group 'new and strange poems' without revealing the poet's name. He left them wondering: Baudelaire? Rimbaud?[3] When he eventually revealed that it was none other than a young dishevelled poet from Syria who was sitting right there among them, their awe and curiosity turned into suspicious whispers.[4] He was Muḥammad al-Maghut, an uneducated young man from the Syrian countryside. It was 1957, and he had just been released from prison in Damascus. He was quite the unlikely attendee at this meeting of the Arab poetic avant-garde.

This staged debut predetermined al-Maghut's role as outsider moving ahead. Its orchestrator, Adonis, who briefly posed as mentor to him, is partly responsible for the perceived unruliness and mystery of the Maghut phenomenon. Since that debut, scholars have approached al-Maghut's work with the assumption or expectation of genius; of something unusually worthy of attention.[5] This assumption is based not on a quality particular to his poems or his prose, but on an interpretation of al-Maghut, the poet and the man, as a phenomenon. The persona he embraced, that of the outsider, the loiterer, the vulgar hobo, is just as integral to his literary fame as his oeuvre. This persona guides and supplements the reading of his work and the perceived achievement of his poetic project.

He had a reputation for being a challenging personality and a very difficult interviewee.[6] Throughout his life, he committedly 'performed' this unruly persona. Yet, 'performance' here does not necessarily imply insincerity or pretence, as much as it reveals his awareness of the power and appeal of the posture he found himself in – a posture at odds with 'institutions' of all kinds and first and foremost the literary institution of his times.

When al-Maghut arrived in Beirut, the Arabic literary scene there was bracing itself for the emergence of the prose poem, and the wave of theorising that was to accompany it. It was 1957; the heated polemics around the prose poem which spilled into broader political and ideological issues of identity, otherness, inclusion/exclusion, history, memory and the possibilities of change were all still on the horizon. After spending several months as a political prisoner in al-Mazza prison in Damascus, al-Maghut escaped to Beirut in search of a refuge. Unsuspecting and probably uninterested in the controversy his poetry would later cause, the young poet was intimidated when Adonis, his former prison mate, invited him to join the *Shiʿr* meetings. He remembers meeting figures such as Unsi al-Hajj, Yusuf al-Khal and the Rahbani brothers at these gatherings. He remembers feeling an outsider:

> I didn't say much in the meetings that were often held at Yusuf al-Khal's house. I heard much discussion about poets and names I hadn't heard of, like Pound, Eliot and Suzanne Bernard. I only knew Arabic. I remained silent during the conversations, and when the food came, I ate.[7]

No one at that first literary meeting could have anticipated al-Maghut's impact on the then-nascent Arabic prose poem. His poetry is both familiar and jarring in its effect. His texts are of a loose, almost unplanned form; nevertheless, they possess evident tension and intensity. His language is simple, almost trite, yet punctuated by unexpected twists that transform the mundane into something seemingly unprecedented.

The Maghutian Poetics of Nonchalance

Al-Maghut's poetic language appeals to both the lay reader and the motivated critic. His poems do not burden the reader with theoretical, formal, or critical concerns. They are accessible, almost entertaining, and his attractively elusive persona as poet and literary figure only adds to their relatability. The majority of his readers are primarily interested in the Maghutian take; they approach the poem sympathetically and find an open, unpretentious text. The priority in al-Maghut's aesthetic remains the 'urgency of lived experiences'. He is of the belief that poetry is ancillary to real experience and thus ought not to take itself too seriously.[8] Rarely did he express investment in a poetic project or theory or political idea or stance. This nonchalance is evident in this account he related about the beginning of his political engagement, which ended with several prison sentences:

> I was a member of the Syrian Nationalist Party. That happened without conviction. It was probably out of poverty. A young poor boy like me needed to belong to something. There were two competing political parties in my hometown of Salamiya, the Baʿth party and the Syrian Nationalist Party. On my way to enlist in one of them, I learned that its headquarters were farther away from my neighbourhood and didn't have

> a fireplace. My limbs were freezing from the cold, so without hesitation I chose the closer one[9] that had a fireplace. Frankly, to this day, I have not read a page of its bylaws. Once the cold season ended, I stopped attending the meetings. I haven't done anything to benefit the party except once when I was asked to collect donations in the village where I worked in the groves. I collected membership fees and donations but used the money to a buy a pair of pants and that was that.[10]

The detached attitude towards organised political activism is equally representative of al-Maghut's poetic stance and posture. He was quick to undermine and mock a position soon after assuming it. That the so-called 'father of the Arabic prose poem' was so little invested in the debates and the discussions around the prose poem is significant. This nonchalance is a dominant feature of his aesthetic. In fact, in later accounts of his early years in Beirut, he identified and embraced a fundamental difference between him and the other *Shiʿr* group members in terms of their attitude toward poetry and its motivations.

> Back then Arabic poetry was drowned in debates about existence and death, and other mysteries that were a hundred light years removed from what was happening on earth. As for me, I was angry and hungry. I spoke about lice in the prison cells and the jailer's stone foot on my heart, about coffins and execution squares [. . .] I was not concerned with labelling what I wrote or categorising it. I only wrote to survive.[11]

When he so deliberately detached himself from the polemics of the prose poem, why is it that later generations of prose poets claimed al-Maghut as their predecessor? What is the meaning of his deliberate recoil from theory, and what is the significance of his meter-less or verse-less poem in the context of Arabic modernist poetics? And more important, what is the influence of the Maghutian text (which I argue here is not a prose poem in the strict sense of the term as it was later developed by its Arab practitioners, especially Adonis and Unsi al-Hajj) on the Arabic prose poem that was written in his wake? After examining salient features of al-Maghut's poetic posture, I will turn to the Egyptian 'Poets of the Nineties' whose poetic attitudes were informed by al-Maghut's poetic detachment and his uninvested relationship with the Arabic poetic heritage. My purpose is not to claim a relationship of linear descendance or direct influence, but rather to suggest possible traceable threads in the development of the Arabic prose poem. If we are to look for networks or clusters in mapping the prose poem in Arabic, one thread is bound to extend from the Maghutian stance of recoil and aloofness to the deliberately detached position of the Egyptian 'Poets of the Nineties'.

Ḥuzn fī ḍaw' al-qamar: Al-Maghut's Poetic Manifesto

When al-Maghut's first poetry collection, *Ḥuzn fī ḍaw' al-qamar*, was published in 1959 by the press of *Shiʿr* journal, it was received as an anomaly. *Shiʿr* had then been publishing for a little over a year, and it had already published three of the poems that were included in the collection.[12] Nevertheless, the collection came as a surprise to readers and, more interestingly, to the poets and critics of the *Shiʿr* group themselves. Unlike many of the other *Shiʿr* group members – such as Yusuf al-Khal, Fu'ad Rifqa, Jabra Ibrahim Jabra and Unsi al- Hajj, who held academic degrees from foreign institutions, who were fluent in at least one foreign language and well versed in other, mainly western, literary traditions – al-Maghut only knew Arabic and was largely self-taught.[13] Still, his first collection was a resounding poetic statement which seemed to come out of nowhere, not aligning with any of the poetic agendas put forth by the major camps of the time, primarily the *Shiʿr* group and the *Ādāb* group.

Reviewing the collection in 1959 under her pen name Khuzāmā Ṣabrī, Khālida Saʿīd expresses an approving, albeit condescending, assessment of the work. Although she recognises merits in the collection, she seemed to believe them accidental and unintended. She portrays al-Maghut as an inexperienced poet who had unknowingly tapped into something very significant. This is obvious in the backtracking comments with which she follows most of her praise of the poems. Of course, her reluctance and holding back in endorsing the young al-Maghut is a political stance more than an aesthetic one. Saʿīd here is a critic committed to the *Shiʿr* agenda, and al-Maghut is a young poet who broke ranks.

After identifying the image as al-Maghut's structuring element, she comments: 'Had al-Maghut been more experienced as a poet, he would have capitalised on this feature as did Jabrā Ibrāhīm Jabrā, who employs scattered-ness and chaos but is able to control it and guide it as he wills'.[14] Although she admits that the reliance on imagery put al-Maghut on the right track, Saʿīd goes on to identify his shortcomings. She postulates that his poetic 'material' does not always succeed in becoming 'modernist images', but rather remains 'primitive and simple, only resembling modernist imagery in its naïveté, strangeness and shock effect'.[15] She concludes that al-Maghut's 'primitiveness and simplicity' come from his overuse of similes (the weakest of figurative tools), because it falls short of transforming its two poles into something new.[16]

Her main point of endorsement, however, comes early in the review, when she expresses a general approval of poetry outside the vessel of meter and rhyme. She does not use the term 'prose poem', which will only be introduced later and canonised as a genre indicator in the 1960 manifestos by Adonis and al-Hajj. She insists, however, that al-Maghut's 'poetic prose' is poetry, emphasising that the challenge of writing poetry without meter and rhyme is greater than what most people might imagine.

> Modern poets broke the vessel and poetry spilled alive unto their hands. They attempt to grasp it and preserve poetry despite what they had done [. . .] Doing away with meter and rhyme, which people often think of as easy, is in fact a challenge only the most talented of poets can overcome.[17]

Although Khalida Saʿid portrayed the collection as a blueprint or a first attempt, with time *Ḥuzn fī ḍawʾ al-qamar* proved itself to be al-Maghut's enduring poetic statement. In his subsequent poetic collections, notably *Ghurfa bi malāyīn al-judrān* (1964) and *al-Faraḥ laysa mihnatī* (1970), al-Maghut does not significantly add to the statement he made in *Ḥuzn*, but rather establishes it further. He made a poetic statement in his first collection, then kept digging into it.

In that sense, *Ḥuzn* serves as a log or an archive, an arsenal almost, of al-Maghut's poetic techniques, techniques he continues to employ until his very last collection, *al-Badawī al-aḥmar*, published a few months before his death. There is a stubborn matter-of-fact-ness about al-Maghut's poetic project, in which he persevered from the very first poem until the end of his life. Despite the simplicity, monotony and expected-ness, his relentlessness sometimes leads to unexpected poetic clearings. His disengaged attitude and his writing of poetry without a literary agenda is probably what canonised him as one of the most prominent figures of modern Arabic poetry's 'other tradition'.[18] He was committed to a less deliberate poetry, a poetry of experience, as he would call it, a poetry that did not rise out of theory or thought. Of course, this view can be read as a political stance. Having distanced himself from the *Shiʿr* group with its apolitical internationalist outlook on one hand and the *al-Ādāb* group with its pan-Arabist, Nasserite agenda on the other, al-Maghut presented his own brand of commitment (*iltizām*), a penetrating social and political criticism delivered through ambivalence and sarcasm. Without delving into the political dimensions of al-Maghut's project, what I am interested in here is his outsider's stance, his poetics of marginality, as well as the attitude and mode they yielded in the works of younger prose poets.

Taking the title poem of *Ḥuzn fī ḍawʾ al-qamar* (Sorrow in the Moonlight) as a launching point, one can detect early yet clear signs of the Maghutian poetic posture. The poem opens as follows:

أيها الربيعُ المقبلُ من عينيها
أيها الكناري المسافرُ في ضوء القمر
خذني إليها
قصيدةَ غرامٍ أو طعنةَ خنجر
فأنا متشرّد وجريح
أحبُّ المطر وأنين الأمواج البعيده
من أعماق النوم أستيقظ
لأفكر بركبة امرأة شهيةٍ رأيتها ذات يوم
لأعاقرَ الخمرة وأقرضَ الشعر
قل لحبيبتي ليلى
ذاتِ الفم السكران والقدمين الحريريتين
أنني مريضٌ ومشتاقٌ إليها
أنني ألمح آثار أقدام على قلبي
دمشقُ يا عربةَ السبايا الورديه
وأنا راقدٌ في غرفتي
أكتبُ وأحلم وأرنو إلى الماره
من قلب السماء العاليه

أسمع وجيب لحمك العاري.

...

ونحن نعدو كالخيولِ الوحشية على صفحاتِ التاريخ
نبكي ونرتجف
وخلف أقدامنا المعقوفه
تمضي الرياحُ والسنابلُ البرتقالية.
وافترقنا
وفي عينيكِ الباردتين
تنوح عاصفةٌ من النجوم المهروله
أيتها العشيقةُ المتغضّنة
ذات الجسد المغطّى بالسعال والجواهر
أنتِ لي
هذا الحنينُ لك يا حقوده.[19]

O Spring looming in her eyes
O Canary traveling in the moonlight,
take me to her
like a love poem or the stab of a dagger.
I am wounded and wandering.
I love the rain and the moaning of distant waves.
From deep sleep, I awaken
to think of the delicious knee of a woman I once desired,
to drink wine and write poetry.
Tell my beloved Layla,
she whose lips are drunken and her feet silk.
Tell her I am sick and longing for her;
tell her I see footprints on my heart.
O Damascus, you rosy caravan of captive women,
Lying down in my room
I write, I dream and watch passers-by.
From the heart of the lofty sky
I hear the pulse of your naked flesh
[. . .]
and we run like wild horses on the pages of history.
crying and shivering,

And behind our crooked feet
Come the winds and orange wheat stalks.
We parted,
a storm of hasty stars weeping in your eyes.
O shrivelled mistress,
with a body covered in coughing and gems,
You are mine.
This longing is for you, you ingrate!

The opening addresses 'O Spring!' and 'O Canary!' set up a romantic mood that is soon undercut by the phrase 'the stab of a dagger'. In fact, the phrase 'a love poem or the stab of a dagger' presents an early example of the unsuspected combinations that characterise al-Maghut's aesthetic. This opening evokes the motif of the beloved Layla, a familiar motif from the Arabic tradition of love poetry, allowing the poem to briefly pose as just another love poem, a guise that is soon thwarted by the turn that the poem takes. This opening is anchored in the two places where the poet swerves away from the expectations he sets. The line 'like a love poem or the stab of a dagger' is one, while 'to think of the delicious knee of a woman I once desired' is another. Here is where the poem begins to reveal its edge.

Al-Maghut's skill in setups and sudden turns is evident in the transition to 'O Damascus, you rosy caravan of captive women'. Neither Layla as a stand-in for Damascus nor the shift from a personal, private tone to a more general public one is new. We had already seen this in the works of the early modern free verse poets, especially in poems burdened with socio-political concerns. It is something beyond that which makes al-Maghut's poem different. He has no interest in the rhetorically textured language of al-Sayyab,[20] nor is he invested in a cause or a political stance, as were al-Bayātī or ʿAbd al-Ṣabūr. Thus, placing al-Maghut in a category of poets is difficult. His seeming withdrawal from the poem he is writing is what allows him to communicate a distinct posture or attitude and succeed in making familiar tropes new. He keeps his readers unsure and anticipating a turn.

'This longing is for you, you ingrate!' is another of these moments which pull the poem above together, imbuing it with a subtext and giving it a dimension that would not have been there had the section ended with 'you are mine'. This allows al-Maghut to de-familiarise exhausted themes of the beloved homeland as ailing, cruel and apathetic. The homeland as the 'shrivelled mistress' comes from the poetic repertoire of free verse poets, reminding us of poets such as al-Bayātī, Ḥijāzī and Ḥāwī and their qualms about cities and homelands. Al-Maghut, however, makes this motif urgent by his resort to a simple direct language, stripped of romanticising loftiness and kept crude by a touch of cynicism which unshakably distinguishes al-Maghut's oeuvre.

Below I will identify two distinctive features of the Maghutian posture: his insistent use of simile and his ambivalent poetic stance. I have chosen to use the term 'posture' rather than 'style' or 'voice' because I believe his approach is one based on juxtapositions, contrasts and manipulations of perspective. More significant than his ideas or his language is al-Maghut's *approach* to ideas and language and, most important, his attitude towards the very act of writing poetry. This attitude often leads to unexpected turns in thought and phrasing, which punctuate and anchor his poems, reining in their otherwise chaotic form and haphazard deluge of ideas.

Wielding the Sword of Simile

Al-Maghut found in the simile a tool that fit his specific attitude and his detached poetic stance. Despite being deemed by Khalida Saʿid as 'primitive and simple', the simile became in al-Maghut's hands a sword that slices through the pretence of figurative language. With his overreliance on simile al-Maghut keeps the workings of poetry on the surface. He capitalises on the disjunction that remains un-mended in the simile to further accentuate his de-familiarising stance. There is something resistant in a simile, a gap that does not relent but remains defiantly visible. Unlike the metaphor's movement towards identification between different things, thus joining them in one, the simile remains two things, constantly signalling each other's differences as well as their similarities.[21]

His early poem '*Janāzat al-nisr*' (The Eagle's Funeral), the first poem in the first edition of *Ḥuzn*, opens with a simile. The poem utilises metaphors and imagery, but the similes are what organise and anchor it.

أظنُّها من الوطن
هذه السحابةُ المقبلةُ كعينين مسيحيتين
أظنُّها من دمشق
هذه الطفلةُ المقرونةُ الحواجب
هذه العيونُ الأكثر صفاءً
من نيرانٍ زرقاءَ بين السفن
أيها الحزن .. يا سيفيَ الطويل المجعَّد
الرصيفُ الحاملُ طفله الأشقر
يسأل عن وردةٍ أو أسير
عن سفينةٍ وغيمة من الوطن
والكلمات الحرّة تكتسحني كالطاعون
لا امرأةَ لي ولا عقيده
لا مقهى ولا شتاء
ضمني بقوة يا لبنان
أحبُّكَ أكثر من التبغِ والحدائق
أكثر من جنديٍّ عاري الفخذين
يشعلُ لفافته بين الأنقاض
إن ملايين السنين الدمويه
تقف ذليلةً أمام الحانات
كجيوشٍ حزينةٍ تجلس القرفصاء
ثمانية شهور
وأنا ألمسُ تجاعيد الأرضِ والليل
أسمع رنينَ المركبة الذليله
والثلجَ يتراكمُ على معطفي وحواجبي
فالترابُ حزين ، والألمُ يومضُ كالنسر
لا نجومَ فوق التلال
التثاؤب هو مركبتي المطهمةُ ، وترسي الصغيره
والأحلام ، كنيستي وشارعي
بها أستلقي على الملكاتِ والجواري
وأسيرُ حزيناً في أواخر الليل.[22]

I think it from the homeland this cloud
approaching like two Christian eyes,
I think she is from Damascus,
this child with hooked eyebrows,

these eyes clearer than
blue fires among ships.
O Sorrow . . . my long, wrinkled sword,
the pavement holding its blond child
asks about a rose and a captive,
a ship and a cloud from home.
Free words sweep over me like the plague.
I have no woman, no creed,
no coffee shop, no winter.
Hold me tight, O Lebanon,
I love you more than tobacco and gardens,
more than a soldier, thighs bare,
lighting a cigarette amid the rubble.
Millions of bloodied years
stand servile at tavern doors,
like wretched armies crouching.
For eight months
I caress the wrinkles of earth and night.
I hear the ringing of the subdued chariot,
snow piling on my coat and eyebrows.
The soil is sad and pain flashes like an eagle,
no stars over the hills.
Yawning is my adorned carriage and my tiny shield;
dreams my church and my street;
in them I lie atop queens and maids,
and walk sad at the end of the night.

The first simile here invites the reader to a leap in reading. The poem does not make the effort to smooth the cloud and the two Christian eyes into one identifiable thing but rather celebrates that unbridged space signalled by the word 'like'. How do Christian eyes approach? And what makes eyes Christian in the first place? These are questions that remain hanging. The evocations of the adjective 'Christian' is left for the readers to sort out. Perhaps the image of a small female child, with clear eyes amid fires, hints at a connection between 'Christian' and childhood or innocence in the face of adversity. In any case, the Christ-like child confronting a burning world is a recurrent image in al-Maghut's work. The child is often associated with the speaker by her shared longing for signs of home, her marginality, her vulnerability and her resignation to sorrow. Obviously, the poet is not invested in pinning down associations. His poems are an unfolding of associations triggered by the un-mended simile.

This poem is a typical Maghutian text thematically and stylistically. It speaks of longing for a distant homeland; it holds up sorrow (*ḥuzn*) as a shield or a cover from the trials of exile and wandering; it evokes Lebanon, as often happens in al-Maghut's world, as both a refuge and a cruel host. The paradox of the relationship with Lebanon paves the way for a sweeping reference to a bloody past now reduced to grovelling broken soldiers. The poem then ends with the typical Maghutian recoil. The poem leaves us with the caricature-like image of the speaker, the cynic, with 'yawning' as 'his mount and small shield'. He throws up his hands and walks away, 'sad into the end of the night', thus ending the poem. The movement of the poem from nostalgia to a mocking defiance and then back to a resigned cynicism is punctuated and signalled by the four similes: a cloud 'like Christian eyes', words 'like the plague', millions of bloody years 'like wretched armies crouching' and pain 'like an eagle'. They allow the poem to maintain an intensity from beginning to end and allow for a layer of meaning that remains latent in the poem. These un-mended similes further lift the poem and guard it from sentimentalism or melodrama.

Al-Maghut's sword of simile exposed the process of image making in the poem, thus keeping the reader alert and the imagery intensive. Rarely do we see al-Maghut use conceits or extended images. He capitalises on the compact intensity of successive similes for a jolting effect.

مخذول أنا لا أهل ولا حبيبه
أتسكع كالضباب المتلاشي
كمدينة تحترق في الليل
والحنين يلسع منكبي الهزيلين
كالرياح الجميلة، كالغبار الأعمى
فالطريق طويله
والغابة تبتعد كالرمح.[23]

Broken
Without kin, without beloved,
I loiter like lifting fog,
like a city burning at night.
Nostalgia stings my lanky sides
like beautiful wind, like blind dust.
The road is long
and the forest grows distant like a spear.

The above excerpt is the opening of a poem titled 'The Wing of Misery'. It showcases al-Maghut's use of successive intensive images to achieve a powerful and disorienting effect. The cascade of similes serves as a reworking of the idea of loitering. The images that follow are all consequences of this 'loitering'. 'A forest becoming distant like a spear' is where the loitering takes us. The simile allows the images to remain discrete. Strung together they create a movement, a thrust forward, saving the images from the finality of symbolism. None of the images is dwelled upon too long. This opening resembles in its restless energy the strolling or the aimless wandering of a loiterer.

Most significantly revealed here, however, is language's ability to visualise without rhetoric, without metaphor. It is a more rudimentary, much simpler capacity of language to visualise verbally, to present images or visualisations not yet layered or complicated by metaphor. This often happens in listing things, naming them, or just merely signalling to them. Through juxtaposition, unexpected contiguities, appositions and positioning, al-Maghut disrupts that familiar process by which language visualises, and he succeeds in producing an unexpected effect. The effect of the images, one after the other, one facing the other, one against the other, is what al-Maghut capitalises on. His similes remain un-representational, and the simile is thus revealed not as a rhetorical tool but rather as a thematic one. Simile in al-Maghut's work is not a way of expressing content, but rather is content itself.[24] Unexpected similitude between disparate things is the idea that al-Maghut relays. He is not invested in elaborating on that idea. His job as an un-invested poet is to signal unlikely connections which disrupt our view of the world rather than explain it or affirm it.

Poetry at Odds

Regardless of the sentiment or the theme of the poem, most of al-Maghut's poetic oeuvre takes as its launching point a sceptical attitude towards poetry and the poet's perspective. Scholars have described this feature and its effect as cynicism, but I contend here that the term 'cynicism' does not encompass the centrality of this posture to al-Maghut's work. The driving force in the Maghutian poem is a belief in the futility of writing a poem in the first place. There is a pivot that then follows, and he goes on to write the poem despite that realisation. He divests himself from the ideal of the poet as visionary as well as the ideal of the poet as romantic recluse. He nevertheless evokes both in order to starkly turn away from them and write poetry at odds with itself and our expectations of it. Much of this is informed, of course, by his unlikely success as a poet early in his career. He wholeheartedly assumes the position of the unlikely poet and incorporates that paradox into his posture as the poet of texts that prove themselves to be poems against all odds.

His often-cited proclamation 'I have had it with you, Poetry, you immortal corpse!' is the opening line in 'The Burning of Words', a poem from his first collection. The poem is a rant against the sad reality of the Arab world. The speaker is angry and frustrated, and he directs that anger at poetry and what seems to him its superfluous nature. He directly addresses poetry (Poetry! O Muse!) and then points to frustrating aspects of the Arab situation, such as the war in Lebanon or the catastrophe of Palestine, but also the submission and aloofness of the Arabs, from whom he does not exclude himself.

سئمتك أيها الشعر، أيها الجيفة الخالده
لبنان يحترق
يثب كفرس جريحة عند مدخل الصحراء
وأنا أبحث عن فتاة سمينه
أحتك بها في الحافله
عن رجل عربي الملامح، أصرعه في مكان ما.
بلادي تنهار
ترتجف عارية كأنثى الشبل

وأنا أبحث عن ركن معزول
وقروية يائسة أغرر بها.[25]

I have had it with you, Poetry, you immortal corpse.
Lebanon is burning.
It jerks like a wounded mare at the mouth of the desert
while I look for a plump girl
to rub against on a bus,
for a man with Arab features
to kill somewhere.
My homeland falls apart,
shivers naked like a cub lioness
while I search in an isolated corner
for a desperate peasant girl to lure.

He mocks the belief that poetry could trigger change. No poetry can stop the onslaught of reality and its devastations. The poem ends on a very sombre note:

لا أشعار بعد اليوم
إذا صرعوك يا لبنان
وانتهت ليالي الشعر والتسكع
سأطلق الرصاص على حنجرتي.[26]

No poetry after this day
if they defeat you, Lebanon,
and the nights of poetry and loitering end,
I shall place a bullet in my throat.

This harsh introspective attitude towards poetry defines al-Maghut's poetic stance. This ostensible disdain for the traditional poet's perspective translates meta-poetically to delineate a vantage point that al-Maghut assumes throughout his career.

The prose poem's discourse of destroying in order to build anew[27] primarily targets a closed-off notion of poetry, as represented by the prescriptive modernism theorised by Nazik al-Mala'ika, for example, and the Arab Nationalist project of the *Ādāb* group. Yet, al-Maghut eventually distanced himself from both *Shiʿr* and their rivals, writing poetry that does not launch itself from a platform of pre-conceived ideas about poetry, but rather charts a poetics embedded in the practice itself.

لقد آن الأوان
لتمزيق شيء ما
للإبحار عنوة تحت مطر حزين حزين...
لا كمغامر
تلفّه سيول من الحقائب والأزهار
كفأر دامع العينين
يستيقظ مذعورا
كلما ناحت إحدى البواخر
وتألقت مصابيحها
كعيون الضباع المبلله.[28]

It is time
to rip something apart
to sail stubbornly under a sad, sad rain . . .
not like an adventurer
encircled by torrents of suitcases and flowers,
like a teary-eyed mouse
waking up, terrified,
every time a ship wailed
and its lamps glittered
like the wet eyes of hyenas.

The prose poetry that was written in the wake of al-Maghut's work was instilled with an attitude of introspection and suspicion towards an established poetic approach. Younger poets influenced by al-Maghut embraced this anti-poetic attitude and, under his influence, set out to write poetry against poetry.[29] The Egyptian 'Poets of the Nineties' are one case in point.

Poetic Detachment: 'The Poets of the Nineties' in Egypt

'The Poets of the Nineties' is a phrase referring to a generation of Egyptian poets who came to prominence in the mid-1990s. A group of them has also been dubbed *al-Jarād* (The Locusts). The nexus of the group was an underground magazine by the same name, founded in 1994 by a few members, most active among them Ahmad Taha (Aḥmad Ṭāhā, b. 1950) and Muhammad Mitwalli (Muḥammad Mitwallī, b. 1970).[30] The magazine introduced a trend of new poetry which claimed to break away from the remnants of the old moulds that continued to restrain the poetry of the first generation of modernists. Professedly detached from the trends and movements which had thus far shaped the poetic discourse, these younger writers were not interested in interrogating language, re-imagining history and redefining their tradition. Disengaging from the motivations of their modernist predecessors, the first two issues of the magazine were an aggressive attack on the Egyptian and Arab poetic scene in its entirety. Like locusts, these poets claimed that their project was self-produced and had no roots in anything prior to it. In the subsequent issues, they toned down their pitch, without abandoning the claim of being a fresh rebooting of Arab and Egyptian poetic life. The introduction of the third issue presents the magazine as …

> … a magazine which claims the ability to shatter all the ready-made traditional frameworks and moulds. Its members do not represent any political parties or trends. They come from themselves, exactly like the locust. They will devour dry dead poetry and produce supple green which will impress even those with traditionalist palate. To these people standing over the *aṭlāl*, we say: Say to one standing, weeping over an abandoned camp site, effaced, What an achievement it would be, had he sat down.[31]

Although their tones, styles and moods vary, all the poets of this group rallied behind the claim of detachment from the continuum of Arabic poetry and all its 'frameworks'; a very Maghutian stance in its deliberate ambivalence and self-distinction. The misquoting of Abu Nuwas's verse[32] in the editorial above, whether intentional or not, is very telling of the indifference with which this group treated the poetic heritage. Clarissa Burt notes in her article 'The Good, the Bad, and the Ugly' the row that this misquotation created among supporters and detractors of the group alike.[33] Hilmi Salem (Ḥilmī Sālim) in a short article in *Nizwa* magazine uses it as an opportunity to point out the shortcoming in these poets' mastery of language and metrics.[34]

The Egyptian poets of the nineties presented themselves as a band of frustrated, self-effacing and cynical anti-heroes. Poetry to them is not the linguistic and cultural conquest of the earlier generation, but rather a symptom of loneliness, boredom and an assumed lack of investment in anything beyond the immediate inescapable graphic and oppressive minutia of the everyday. In a poem titled '*Aṣdiqāʾī*' (My Friends) from his last collection *ʿAyn sāriḥa ʿayn mundahisha* (*A Wandering Eye, A Perplexed Eye*, 2003), Usāma al-Danāṣūrī (1960–2007) speaks of the feelings of inadequacy and loneliness that motivate him to write:

ما أحوجني الآن لكتابة قصيدة
ليس لأن شيطان الكتابة يتلبّسني
ولا لأني أهيم عشقًا بحبيبٍ لا مبالٍ.
لا...
فقط لأني وحيد
ولكوني خجولاً
أحجم، عادة، عن مبادرة أصدقائي.
«كان لي صديق
أكلّمه وقتما أشاء
لكنه الآن خارج البلاد».

بينما لو كتبتُ قصيدة جديدة
لكان من حقي إذن
أن أباغت أيًا منهم في أي وقت
وأن انتزعه من النوم
بلا أدنى شعور بالخجل
بل بغبطة كافية
لجعله يجلس مقرفصًا لساعاتٍ طويلة
مشغولاً باقتسامها معي.

لست سيئًا
أنا أكتب القصائد من أجل أصدقائي.

(.. إن شئتم الصدق
أكتبها في الحقيقة من أجل نفسي.)

كتبتُ ذات مرة عن الكلاب
لا لأن الكلاب أصدقائي كما قد تظنون
بل لأن أصدقائي كلاب..

هل أكتب إذن عن أصدقائي؟
لكنني حتى الآن
ما زلت أجهل عنهم الكثير
آآه.. ليت أصدقائي
كلاب.[35]

How I need to write a poem now,
not because the demon of poetry has possessed me
or because I'm infatuated with an indifferent beloved.

No.
It's just because I am lonely.
Because I'm shy
I usually refrain from approaching my friends

'I used to have a friend
I talked to all the time
but he is abroad now'.

Whereas if I wrote a new poem
I'd have the right
to surprise any of them at any time
and snatch him from his sleep
without a hint of shame
but with enough joy
to make him crouch down for hours,
busy sharing it with me.

I am not bad.
I write poems for my friends.

(if you want the truth . . .
I actually write them for myself)

I once wrote about dogs
not because dogs are my friends, as you might have thought.

but because my friends are dogs . . .
Should I write about my friends then?

But even, now I still don't
know much about them
Oh . . . if only my friends
were dogs.

The introduction of 'dogs' at the end of this piece not only expresses the speaker's resentment towards his 'friends', his readers, but also a bitterness and frustration towards the creative engagement itself. With cynicism, al-Danāṣūrī exposes the immediate and self-involved motivations of the poem. Beyond poetry being a record or a manifestation of an individual's immediate experience, there is no point in writing poetry. This disillusionment reflects al-Maghut's position against poetry from which he then proceeds to write self-reflexive, self-mocking poems. Cynicism[36] towards poetry itself guarantees these poets their outsider's position even vis-à-vis the creative process in which they are engaged. This further manifests itself in the simple unassuming and rhetorically minimalist language they adopt.

Iman Mersal is another member of this group and probably the best-known outside the Arab world, with a substantial portion of her work translated into English.[37] She takes on the defiant cynical woman's perspective, often pointing out ironic and devastating contradictions in social norms and expectations. Assuming the vantage perspective of the outsider, her work centres on the experience of displacement and the struggle to find one's place among languages, countries, selves and others. Her recent work exhibits an insightful attention to details and a reliance on intensive imagery which Khaled Mattawa described as 'imagistic'.[38]

تبويب صارم للشهيق،
سنواتٌ على الشاشة، الشهاداتُ قبل الوظائف،
واللغاتُ بكل عذابها تحت خانة اللغات.
أين ذهبت كل تلك الأيام الضائعة، تجريب العمى
هلاوس تخبُّ على جدران الغرفة
أين الذنوب
والحزن المفاجئ أمام تل من الفاكهة على عربة يد في شارع منسيّ.

سنواتٌ بلا انتظار ولا جنازات،
خالية من الإحباط المقرف، من قضْم الأظافر
ومن نسيان مفتاح البيت داخل البيت.
ليس فيها حتى نافذة واحدة مفتوحة
ولا رغبة مؤجلة في القفز إلى الغياب
حياة متخمة بالإنجازات،
مغسولة من علكّ الحياة نفسها
كدليل قاطع على أنّ صاحبها
طمس أخيرا علاقته بالطين.[39]

CV

A strict categorisation of inhales
years of the screen, degrees before jobs
and languages with all their torments under the heading: Languages.
Where did all the lost days go? The testing of blindness,
the hallucinations creeping up the walls?
Where are the sins
and the sudden grief brought on by a heap of fruit on a hand cart in a forgotten street?
Years without waiting or funerals,
empty of sickening frustration, nail-biting
and forgetting the house keys inside the house.
Not a single window is opened here,
no postponed desire to leap into oblivion.
A life chockfull of achievement,
cleansed of the mess of life,
to definitively prove that its owner
has finally overcome his relationship to mud.

In this piece titled 'CV', she relies on flashes of details and rhetorical minimalism to portray and comment on the violence of language and the written text, as well as their ultimate failure in capturing all the dimensions of experience. A poem is ultimately as reductive as a CV in reflecting all of reality or experience. The poem is nevertheless written with that realisation of ultimate distortion or failure.

Of this generation of Egyptian poets, however, Imad Abu Salih

(b. 1967) remains one of the most singular yet undiscovered representatives. Like al-Maghut, Abu Salih jealously guards his position as outsider. Never enlisted in any collective literary effort, he has deliberately placed himself on the margins of the Egyptian and Arab literary scene. His poetic career, which began in 1995 with the collection *Matters Already Decided*, has thus far been unusual, idiosyncratic and punctuated by periods of self-imposed silence. He chooses to self-publish and distribute all his works at his own expense,[40] even after establishing himself as one of the prominent prose poets of his generation.[41]

Abu Salih is fascinated by the graphic, the ugly and the jarring details of the mundane. He, like al-Maghut, writes 'poetry of experience' and is ultimately sceptical about poetry's ability to change the world. In the following self-portrait titled 'I Grew Up to Be A Poet', Abu Salih mocks the assumed role of the poet by juxtaposing it with the oppressive realities of poverty, disease and complicated family dynamics.

طلعت شاعرا
علبة سالمون . . . كوبي
ولحافي شوال قديم.

دوبارة رباط جزمتي
وحبيبتي كلبة الجيران.

الناموس فراشات دارنا
نجفة السقف عنكبوتة
حفلة السواريه صوت الصرصار
شجرة الصفصاف شمسية
شاطئ الترعة البلاج
وسحابة آيس كريم.

عمي بنته البلهارسيا
أمي ملكة شعب الدجاج
أبي،
آه من أبي،
رباني
بكل خبرته
في تربية البهائم.[42]

I Grew Up to Be a Poet

A salmon can… my cup
and my blanket an old burlap sack.

My shoelace is twine
and my beloved is the neighbours' dog.

Mosquitoes are our house's butterflies,
a spider our ceiling chandelier,
a cricket's song our *soiree*,
a willow tree an umbrella
the canal-bank a beach
and a cloud ice-cream.

My uncle's daughter is Bilharziasis;
My mother, the queen of the chicken people;
and my father,
O my father,
he raised me
with all his experience
in raising cattle.

The curtness of his texts, the feigned naivete in tone and the sarcastic edge with which he portrays disparities of daily life are what make his writing 'poetic' in its overall effect. He builds his poems as one sets up a joke; all the details serve a purpose. And then, like a tower of blocks, it all comes crumbling down, with a final revealing twist.

Abu Salih's most recent collection, *He Was Asleep When the Revolution Came*, appeared in 2015, after ten years of silence. Motivated by a combination of anger and resignation, the collection is an antagonistic stance. From the very title, and in a single blow, he acknowledges, criticises and dismisses the post-Arab spring as a socio-political moment. The collection is an *anti*-manifesto, disparaging, rejecting and marking decisive positions in praise or attack of grand exhausted abstractions that dominate the public discourse. Built on binaries, the collection opens and closes with a Cain and Abel motif. Most of the texts that follow are declarations with or against something, such as ‘In Praise of Error’, ‘In Praise of Emptiness’, ‘In Praise of Nothing’, ‘In Praise of Darkness’, ‘Against Revolution’, ‘Against Freedom’, ‘Against Love’. In ‘Against Poetry’, he says:

-أعطني سيجارة
*تفضّل
-من انت
*شاعر
-لماذا تجلس في الحديقة؟
*أنتظر الشعر
-لا يسكن هنا.
*تعرف مكانه؟
-المزبلة
*كيف؟
-حين يعثر جائعان
على تفاحة كاملة
هربت من أسنان عائلة سعيدة
*أكلاها معا؟
-كانا سيتقاسمانها فعلا
لكن سكين
لمعت فجأة
من البيت نفسه
وحسمت الصراع
لصالح فم واحد
*أنت شاعر؟
-المذبحة
حين يتدحرج ذراع قديس
ويحضن عاهرة
في مصالحة حقيقية
بعد فوات الأوان
*أنت شاعر؟
-كنت.
*تركته؟
-أغواني وهجرني.
*لماذا تجلس في الحديقة؟

-لأنصح الأطفال.
*ماذا تقول لهم؟
-احذروه
يتخفى، أحيانا، في الحلوى.
*وللشعراء الجدد؟
-أمامكم فرصة للهرب
سيحولكم إلى كلاب
تلهثون وراء خطواته
اكتبوا الروايات.[43]

-Give me a cigarette
*There you go.
-Who are you?
*A poet.
-Why do you sit in the garden?
*I'm waiting for poetry.
-It doesn't live here.
*Do you know where?
-The dumpster.
*How?
-When two hungry people find one whole apple that has slipped from under a happy family's teeth.
*Do they eat it together?
-There were going to split it but suddenly
a blade gleamed
from the same house
and ended the conflict
in favour of one mouth.
*Does it live anywhere else?
-The slaughterhouse,
when the arm of a saint tumbles
and wraps around a whore
in a sincere reconciliation
that comes too late.
*Are you a poet?

-I was.
*Not anymore?
-It lured me and then abandoned me.
*Why do you sit in the garden?
-To advise the children.
What do you say to them?
-Beware of it.
It sometimes hides in candy.
*And to young poets?
-You still have a chance to escape.
It will turn you into dogs
panting in its footsteps.
Write novels instead.

This piece turns onto itself. The disillusioned poet is in conversation with his younger starry-eyed self. And where the younger poet insists on seeing hope – 'Did they eat it together?' – the older poet can only see the futility of hope and the vainness of poetry in the face of harsh reality. The abrupt lines 'but a knife/ suddenly gleamed' have a jolting effect. Ultimately, one hungry mouth gets to eat, regardless of what the young poet likes to imagine or hope for. The final advice is drenched in sarcasm and self-mockery. Poetry 'will turn you into dogs/ panting behind it./ Write novels instead'. The effect of the piece is made even more devastating through Abu Salih's mastery of the short lines. He capitalises on the question-and-response format to create an extremely simple yet intense piece.

Reminding us of al-Maghut's frustration with poetry, that 'immortal corpse', Abu Salih and his generation of poets have adopted his insistence on the primacy of experience, his rhetorical minimalism and his poetics of marginality. They write poetry that distances itself from poetic and critical concerns and turns towards the immediate lived reality. This 'poetics of the mundane' which finds the poetic in the most unexpected and 'non-poetic' details of life can be traced to al-Maghut. Yet, most significant in his legacy is his attitude towards poetry itself, its motivations and its claims.

The distance that al-Maghut maintained, even from his own art, developed into a distinct poetic statement voiced through a simple yet unexpectedly resonant poetic language. His significant intervention ultimately stems from his opening up the boundaries of the poetic text beyond the expectations of meter, subject matter, diction and register. He demonstrates a vision of poetry rooted in practice, not in pre-conceived theoretical expectations.

Throughout his career, al-Maghut adamantly adhered to a rebellious anti-establishment posture in his poetry and outside of it. The resonance of his work does not arise from anything particularly related to the prose poem as a form or as a theoretical practice, but it rather rises from his deliberate detachment from the prose poem as a project or a trend or an institution. When scholars trace lineages on the Arabic prose poem in the works of later generations, they often cite al-Maghut as the founder of a poetics of 'the ugly' (*al-qabīḥ*) or the mundane or the non-poetic;[44] however, it is his poetics of indifference or detachment that more drastically shaped the prose poem on levels beyond subject matter or tone. He was easily willing to give up the claim of poetry of the poem. His 'texts' invite both poets and their readers into an open space where long-standing prescriptions for and expectations from Arabic poetry are shaken and perhaps ultimately relinquished. He thus paved the way for a generation of younger poets who set out to 'destroy the temples of poetry',[45] as the critic Subhi Hadidi (Ṣubḥī Ḥadīdī) puts it. They are poets not concerned with signalling allegiances or claiming poetic lineages, as much as they are concerned with opening up the purview of Arabic poetry through individual experiences which in turn produce multiple individual definitions of what Arabic poetry can be.

Notes

1. For more on al-Maghut's relationship to the *Shiʿr* group, see Haidar, pp. 168–71, and Subhi Hadidi, 'Al-Maghut wa-shiʿr: tawqīr wa-taḥqīr', *al-Quds al-ʿArabī*, 4 April 2016, http://www.alquds.co.uk/?p=510578 (last accessed 26 November 2017).
2. Abbas Baydoun, 'Al-Sulālah al-Maghūṭiyyah: qirāʾa fī shiʿr sūrī ḥadīth', *al-Nāqid* 30 (1990), pp. 30–38; Sayed Elsisi (Sayyid al-Sīsī), *Mā baʿda*

qasīdat al-nathr: naḥwa khitāb jadīd lil-shi'riyya al-'arabiyya (Beirut: al-Mu'assassa al-'Arabiyya, 2016), p. 94; Muhammad Jamal Barut (Muḥammad Jamāl Bārūt), *Al-Shi'r yaktubu ismahu* (Damascus: Manshūrāt Ittiḥad al-Kuttāb al-'Arab, 1981), pp. 89–120.

3. Saniya Ṣāliḥ, 'Introduction', *Dīwān Al-Maghut* (Beirut: Dār al-'Awda, 1978), p. 8.
4. Ibid.
5. For more on al-Maghut's place vis-à-vis other early Arab modernists see S. Khadra Jayyusi's introduction to May Jayyusi and Naomi Shihab Nye, trans., *The Fan of Swords*, ed. Salma Khadra al-Jayyusi (Washington, DC: Three Continents Press, 1991), pp. ix–xxi.
6. Khalil Suwaylih (Khalīl Ṣuwayliḥ), *Ightiṣāb kāna wa-akhwātihā* (Damascus: Dār al-Balad), pp. 5–7.
7. Suwaylih, p. 50.
8. Ibid. p. 53.
9. He intentionally avoids naming the party he joined. We know from his biography that he ended up joining the Syrian Nationalist party for a short while.
10. Ibid. p. 37.
11. Ibid. pp. 48–51.
12. Haidar, p. 173.
13. Subhi Hadidi, 'Al-Maghut: waṣīt al-nathr, adā' al-shā'ir, wa jadal al-qaṣīda (Al-Maghut: The Medium of Prose, the Poet's Performance, and the Controversy of the Poem)', http://www.arabworldbooks.com/Readers2009/articles/maghut_hadidi2.htm (last accessed 26 November 2017).
14. Khalida Sa'id (Khuzāmā Ṣabrī), '*Ḥuzn fī ḍaw' al-qamar* li-Muhammad al-Maghut', *Majallat Shi'r* 11 (1959), pp. 98–99.
15. Ibid. p. 96.
16. Ibid.
17. Ibid. pp. 94–95.
18. Perloff, *Poetics of Indeterminacy*, p. vii.
19. Muhammad al-Maghut, *Al-A'māl al-shi'riyya*, 3rd edition (Beirut: Dār al-Madā, 2003), pp. 11–12.
20. For comparison, consider the iconic opening of al-Sayyab's '*Unshūdat al-maṭar*' (The Song of Rain) as an example of textured rhetoric:

    Your eyes are two palm tree forests in early light
    Or two balconies from which the moonlight recedes
    When they smile, your eyes, the vines put forth their leaves,

And lights dance . . . like moons in a river
Rippled by the blade of an oar at break of day;
As if stars were throbbing in the depths of them.

Translated by Lena Jayyusi and Chris Middleton, in S. Khadra Jayyusi (ed.), *Modern Arabic Literature: An Anthology* (New York: Columbia University Press, 1987), p. 427.

21. For more on simile, see Zachariah Pickard, *Elizabeth Bishop's Poetics of Description* (London: McGill-Queen's University Press, 2009), pp. 14–37; and Jacqueline Vaught Brogan, *Stevens and Simile: A Theory of Language* (Princeton: Princeton University Press, 1986), pp. 117–66.
22. Al-Maghut, p. 16.
23. Ibid. p. 42.
24. For more on simile as content see Lara Harb's summary of al-Jurjani's take on simile in Harb, 'Form, Content, and the Inimitability of the Qur'ān', pp. 310–12.
25. Al-Maghut, p. 50.
26. Ibid.
27. For the notion of destroying to build anew and the prose poem, see Adonis, 'Fī qaṣīdat al-nathr', pp. 75–83; al-Hajj, 'Introduction', *Lan*; Bazzun; al-Janabi, 'Introduction', *Dīwān ilā-l-abad.*
28. Al-Maghut, p. 92.
29. Elsisi, p. 94.
30. See Clarissa Burt, 'The Good, the Bad, and the Ugly: The Canonical Sieve and Poems from an Egyptian Avant Garde', *Journal of Arabic Literature* 28. 2 (1997), pp. 142–43, and Maghed Zaher, 'Three Egyptian Poets', *Jacket* 36 (2008), http://jacketmagazine.com/36/egyptian-poets.shtml (last accessed 20 October 2020).
31. Muhammad Mitwalli, et al. (eds), *Al-Jarād* 3 (1996), p. 1.
32. The verse evoked here is the Abbasid poet Abu Nuwas's (al-Ḥasan b. Hānī Abū Nuwās, d. 814) famous mocking of the convention of standing upon the ruined abode (*aṭlāl*). (Tell him who weeps over ruined abodes, standing, what harm would it have done had he sat down):

قل لمن يبكي على رسم درس   واقفا ما ضرّ لو كان جلس

The line is paraphrased or misquoted or distorted in the *Jarād* editorial. It also includes a misspelling of the verb ḍarra as darra:

قل لواقف يبكي على طلل درس ما دره لو كان جلس

See Mitwalli, et al., p. 1.

33. Burt, 'The Good, the Bad, and the Ugly', p. 143.
34. Hilmi Salem, 'Laqatat min lawha', *Nizwa*, 1 June 1996, http://www.nizwa.com/لقطات-من-اللوحة/ (last accessed 20 October 2020).
35. Usāma al-Danāṣūrī, *Al-A'māl al-kāmila (Collected Works)*(Cairo: Dār Mīrīt, 2009), pp. 111–12.
36. For more on the recurrent theme of dogs in the poetry of this generation of poets and its connection to an overwhelming cynicism (*al-naz'a al-kalbiyya*) which characterises their tone and approach, see Chapter Five of Sayed Elsisi's book *Mā ba'da qasīdat al-nathr*, pp. 251–53.
37. See Iman Mersal, *These are not Oranges, my Love*, trans. Khaled Mattawa (New York: The Sheep Meadow Press, 2008).
38. Khaled Mattawa, trans., 'Introduction', *These are not Oranges, my Love* (New York: The Sheep Meadow Press, 2008).
39. Iman Mersal, *Ḥattā atakhallā 'an fikrat al-buyū*t *(So I May Give up on the Idea of Houses)* (Cairo: Dār al-Tanwīr, 2013), p. 35.
40. Gaining access to Abu Salih's work is challenging. His self-published collections are not sold in bookstores or held in public collections; they are only privately circulated. I have relied on images and scans acquired through friends who have access to the limited printed editions.
41. Subhi Hadidi, *Shi'riyyāt al-ta'āqud al-'asīr* (Beirut: Al-Ahliya lil-nashr, 2017), pp. 92–93.
42. Abu Ṣaliḥ, *Jamāl kāfir (Heretic Beauty)* (private publication, 2005), p. 6.
43. Abu Salih, *Kāna nā'iman hīna qāmat al-thawra (He was Asleep when the Revolution Came)* (private publication, 2015), pp. 85–86.
44. See Jabir 'Asfur (Jābir 'Aṣfūr), *Rū'ā al-'ālam: 'an ta'sīs al-ḥadātha al-'arabiya* (Morocco: al-Markaz al-Thaqāfī al-'Arabī, 2008), pp. 186–93.
45. Hadidi, *Shi'riyyāt al-ta'āqud al-'asīr*, p. 93.

5

Mahmoud Darwish as Middleman

The large hall of *Qaṣr al-thaqāfa* in Amman was packed, as expected. It was the 23rd season of the Jarash Festival. '*Ḥāṣir ḥiṣarak lā mafar*' (Tighten your siege. There is no escape), Mahmoud Darwish (1941–2008) begins to read.[1] The audience reacts with fervour, not only in acknowledgement of the iconic poem, but also in gratitude that their expectations were satisfied. For that is the Darwish they flock to listen to in all the cities of the world. And, here in Amman, a stone's throw away from Palestine, it was only fitting that he read one of the poems that had consecrated him as the voice of the Palestinian cause. But Darwish was uneasy, especially as he stood receiving the wave of applause which swept across the hall. Perhaps he felt unsettled in his role as the poet of the cause, perhaps he had begun to find that role inadequate or limiting as a poetic aesthetic. Just as the applause begins to recede, he leans into the microphone with a disclaimer: 'This is just so I can read what I want later', he tells the audience. 'We have a pact, don't we?'

This incident was in 2004; earlier that year Darwish had published his collection *Lā taʿtadhir ʿammā faʿalt* (Don't Apologise for What You Have Done) in which he had begun to grapple with questions at the core of his poetic experience, his relationship with language, with other poets and with his subject matter. In that collection, he is openly preoccupied with the making of poetry and its possibilities in an abstract sense. In that collection, he particularly addresses his readers or his poetic interlocutors, not the crowds of unquestioning sympathising followers. Beyond the crowds of fans, he appears eager to engage the smaller group of discerning readers and listeners.

Darwish's uneasiness with the audience's immediate almost impulsive reaction to the poem in the scene above marks a meta-poetic introspective turn in his career. It also signals a shift in the poetic stakes he wanted to set up for himself and his audience. Sometimes apologetic and sometimes confrontational, with every reading and every publication after 2004, Darwish faced his audience intent on creating a shift in or an adjustment to both his perspective on his craft and their reception of it. The publication of *Lā taʿtadhir* presented Darwish in a deliberate late-style meditation on the aesthetics of his poem and the secret of the poetic in it. And we see him urgently pushing the boundaries which had informed and shaped his aesthetic thus far.

Both his professional audience and his wider following or fans were trained or conditioned in the Darwishian language and style. To the wider audience, the Darwishian text carried with it a specific mood and a recognisable ambiance. Reading his work, and especially listening to him read in a public setting, automatically conjured up an imagined shared experience which might be triggered by the poem, but which garnered the power of its effect from the political and cultural stance he came to be associated with or to represent. This is not to say that Darwish exploited political rhetoric in his work. He rarely did. This is to say that, in the poetic world he builds, a familiar poignant reality remains readily accessible. Multifaceted as the Darwishian text maybe, one of its dimensions is easily recognisable, relatable and immediately relevant to multitudes of readers/listeners. And, although his later work reveals a certain degree of exasperation with this 'status', he was well aware that he will remain indebted to the multitudes and that their expectations will continue to inform his evolving poetic project. However, he was not happy to settle in his audience's expectation, but instead eager to challenge and expand them.

Darwish is probably one of the last widely popular poets in Arabic, one of the last poets recognised and 'loved by millions'.[2] He enjoyed a high standing in the professional literary circles of poets, critics and academics, as well as wide popularity and celebrity in the public sphere in its broadest sense. His name is one of the most recognisable Arab names outside the Arab world. He makes us want to think, as does John Berger, about 'why millions of people love a poet'. At the core of this question is another more relevant one in our case here: What does poetry mean to millions who love a poet? And how does the poet balance between the expectations of millions on one hand and his commitment to his evolving poetic craft and his growing critical and meta-poetic concerns on the other? This is Mahmoud Darwish's dilemma, which he voluntarily and sincerely took on in the later part of his life.[3] Confronting this dilemma drove his later work and imbued it with an impressive self-critical edge to which poets of Darwish's status rarely feel the need to subject themselves. He reimagined his career as an 'on-going birth' and a perpetual search for 'another form of writing'.[4]

At the centre of Darwish's poetic fantasies and critical exercises was the prose poem. Darwish had experimented with poetic prose earlier in his career, most notably in his 1982 memoir of war-torn Beirut, *Memory for Forgetfulness*. Even though the work is sometimes referred to as a 'sequence of prose poems',[5] Darwish deliberately labelled it a 'memoir', keeping himself outside the ranks of Arabic prose poets. It is in this later phase, post-2004, that Darwish begins to intentionally blur the dividing line between poetry and prose and to consciously draw attention to the evasiveness of genre labels such as memoir, diaries and texts. However, these experimentations and critical meditations were both guided and restrained by his 'pact' with his audience, as he referred to above.

This audience which, throughout his career, had hailed him as a poet and received his work as poetry was the barometer by which he guided his experiments, especially those at the intersection of poetry and prose. He realised that his audience was trained in receiving his words with specific expectations of poetry. Perhaps relating to what we might call the 'orthodoxy of genre classifications' and the reading practices they engender,[6] the audience is trained in receiving everything Darwish writes as poetry. This allowed him room to push the boundaries of the poem to some extent, without the risk of falling out of the purview of poetry and out of his audience's expectations of it.[7] He was at the same time aware that his brand and his voice were intimately associated with a certain lyrical, performative and musical aesthetic from which he could not stray too far. Thus, it is from his vantage point as a poet of form and meter in Arabic that Darwish courted the prosaic and lured it into his poem.[8]

On the Road between Poetry and Prose: *Don't Apologise* and *Like Almond Blossom and Beyond*

In *Lā taʿtadhir ʿammā faʿalt* and the subsequent *Ka-zahr al-lawz aw abʿad*, Darwish actively scrutinises his own definition of poetry and his sources of inspiration. He places himself in a poetic tradition but acknowledges its evolving nature. In a poem titled '*Tunsā ka'anaka lam takun*' (Forgotten As If You Never Were), Darwish contemplates his positionality vis-à-vis those who came before and those who shall follow. He contemplates the distance between him and them, while they both travel the same road.

أَنا للطريق... هناك من سَبَقَتْ خُطَاهُ خُطَايَ
مَنْ أَمْلَى رُؤاهُ على رُؤَايَ. هُنَاكَ مَنْ
نَثَرَ الكلام على سجيَّتِه ليدخل في الحكايةِ
أَو يضيءَ لمن سيأتي بعدَهُ
أَثراً غنائياً...وحدسا

...

أَنا للطريق... هناك مَنْ تمشي خُطَاهُ
على خُطَايَ، وَمَنْ سيتبعني إلى رؤيايَ.
مَنْ سيقول شعراً في مديح حدائقِ المنفى،
أمامَ البيت، حراً من عبادَةِ أمسِ،
حراً من كناياتي ومن لغتي، فأشهد
أَنني حيٌّ
وحُرٌّ
حين أُنْسَى![9]

... I am for the road . . . there are those whose footsteps preceded mine
Those who dictated their visions onto mine. There are those
who scattered speech at ease, so it may enter the story,
or illuminate a lyrical effect or intuition
for those who shall come after
[. . .]
I am for the road . . . there are those whose steps
fall on mine, those who follow in my visions,

> those who will compose poetry praising the gardens of exile.
> In front of the house, free of the worship of yesterday,
> free of my metonymies and my language, I attest
> that I will be alive
> and free
> once forgotten.

This view of a poetic tradition as a road being travelled portrays both predecessors and the successors in motion and keeps the distance between them dynamic as well. The excerpt above speaks to a host of concerns from anxiety of influence (those whose footsteps precede mine/ those who dictate their visions unto mine) to awareness of legacy (there are those whose steps/ fall on mine, those who follow in my visions) to fear of settling or creative stagnation. An obvious subtext that directly speaks to this last concern is Darwish's constant challenging of himself and his aesthetic. The grand metaphor in this poem is the road that a poet travels throughout his career, and Darwish seems preoccupied with the way in which his road will end. He likes to imagine himself once he finally arrives 'in front of the house' as free and new. This is not a desertion of past selves or past causes, but rather a fear for them and a dread of them growing old and flat. Darwish likes to imagine his poetic voice evolving on a road, constantly emerging from itself, from its metonymies and language, and stepping forward.

Prose is one of the tools on which Darwish consciously relied to challenge himself and his poetic voice. The poem above indirectly hints at the new possibilities of poetry when speech is 'scattered at ease'. A lyrical effect instead of overt lyricism and a poetic intuition instead of an acquired knowledge are what Darwish stands considering at this crossroad. And, in his later work, beginning with *Lā taʿtadhir*, he chooses to walk the more challenging road, moving away from his comfort zone in the *tafʿīla* poem toward its frontier with *qaṣīdat al-nathr*, even though he does not jump the fence of meter, just yet.

The first section of *Lā taʿtadhir* titled 'On the Desire for Rhythm' (*Fī shahwat al-ʾīqāʿ*) reveals a pointed interest in interrogating the notion of rhythm or cadence, a major point of debate between prose poets and their contenders.

يختارني الإيقاع، يَشْرَق بي
أنا رجع الإيقاع، ولست عازفه
أنا في حضرة الذكرى
صدى الأشياء تنطق بي
فأنطق...[10]

The rhythm chooses me and chokes.
I am the rhythm's echo, not its player.
In the presence of memory
I am an echo; things speak me
So I speak . . .

Darwish here relinquishes the role of the poet as agent and designer. A poet is an echo, not a player; before he speaks, a poet is spoken to and listens. The poem thus has the potential to be as varied as the things that speak to the poet. This is not only a statement relating to subject matter but also to form. Echoing a line by al-Maʿarri on a later poet's ability to bring forth something new,[11] Darwish moulds the poem in all forms and shapes:

وأنا، وإن كنت الأخير،
وجدت ما يكفي من الكلمات...
كل قصيدة رسم
سأرسم للسنونو الآن خارطة الربيع
وللمشاة على الرصيف الزيزفون
وللنساء اللازورد...[12]

I, even though I'm last,
have found enough words …
Every poem is a tracing.
I will now trace for the swallow a map of spring
and for pedestrians on the sidewalk a jujube tree
and for women lapis lazuli …

In this metrically exact *tafʿīla* poem, Darwish rejects the formulaic and the designed. To stay alive 'every poem is mother' which gives birth to its alternatives. He embraces the poem as a dream, the dream of a dream, which poets continue to pursue until 'the last line/ on the marble of the grave':

كل قصيدة أم
تفتّش للسحابة عن أخيها
قرب بئر الماءِ:
«يا ولدي! سأعطيك البديلَ
فأنني حبلى...»/
وكل قصيدة حلمٌ:
«حلمت بأن لي حلماً»
سيحملني وأحمله
إلى أن أكتب السطر الأخير
على رخام القبر:
نمت...لكي أطير»[13]»

Every poem is a mother
seeking a brother for the cloud
near the water well:
'My son, I will give you the alternative,
for I am pregnant . . . '
And Every poem is a dream:
'I dreamt I had a dream'
It will carry me and I will carry it
until I write the last line
on the marble of the grave:
'I have fallen asleep . . . so I may fly'.

This poem's final line echoes the sentiment which ended the earlier 'Forgotten As If You Never were'. For Darwish, more terrifying than death is dying without having changed, dying without having broken free of earlier sounds. More terrifying than the end is having arrived at it the same as one had set out.

In another poem incitingly titled '*Qul mā tashā*'' (Say What You Want), Darwish arrives at a new personal *ars poetica*. He does not prescribe as much as records private notes, motivated by a question he asks himself: 'Did you write a poem?' This allows him to reflect on the alchemy of the poem and the poetic, returning to the question of rhythm:

قل ما تشاءَ. ضَعِ النقاطَ على الحروفِ.
ضَعِ الحروفَ مع الحروف لتُولَدَ الكلماتُ،
غامضةً وواضحةً، ويبتدئَ الكلامُ.
ضَعِ الكلامَ على المجاز. ضَعِ المجازَ على
الخيال. ضَعِ الخيالَ على تَلفُّته البعيد.
ضَعِ البعيدَ على البعيد.... سَيُولَدُ الإيقاعُ
عند تَشَابُكِ الصُّوَرِ الغريبةِ من لقاء
الواقعيِّ مع الخياليِّ المُشَاكسِ[14]

Say what you want. Place the dots on the letters.
Place letters along letters so that words may be born,
mysterious and clear, and then speech will begin.
Place speech on metaphor and metaphor on imagination.
Place imagination on its glancing in the distance.
Place the distant on the distant . . . and rhythm will be born
upon the entangling of strange images; from the joining
of the realistic with the quarrelsome imaginary

Very Abu Tammamian[15] in tone, this recipe for rhythm calls for the 'strange' (*gharīb*) and the 'petulant' (*mushākis*) or resistant 'distant' (*baʿīd*) summoned from afar. 'Did you write a poem?' is a very urgent question, especially when a poet in a long formal poetic tradition asks it to himself.

هل كتبت قصيدة؟
كلا!
لعل هناك ملحاً زائداً أم ناقصاً
في المفردات. لعلّ حادثة أخلّت بالتوازن
في معادلة الظلال. لعلّ نسراً
مات في أعلى الجبل. لعلّ أرضَ
الرمز خفّت في الكناية فاستباحتها
الرياح. لعلّها ثقلت على ريش الخيال.
لعل قلبك لم يفكر جيدا، ولعلّ
فكرك لم يحسَّ بما رجّك.[16]

Did you write a poem?
No!

Perhaps there's too much or too little salt
in the words. Perhaps some incident disturbed the balance
in the equation of shadows. Perhaps an eagle
died on the mountain top. Perhaps the ground of symbol
became lighter in the metonymy and was carried away by the winds.
Perhaps it was too heavy for the wings of imagination.
Perhaps your heart did not think straight.
Perhaps your thoughts did not feel that which shook you.

Darwish here dispels the comfort in prescribed form, in meter and rhyme, and returns the word *qaṣīda* to its abstract illusive meaning. The *qaṣīda* is not a formula but a dream and aspiration, like poetry. The *qaṣīda*, the poem, is the miraculous delicate configuration of elements, known and unknown, conscious and unconscious. It is an irreducible magical recipe, paradoxical in the ingredients it calls for and in the energies it requires: 'salt in words', 'equation of shadows', 'feather of imagination', the degree of a metonymy's exposure to the wind, thinking straight enough, feeling profound enough.

In the final section of the poem, Darwish once again indirectly draws out the issue of prose, an avenue of thought that is obviously a preoccupying subtext in this collection. He sets up two central dichotomies: tomorrow and yesterday, writing and speech. But he complicates the binaries by placing the poem/poetry in an obscure place between their two poles.

فالقصيدة ،
زوجة الغد وابنة الماضي، تخيّم في
مكان غامض بين الكتابة والكلام /
فهل كتبت قصيدة ؟
كلا!
إذن، ماذا كتبت؟
كتبت درساً جامعياً،
واعتزلت الشعر منذ عرفتُ
كيمياء القصيدة . . . واعتزلت![17]

[. . .] For the poem,
wife of tomorrow and daughter of yesterday, camps

in an obscure place between writing and speech/
So, have you written a poem?
No!
What have you written then?
I have written a university lecture,
and retired from poetry once I figured out
the chemistry of the poem . . . and I retired!

Once again, this poem ends by situating the contemplation of personal poetics and the possible alternative poetic roads in a moment of personal resignation and the awareness of an approaching end. It is as if figuring out the 'chemistry of the poem' becomes more pressing when the poet confronts his own death. The closer the poet is to the end of his career, the more invested he becomes in interrogating poetry at its very limit or edge, where it is at risk of disintegrating into its other (prose) or at the potential of being set 'free' of the juxtaposition all together.

Similarly, in *Like Almond Blossom or Beyond*, Darwish definitely has prose on his mind. His choice of epigraph is most telling. From the twenty-fifth night of Abū Ḥayyān al-Tawḥīdī's *al-Imtāʿ wa al-muʾānasa*, he selects this often-quoted statement, announcing the aesthetic stakes of the collection:

> The best speech (*aḥsan al-kalām*) is that [. . .] whose form (*ṣūra*) takes a middle position between poetry that is like prose and prose that is like poetry.[18]

This epigraph colours the reader's reception of the poems that follow. Although all of them are formal poems abiding by the *tafʿīla* system, Darwish plants the idea of prose in his reader's head.

The book is divided into eight sections, the first four of which are respectively titled 'You', 'He', 'I' and 'She'. The remaining four sections are all titled 'Exile' (*manfā*). This design reveals a heightened awareness of positionality. By grouping poems under the headings of the four pronouns, Darwish examines his poetic voice from different angles. All the pronouns are lenses through which the poet scrutinises himself. The collection, thus, reads like a confessional in which the poet assesses his relationship to past selves, others, beloveds, addressees and interlocutors – and prime among them is exile. In a poem titled 'Now in Exile', we hear the voice of the veteran poet pondering final statements:

قُلْ للحياةِ، كما يليقُ بشاعرٍ متمرِّس:
سيري ببطء كالإناث الواثقات بسحرهنَّ
وكيدهنَّ. لكلّ واحدةْ نداءُ ما خفيٌّ:
هَيْتَ لَكْ / ما أجملَكْ!
سيري ببطءٍ، يا حياةُ ، لكي أراك
بِكامل النُقصان حولي. كم نسيتُكِ في
خضمِّكِ باحثاً عنّي وعنكِ. وكُلَّما أدركتُ
سرَاً منك قُلتِ بقسوةٍ: ما أَجهلَكْ!
قُلْ للغياب: نَقَصتني
وأنا حضرتُ ...لأُكملَكْ![19]

Say to life, as befits an experienced poet:
Proceed slowly like females confident in their charm
and their wiles. For each has a secret call:
Come here/ How beautiful you are!
Proceed slowly, O life, so I may see you
through the complete lack that surrounds me. How I have forgotten you
when I was in your midst, seeking you and myself. Every time I
grasped
a secret of yours, you'd harshly say: How ignorant you are!

Say to absence: I lack you
and here, I have come to complete you.

In a conversational tone, prevalent in *Almond Blossom*, Darwish makes room for other voices to inhabit his own. He invites other voices to challenge his voice and push it in new directions. Fond of deconstructing binaries and blurring opposites with each other, the dialogue technique becomes, at Darwish's hands, the most honest and intimate form of self-confrontation or confession.

In the 'Exile' sections of the book, the meta-poetic concerns are foregrounded. Darwish engages two major interlocutors: an abstracted pre-Islamic poet and Edward Said. His conversation with the abstracted 'pre-Islamic poet' (*shāʿir jāhilī*) in '*Ka-washm yadd fī muʿallaqat shāʿir jāhilī*' (Like a Hand Tattoo in a Pre-Islamic Poet's Ode) allows him to soliloquise some of his haunting poetic concerns. He meditates on poetic origins and their evolution as the poet approaches the end. 'I am he', the poem opens, allowing Darwish to contemplate his evolving definition of poetry, his relationship to his Arabic tradition and the new directions he feels compelled to move in. He acknowledges the pre-Islamic poet as his partner in his poetic journey which begins with Darwish following in the pre-Islamic poet's steps.

أَنا هُوَ، يمشي أَمامي وأَتبعُهُ
لا أقول له: ههنا، ههنا
كان شيء بسيط لنا:
حَجَرٌ أَخضَرٌ. شَجَرٌ. شارعٌ.
قَمَرٌ يافعٌ. واقعٌ لم يعد واقعاً.
هو يمشي أمامي
وأمشي على ظلّه تابعاً ...

...
ألم نفترق؟ قلتُ، قال: بلى.
لك مني رجوعُ الخيال إلى الواقعيّ
ولي منك تُفَّاحة الجاذبيَّة
قلت: إلى أَين تأخذني؟
قال: صوب البداية، حيث ولِدْتَ
هنا، أنت واسمك [20]

I am he. He walks ahead of me and I follow.
I don't say to him: here, here.
Simple things were ours:
A green stone, trees. A street
a young moon. A reality no longer real.
He walks ahead of me
And I walk following his shadow …
Have we not parted?: I asked. He said: yes.
I'll give you the return of imagination to the real,
and I'll take from you the apple of gravity.
I said: Where are you taking me?

He said: Toward the beginning, where you were born
Here, you and your name

But the later poet is not always the one following, as their paths converge and diverge, and they stand speaking to each other across the widening and closing divide.

أنا هو، يمشي عليّ، وأسأله:
هل تذكرتَ شيئاً هنا؟
خَفِّف الوطءَ عند التذكُّر،
فالأرض حبلى بنا.[21]

I am he, he walks over me, and I ask:
Do you remember something here?
Tread lightly when you remember
For the earth is pregnant with us.

Darwish addresses the pre-Islamic poet: 'I am you . . . I am us . . . I am the love poem you will write . . . '[22] He recognises himself as the 'present moment' of a past he invents or conjures up. 'How am I born from something . . . that I make',[23] he wonders. It is the temptation of poetry that deceives them both,[24] he and his predecessor, and lures them towards an impossible that summons from the distance. Whether they merge into one or stand facing each other as strangers, the pre-Islamic poet leaves Darwish with the following advice:

دع الاستعارة وامش معي. هل
ترى أثراً للفراشة في الضوء؟
قلت: أراك هناك أراك تمرُّ
كخاطرة من خواطر أسلافنا
قال لي: هكذا تستعيد الفراشة
أشغالها الشاعرية: أغنية لا
يدونها الفلكيون إلا دليلاً
على صحة الأبدية / [25]

Leave the metaphor and follow me.
Do you see a trace of the butterfly in the light?
I said: I see you there passing
Like an ancestor's thought

He said: That is how the butterfly
Remembers its poetic tasks: a song
Not recorded by astronomers except to prove
the soundness of eternity.

Poetry here appears as the trace of subtle movement, as a passing thought, as a song only recorded to prove the impossible are the bequest with which Darwish walks away.

In his conversation with Edward Said, his personal friend, his fellow exile and political ally, Darwish foresees a poetic break on the horizon, a challenge. The 'impossible' appears again in the advice Edward Said entrusts Darwish with at the end of this monumental elegy, '*Ṭibāq*' (Antithesis or Counterpoint).[26]

قال: إذا متّ قبلَكَ
أوصيكَ بالمستحيْل!
سألتُ: هل المستحيل بعيد؟
فقال: على بُعْد جيلْ
سألت: وإن متُّ قبلك؟
قال: أُعزّي جبال الجليلْ
وأكتبُ: «ليس الجماليُّ إلاّ
بلوغ الملائم». والآن، لا تَنْسَ
إن متُّ قبلك أوصيكَ
بالمستحيلْ![27]

He said: If I die before you
I entrust you with the impossible?
I asked: Is the impossible far?
He said: A generation away.
I asked: And what if I die before you?
He said: I will console the mountains of Galilea
and will write: 'The aesthetic is nothing
but finding the appropriate'. And now don't forget.
If I die before you, I entrust you with the impossible.

As is often the case in the Arabic genre of elegy, the poet contemplates his own mortality as he laments the loss of his friend. Again, here, the poem takes the form of a dialogue, a conversation in which the speaker addresses himself in the mourned other. Mourning Said, Darwish also foresees a new phase in his poetic journey. The poem and with it the entire collection end with bidding farewell to 'the poetry of pain' and the echo of Edward Said's voice urging Darwish towards the impossible.

كان كالبطل الملحميّ
الأخير يدافع عن حقّ طروادةٍ
في اقتسام الروايةِ /

نَسْرٌ يودِّعُ قمَّتَهُ عالياً
عالياً،
فالإقامةُ فوق الأولمب
وفوق القِمَمْ
تثير السأمْ

وداعاً،
وداعاً لشعر الألَمْ![28]

He was like the last epic hero
defending Troy's right in sharing the narrative.

An eagle soars higher and higher, bidding farewell to his peak,
for dwelling on Olympus
and over heights
is tedious.

Farewell,
farewell poetry of pain!

Prompting the epigram from al-Tawhidi which opens the entire collection, Darwish's parting with one poetic mode signals the venturing into another. Motivated by his awareness of an approaching end, he sets out in search of that impossible middle point in the antithesis (*ṭibāq*) of poetry and prose. He sets out to write the text that sits exactly at the counterpoint to which al- Tawhidi points.

After the elegiac and reflective stance prevalent in *Almond Blossom and Beyond*, Darwish becomes more adventurous in his courting of prose.

The two major works that foreground his deliberate walking of the tight rope between genres are *In the Presence of Absence* (2006) and his final work *The Butterfly Effect* (2008). Both works appeared after a phase marked by Darwish's two brushes with death due to cardiac problems. These are experiences he recorded in *Mural* (2000) and *In the Presence of Absence*.

Darwish's writing in the period bookended by *Mural* and *In the Presence of Absence* is urgently motivated by the contemplation of death and, with it, the end of poetry. When the poet confronts his own death or eternal silence, he urgently returns to question his voice and to examine the avenues of speech that he had adopted, seeking to open new undiscovered ones. This connection between personal death and a poetic dead-end is what seems to have tempted Darwish to his more daring experimentations in conflating poetry and prose.[29]

If the search for poetry is one that haunts all poets, it is more pronounced in the works of Arab poets like Darwish who committed themselves to the *tafʿīla* poem but found themselves, especially later in their careers, eager to push the boundaries of the form upon which they insisted. Here is where the technical dilemma of meter takes on added symbolic significance.

A Final Journey towards Poetry as Effect

Not merely an autobiographical text, Sinan Antoon describes *In the Presence of Absence* as a 'poetography . . . the genesis and maturation of a poet and a life in and for poetry'.[30] In this self-elegy, Darwish bids farewell to himself and his others and clearly signals his 'search for another form of writing'. Consisting of blocks of metered and rhymed poetry, as well as unmetered yet highly rhythmic and musically charged prose, Darwish chooses to label this convergence of poetry and prose 'a text'. By that, he deliberately distances himself from the practice of the Arabic prose poem, while at the same time inserting himself in the polemics that surround it.

In his book *In the Presence of Absence*, Darwish takes the poet's monologue, his dialogue with the self, to an abstracted extreme. The book opens with the poet addressing himself in the second person, however the address, at that conjuncture in Darwish 's career, could easily be directed at poetry, the elusive ‘impossible’ he had committed himself to track down, no matter where this ‘alluring conquest’ will take him.

سطراً سطراً أنثرك أمامي بكفاءة لم أوتها إلا في المطالع /
وكما أوصيتني، أقف الآن باسمك كي أشكر مشيّعيك إلى هذا السفر الأخير، وأدعوهم إلى اختصار الوداع،
والانصراف إلى عشاء احتفالي يليق بذكراك /

فلتأذن لي بأن أراك، وقد خرجت مني وخرجت منك، سالماً كالنثر المصفّى على حجر يخضرّ أو يصفرّ في غيابك. ولتأذن لي بأن ألمّك، واسمك، كما يلمّ السابلة ما نسي قاطفو الزيتون من حبّات خبّأها الحصى. ولنذهبنّ معاً أنا وأنت في مسارين:

أنت، إلى حياة ثانية، وعدتك بها اللغة، في قارئ قد ينجو من سقوط نيزك على الأرض.

وأنا، إلى موعد أرجأته أكثر من مرة، مع موت وعدته بكأس نبيذ أحمرَ في إحدى القصائد. فليس على الشاعر حرج إن كذب. وهو لا يكذب إلا في الحبّ، لأن أقاليم القلب مفتوحة للغزو الفاتن.[31]

I scatter you before me line by line with a mastery I possessed only in the beginnings.

Just as you asked me, I stand now in your name to thank those who have come to bid you farewell before this final journey and to call on them to hasten their farewell and go on to the banquet befitting your memory.

Allow me to see you, now that you have left me and I have left you, safe and sound like pure prose on a stone that may turn green or yellow in your absence. Allow me to gather you and your name, just as passersby gather the olives that harvesters forgot under pebbles. Let us then go together, you and I, on two paths:

You, to a second life promised to you by language, in a reader who might survive the fall of a comet on earth.

I, to a rendezvous I have postponed more than once with a death to whom I had promised a glass of red wine in a poem. A poet is at liberty to lie, but he only lies in love because the heart’s provinces are open to alluring conquests.[32]

The 'I' here addresses itself, its 'you', as poetry. Heading towards a remainder of life spared by death, Darwish also sees his poetry heading towards 'a second life in language, scattered line by line . . . like pure prose on a stone'. Poetry here, too, confronts its absence and the possibility of second life in its other.

Mahmoud Darwish is fond of paradoxes: memory and forgetfulness, self and other, home and exile, here and there, victim and oppressor . . . For his entire career, he too easily drew upon some of these oppositions, so that they lost their charge and became expected fixtures of his poetic repertoire. The opposition of poetry and prose, however, is one he confronted with the urgency of realising that his life was not spent in poetry but in search of it, a constant movement towards poetry that looms on the horizon of the impossible. In *The Butterfly Effect,* Darwish sets out towards that horizon.

Many critics and translators have used the term 'prose poem' to describe texts by Darwish as early as *Dhākira lil-nisyān* (*Memory for Forgetfulness*, 1982). The term in these cases is probably not a genre marker as much as it is a way of expressing admiration towards the aesthetic qualities of Darwish's prose. However, the term becomes misleading and wrong, when used to describe the later texts, especially *The Butterfly Effect*. For it fails to acknowledge the juxtapositions of verse and prose in all its technical detail, and poetry and prose in the abstract sense, which were at the forefront of Darwish 's concerns in that work. As is the case with *In the Presence of Absence*, in *The Butterfly Effect*, Darwish was writing on the edge of verse, at the limits of the *taf'īla* system, with prose on his mind. He consciously labelled the former 'text' and the later 'diaries'. Regardless of what these labels indicate or how accurate they are in describing the texts that ensue, both labels disturb or complicate the assumptions of 'poetry' and 'poems' which are easily made about any texts that Darwish presents.

It is reductive to describe *The Butterfly Effect* as a collection of prose poems because most pronounced in this book are two things: Darwish's motivating preoccupation with the prose poem in these texts and his insistence on not using the term prose poem to describe any of them. The dilemma of *qaṣīdat al-nathr,* both on an abstract level relating to what poetry is and can be, and on a specific level relating to the technicalities of Arabic prosody, is one of the determining impetuses in *The Butterfly Effect*. Furthermore, it is a dilemma that Darwish is not eager to resolve.

The work consists of prose entries and metered *taf'īla* pieces which are almost always lineated and signalled as verse. However, both metered and unmetered texts are included under the label of 'diaries'. They are all entries or installations in what we assume to be the poet's private thoughts or notes. The guise of 'diaries' (*yawmiyyāt*) allows for a text that flirts with several genres: the poem, the short story, the journalistic report, the epigrammatic note, the manifesto. The label 'diaries' also alters the reader's relationship to the text. Not an addressee as much as an accidental listener or eavesdropper, the reader of *The Butterfly Effect* is privy to Darwish 's exercises in or around the prose poem, exercises he has not fully intended or committed to writing yet. The entry titled 'Like a Prosaic Poem' is most striking among these exercises.

> صيفٌ خريفيٌّ على التلال كقصيدة نثرية. النسيم إيقاعٌ خفيف أحسُّ به ولا أسمعه في تواضع الشجيرات. والعشب المائل إلى اصفرار صورٌ تتقشف، وتغري البلاغة بالتشبه بأفعالها الماكرة. لا احتفاء على هذه الشعاب إلا بالمتاح من نشاط الدوريّ، نشاط يراوح بين معنى وعبث. والطبيعة جسد يتخفف من البهرجة والزينة، ريثما ينضج التين والعنب والرّمان ونيسانُ شهوات يوقظها المطر. «لولا حاجتي الغامضة إلى الشعر لما كنت في حاجة إلى شيء» – يقول الشاعر الذي خفّت حماسته فقلّتْ أخطاؤه. يمشي لأن الأطباء نصحوه بالمشي بلا هدف، لتمرين القلب على لامبالاةٍ ما ضرورية للعافية. وإذا هجس، فليس بأكثر من خاطرة مجانيّة. الصيف لا يصلح للإنشاد إلا في ما ندر. الصيف قصيدة نثرية لا تكترث بالنسور المحلّقة في الأعالي.[33]

> An autumnal summer on the hills, like a prose poem. The breeze is a light rhythm I feel but do not hear in the modesty of trees, and the yellowing grass is images becoming austere and luring rhetoric to emulate its sly deeds. Nothing celebrated in these parts except what activities the swallow offered, activities alternating between meaning and absurdity. Nature is a body shedding adornments and decoration while the fig, the grape, the pomegranate ripen; and April: desires awoken by rain. 'If it weren't for my mysterious need for poetry, I wouldn't have needed anything', says the poet whose enthusiasm has waned and thereby his mistakes are scarce. He walks because the doctors recommended that he

> walk aimlessly to train the heart in a carelessness necessary for health. If he thinks, it's only with a gratuitous thought. Summer is rarely fit for song. Summer is a prosaic poem indifferent to the eagles soaring high above.

Darwish stands at arm's length from the idea of a prose poem, contemplating it. He keeps his distance with the use of the simile, 'like' and with the adjective prosaic (*nathriyya*). This is not a prose poem but an imitation of one. Indeed, delving too deeply into the weave of the technicalities here will not amount to much. Nevertheless, it can shed light on Darwish's reservations when writing this piece with the word *qaṣīda* in its title. Rather than writing a prosaic (or prose) poem, Darwish wants to think about it as a hypothesis.

It is not a thing as much as a transition from one thing to another, like an 'an autumnal summer', coming out of itself and disintegrating into something else. Right at that moment of transformation, Darwish imagines the prosaic poem. It is something latent and in the process of forming, not yet achieved, felt but not yet heard, yellowing, alternating, stripped of embellishment, waiting. Darwish's hypothetical poem sits right at the counterpoint where direction begins to change from one thing to its opposite. Even if sceptical about this new direction, it is healthy for the experienced poet to walk aimlessly, even if hesitantly, down the path of prose. Something is rejuvenating, even if agitating, in occupying oneself with a 'gratuitous thought', surrendering to the summer and forgetting about the 'eagles soaring high above'.

In pieces like 'The Horse Has Fallen Off the Poem' and in 'The Critics Assassinate Me Sometimes',[34] Darwish hints at a repositioning in his poetic stance. The core movement of this shift is a loosening up or a certain degree of abandon, not on a technical level, but on the ontological level of thinking about poetry. The theme of turning away from the established 'purposes of poetry' and 'taking a side road' is recurrent in later works. As early as the collection *Why Did You Leave the Horse Alone* (1995) and especially the poem 'A Rhyme for the Mu'allaqāt',[35] Darwish begins gesturing towards prose as an inevitable poetic challenge. The poet's excursion into prose, even when Darwish portrays it as a playful straying off the path, is always haunted by the spectre of Arabic 'divine prose'[36] which can surpass verse as poetry. And hence, the nod to the Qur'ānic is hard to miss in 'Like a Prosaic Poem' (while the fig, the grape, the pomegranate ripen). In later works, and especially in *The Butterfly Effect*, it becomes clear that prose as a poetic challenge is at the core of Darwish's late style. Eager for a dialogue with the other side, as Darwish always is, he lures prose and the more problematic 'prose poem' into a conversation.

A Prose Poet by Proxy: Mahmoud Darwish Channels Salim Barakat

Darwish's conversation with his friend Salim Barakat (b. 1951), the Kurdish-Syrian poet and novelist, is the closest he gets to admittingly writing a prose poem. Through Barakat's intercession, Darwish discovers a conviviality with the prose poem. Marvelling at his friend's ability to render the 'impossible' seemingly probable, he more daringly interrogates the poetic possibilities of prose.

Darwish composes two poems dedicated to Salim Barakat inspired by the latter's unique style in achieving the poetic. The first poem 'The Kurd Has Nothing But the Wind' is the last poem in *Don't Apologise for What You Have Done*. In this *taf'īla* poem, Darwish proves himself to be an exceptionally attentive reader of Barakat's 'magical' prose. Alert to the subtleties of Barakat's language, diction, attitude and posture, Darwish captures what renders the prosaic 'magical' in Barakat's texts. He distils the Barakatian lexicon to its key elements and uses them to build this poem; a tribute to Barakat the man, the writer and the poetic voice.

يتذكّرُ الكرديُّ حين أزورُهُ، غَدَهُ ..
فيُبعدُهُ بُمكْنسة الغبارِ: إليك عنّي!
فالجبالُ هِيَ الجبالُ. ويشربُ الـڤودكا
لكي يبقي الخيال على الحياد: أَنا
المسافرُ في مجازي، والكراكيُّ الشقيَّةُ
إخوتي الحَمْقىَ. وينفُضُ عن هُويَّتِهِ
الظلالَ: هُوِيَّتي لُغتي. أنا.. وأنا.
أنا لغتي. أنا المنفيّ في لغتي.
وقلبي جمرةُ الكُرْديِّ فوق جبالِهِ الزرقاء ...

نيڤُوسْيا هوامِشُ في قصيدته،

ككُلّ مدينةٍ أخرى. على درّاجةٍ
حمل الجهاتِ، وقال: أسْكُنُ أَينما
وَقَعَتْ بيَ الجهةُ الأخيرةُ. هكذا
اختارَ الفراغَ ونام. لم يَحْلُمْ
بشيء مُنْذ حَلَّ الجِنُّ في كلماتِهِ،
[كلماتُهُ عضلاتُهُ. عضلاتُهُ كلماتهُ]
فالحالمون يُقَدِّسون الأمسَ، أَوْ
يَرْشُون بوَّاب الغد الذهبيِّ...
لا غَدَ لي ولا أمسِ. الهُنَيْهَةُ
ساحتي البيضاء.../[37]

When I visit him, the Kurd remembers his morrow
and waves it away with a duster: Away!
The mountains are the mountains. He drinks vodka
to keep the neutrality of imagination: I travel in my metaphor
and the mischievous cranes are my foolish brothers.
He dusts the shadows off his identity:
my identity is my language. I . . . and I.
I am my language. I am exiled in my language.
My heart is the Kurd's coal, burning on his blue mountains.

Nicosia is a margin to his poem,
like every other city. On a bicycle
he carried the directions and said: I settle wherever
the last direction places me. Thus,
he chose emptiness and fell asleep. He has dreamt
of nothing since genies have settled in his words
[His words are his muscles. His muscles, his words]
For Dreamers worship yesterday or
bribe the doorman of the golden morrow …
No morrow for me, no yesterday. This instance alone
is my white piazza.

On one level the poem is a biography, capturing the most fundamental experience in Barakat's life, the itinerant, the Kurd, the traveller on the margins of place and time. However, the poem succeeds in capturing

Barakat's particular Kurdish experience without exploiting the all too exhausted theme of the exile or the outsider. Taking cues from Barakat himself, Darwish turns the theme inside out. Place becomes the margin to the marginalised subject. Directions do not take him, but rather 'on his bicycle he carried directions'. As an outsider shunned by and consequently unburdened by past and future, the Barakat of Darwish's poem defiantly claims the present moment and from that only certainty deals his revenge on time, place and their politics of inclusion and exclusion.

Darwish paints a penetrating profile of Barakat the erratic, violent and linguistically reckless man, 'His words are his muscles. His muscles are his words'. Still, more important than the biographical portrait is Darwish's employing of the biographical to highlight and pay tribute to the most defining feature of Barakat's personality and his texts: his unique way of contending with language. Darwish captures Barakat's unique oppositional stance in time and place as it manifests itself in his poetic language. The achievement of Darwish's poem, thus, is that it is itself a commentary on the poetic 'miracle' of Barakat's prose and a translation of it into verse.

منزله نظيفٌ مثلُ عَيْن الديكِ ..
منسيٌّ كخيمة سيّد القوم الذين
تبعثروا كالريش. سَجَّادٌ من الصوف
المجعَّد. مُعْجَمٌ مُتآكل. كُتُبٌ مُجَلَّدةٌ
على عَجَل. مخدّاتٌ مطرَّزَةٌ بإبرة
خادم المقهى. سكاكينٌ مُجَلَّخةٌ لذبح
الطير والخنزير. فيديو للإباحيات.
باقاتٌ من الشوك المُعَادِلِ للبلاغةِ.
شُرْفَةٌ مفتوحةٌ للاستعارة. ها هنا
يَتَبادَلُ الأتراكُ والإغريقُ أدوارَ
الشتائم. تلك تَسْلِيَتي وتَسْلِيَةُ
الجنود الساهرين على حدود فُكاهةٍ
سوداء../

ليس مسافراً هذا المسافرُ، كيفما اتَّفَقَ..
الشمالُ هو الجنوبُ، الشرقُ غَرْبٌ
في السراب. ولا حقائبَ للرياح،
ولا وظيفة للغبار. كأنه يُخفي

الحنينَ إلى سواهُ، فلا يُغنّي . . . لا
يُغَنيِّ حين يدخُلُ ظلُّه شَجَرَ الأكاسْيا،
أو يبلِّلُ شَعرَهُ مَطَرٌ خفيفٌ...
بل يُناجي الذئبَ، يسأله النزالَ:
تعال يا ابن الكلب نَقْرَعْ طَبْلَ
هذا الليل حتى نوقظ الموتى. فإنَّ
الكُرْدَ يقتربون من نار الحقيقة،
ثم يحترقون مثل فراشة الشُّعَراء/

عرفَ ما يريد من المعاني. كُلُّها
عَبَثٌ. وللكلمات حيلَتُها لصيد نقيضها،
عبثاً. يفضّ بكارةَ الكلمات ثم يعيدها
بكراً إلى قاموسه. ويَسُوسُ خَيْلَ
الأبجدية كالخراف إلى مكيدته، ويحلقُ
عانَةَ اُللُغةِ: انتقمتُ من الغياب.
فَعلْتُ ما فعل الضبابُ بإخوتي.
وشَوَيْتُ قلبي كالطريدة. لن أكون
كما أريد. ولن أحبَّ الأرض أكثر
أو أقلَّ من القصيدة. ليس
للكرديِّ إلاّ الريح تسكنُهُ ويسكُنُها.
وتُدْمِنُه ُويُدْمنُها، لينجوَ من
صفات الأرض والأشياء .../[38]

His house is as clean as a rooster's eye …
Forgotten like the tent of a chief whose people
have scattered like feathers. Rugs of
wrinkly wool. A tattered dictionary. Books hurriedly
bound. Cushions embroidered with the café servant's
needle. Knives sharpened for the slaughter
of bird and pig. Pornographic videos.
Bouquets of thorns that equal eloquence.
A balcony open onto metaphor: right here,
the Turks and Greeks exchange
curses. This is my entertainment and that
of soldiers keeping vigil on the borders of black comedy . . . /

This is no traveller who travels any which way ...
North is south and east is west
in the mirage. No luggage for the wind,
no vocation for dust. As if he hides
his longing for others and doesn't sing.
He does not sing when his shadow enters the acacia tree,
nor when light rain wets his hair.
He calls to the wolf instead, and invites him to a duel:
Come, you son of a dog, let's sound the drums
of this night and wake the dead. The Kurds
approach the fire of truth and then
burn like the poet's butterfly/

He has learnt all the meanings he wanted, all
nonsense. And words have tricks to trap
their opposites, all nonsense. He deflowers words
then returns them as virgins to his dictionary. He herds
the cavalry of the alphabet like sheep into his trap, and shaves
the pubis of language: I have avenged myself of absence.
I did what fog had done to my brothers
and roasted my heart like prey. I will not be
as I wish. I will not love the land more
or less than the poem. The Kurd has nothing
but the wind living in him as he in it,
addicted to him as he to it,
that he may be spared the attributes of land and things.

'Feathers', 'knives', 'vain', 'slaughter', 'deflower', 'trap', 'pubis', 'prey' . . . these are just a few of the quintessentially Barakatian words that Darwish employs here. The poem is an inventory of words, motifs and constructions not just recurrent in Barakat's work, but foundational to the linguistic world that Barakat carves into the body of Arabic. And, this, the claim on the Arabic language that Barakat undeniably succeeds in making is what draws Darwish to Barakat's poetic project in prose and motivates him to emulate it or co-opt it or pay tribute to it, or simply engage it in conversation.

The poem ends with a powerful statement in which Darwish points to the seat of poetry in a text, whether in verse or in prose. The crutch of identity politics does not make poetry, nor do themes or worthy causes. Darwish recognises in Barakat's duelling with language a confrontation which yields poetry needless of proofs;[39] a confrontation Darwish himself had deliberately taken on later in his life. Addressing himself as much as Barakat, Darwish ends his poem with two notions that have shaped both his and Barakat's poetic experiences: identity and absence. And, poetry, he concludes, is a negation of defeat of both in language.

باللغة انتصَرْتَ على الهُوَيَّةِ
قُلْتُ للكرديِّ، باللغة انتقمتَ
من الغيابِ
فقال : لن أَمضي إلى الصحراءِ
قُلْتُ ولا أَنا...
ونظرتُ نحو الريح/
– عِمْتَ مساء
– عمت مساء[40]

With language, you triumphed over identity,
I told the Kurd, with language you have taken your revenge
on absence.
He said: I will not retreat to the desert
I said: Neither will I …
and I glanced toward the wind/
-Good night
-Good night

Despite the many resonances Darwish finds with Barakat's text, in 'The Kurd Has Nothing But the Wind', he comments on Barakat's recipe for poetry from the other side of the fence. With admiration bordering on fascination, he *counterparts* Barakat's poetic world in a *taf'īla* poem, he translates it into verse, the poetic mode he masters. In 'Skogas', a diary entry in *The Butterfly Effect*, Darwish is tempted to try out Barakat's poetic recipe. Taking advantage of the space allowed him by the claim of 'diaries', he *contrafacts* the Barakatian prose poem. Insightfully following Barakat's cues, he composes a prose piece which functions as a manifesto: a statement on Barakat's poetry, on prose as a medium for poetry and on poetry as the impossible that forever eludes and recedes into the horizon.

This block of prose is structurally designed around three focal points, all borrowed from Barakat's poetic world: the scene (the raw material), the hunt (the approach) and the cooking (the art). By selecting these three key motifs, Darwish reveals his understanding of the poetic function of themes in Barakat's work and perhaps the prose poem in general. Themes are transformed, by insistent repetition, into elements of form. They contribute to the music and design of the text more than they contribute to its meaning. Meaning is the least of Barakat's concerns. He is willing to subdue it or sacrifice it for the sake of creating the effect, the sound and echo, the thunder (*dawiyy*) of poetry. Darwish performs this understanding in the opening of 'In Skogas', in which he sets the scene (*al-mashhad*):

> سكوغوس، من ضواحي ستوكهولم. غابة من أشجار البتولا والصنوبر والحور والكرز والسرو. وسليم بركات في عزلته المنتقاة بمهارة المصادفة التي تهبُّ بها الريح على المصائر. لا يخرج منها منذ صار جزءاً من المشهد، محاطاً بطيور الشمال: العقعق والغراب وكسّار الجوز ونقّار الخشب والزرياب والقُرْقُف والشحرور الأسود والسمّان والذيل الحرير. صادقها ريشاً ومنقاراً وذيلاً وهجرة، ومنحها صفاتٍ كردية من مشتقات القلق، لا ليكسر العزلة، بل ليؤثث شروط الإقامة في البعيد...بعيدا عما يفعل الكُتّاب بالكتاب إذا غاروا من بلاغة المنفي... وقريباً من أُلفة السناجب، والأرانب والغزلان والثعالب التي تلقي عليه التحية عبر النافذة، وتهرب وتلعب خلف تمارينه اللغوية.[41]

> Skogas, a suburb of Stockholm, a forest of birches, pines, poplars, cherries and cypresses. And Salim Barakat, in his isolation, an isolation chosen with the skill of coincidence brought about by the winds of fate. He hasn't emerged from it since he had become part of the scene, surrounded by the birds of the North: magpies, crows, nutcrackers, woodpeckers, jays, blue tits, blackbirds, pheasants and waxwings. He has befriended them in feather, beak, tail and migration and has bestowed upon them Kurdish traits derived from worry. This he did not to disrupt his isolation but to better furnish the conditions for settling in the distance, away from what writers do with other writers when they are jealous of exile's eloquence, but close to the familiarity of squirrels,

> rabbits, deer and foxes who greet him from the window and scurry to play behind his linguistic exercises.

Scene (*mashhad*) is one of Barakat's buzzwords. Darwish here paints an overwhelming abundant scene with lists of trees, birds and animals all extracted from the Barakatian poetic space. The lists and their constituting words scurry one behind the other to 'play behind his linguistic exercises'. Each list functions as one strain of the complex melody constructed here. The names of trees, animals and birds pick up the pace of the piece and propel it forward in form, sound and poetic charge. After setting a distinctly Barakatian scene populated with the raw material from which a poem may emerge, Darwish turns to Barakat the hunter, the trapper, the butcher of the wild (*al-mutawaḥḥish*).

> يستيقظ على تحرُّشات الطير بزجاج البيت المبنيّ بالطوب والخشب.. يجرُّ عربته الصغيرة إلى سوق اللحم: نداءِ الحسّيّ للحسّيّ. يختار منه الصريح المتعطش إلى تدريب المتوحش على آداب الطهو. ويختار، لتأجيج الرغبة بين الآكل والمأكول، توابلها الحارقة الحاذقة... الفُطْر المخصص لمذاق التورية، ونبيذاً شيرازي النَّسَبِ يوقظ في الشاعر نزعته إلى الطرب في خريف المنفى. يجر عربته الصغيرة وسط الغابة برفقة طيور الشمال التي تعرفه من فانيلته المبللة بالمطر والعرق. فلا أحد سوى كرديّ مثله يتجاسر على مناخ البلطيق.[42]

> He wakes up to the birds pecking at the glass of brick and timber house. He drags his small cart to the meat market: the call of flesh to flesh. There he chooses the unabashed, thirsting for training the wild in the art of cooking. For igniting the desire between eater and eaten, he chooses its hot pungent spices . . . and mushrooms to accentuate the taste of dissimulation and wine of Shirazian lineage to awaken in the poet the urge to ecstasy in the autumn of exile. He drags his small cart through the forest accompanied by the birds of the North that recognize him from his undershirt, wet with rain and sweat. Nobody but a Kurd like him could brave the Baltic climate.

Building on idiosyncrasies of Barakat's personality, his undershirt, his fascination with knives and his love of cooking, Darwish transforms the biographical tidbits into correlatives of Barakat's poetic project. He captures the graphic, violent, aggressive approach in the image of Barakat dragging his cart to the meat market. The prose poet hunts his words and ensnares them in a lexicon whose logic corresponds to 'the call of flesh to flesh'. The meat of a word, its flesh speaks to the flesh of that next to it. Together they contribute to a design that functions very much like a web or net, which holds the wild and chaotic within a form shaped by the unruliness of the elements trapped in it. In this hunt, Darwish describes Barakat's process as a hunt scene[43] in which the poet recognises and engages the raw material of poetry.

In the final movement of this piece, Darwish turns to Barakat the cook, the skilled master who holds the magic wand of language stirring the unsuspecting ingredients into poetry. This is the moulding phase, the work of the skilful hand which interprets, transforms, arranges and creates:

وهو إذ يهجس الآن فلا يهجس إلا بالطهو: قصيدة نهاره المرئية. الطهو موهبة اليد المدربة على وضع الملائم في الملائم، وعلى إدراك المتخيل الشعوري بالرائحة والطعم، وعلى إبداع المعنى الحسي مما كان بدائي الشكل. الطهو شعر الحواس إذا اجتمعت في يد... قصيدة تؤكل ولا تتحمل خللاً في التوازن بين العناصر. وسليم بركات لا يتحمل الثناء، منذ صار سريع البكاء![44]

> His only obsession now is cooking: the visual poem of his day. Cooking is the talent of a hand skilled at pairing things together, at achieving the imagination of emotion in taste and smell, at creating sensuous meaning from primitive form. Cooking is the poetry of the senses combined in a hand . . . an edible poem that doesn't tolerate imbalance in ingredients. And Salim Barakat no longer tolerates praise since he has become prone to tears.

A visible, edible poem is an evident poem, in no need of proof. And the secret lies in the balance: 'pairing things together', 'achieving' smell and taste of the imaginary, and innovating tangible, sensuous meaning from 'primitive form'. The secret to poetry, thus, is in the mix, the recipe and the interpretation of the recipe which holds the whole together. Form and meaning are the fruit of that intricate process. There is no way of anticipating how it will cook. It all depends on the art and intuition of the hand that finds, grabs and moulds.

The definition of poetry we find in one poem is a dimension of its organic structure or makeup. There is no way of comparing poetry in one text to poetry in another, except by using an abstraction that has nothing to do with either. The term poetry itself is, therefore, such an abstraction. If our investigation of poems is launched from abstraction, it is then bound to miss or disregard specific manifestations or disclosures of poetry born out of poets' mishaps, their dodging of the abstraction and their contention or unease with it. 'What is poetry?' Darwish asks himself in his late style mode. 'It is that which once we hear or read drives us to say: This is poetry and there is no need for proof',[45] he answers. And, setting out, *a priori*, to write a poem that fits an already existing definition is impossible. Poetry can only be achieved after the fact, that is the poem.

On his quest for poetry, with Edward Said and Salim Barakat as guides, Darwish accepts poetry as the impossible, as an end beyond reach. Texts that strive to achieve that impossible are poems, needless of proof, regardless of how they make their claim. For when the end goal is placed in the realm of the impossible, everything before it, on the way to it, becomes allowed, attainable and at the disposal of the hand that reaches.

Notes

1. www.youtube.com/watch?v=yqXBR8TUy38&t=11s
2. John Berger, https://www.youtube.com/watch?v=Jvqa5QfgCKk
3. Sinan Antoon, 'Preface', *In the Presence of Absence* (New York: Archipelago books, 2011), p. 8.
4. Ibid.
5. Ibrahim Muhawi, 'Introduction', *Memory for Forgetfulness*, by Mahmoud Darwish (Berkley: University of California Press, 1995), p. xxviii.
6. Perloff, *Dance of the Intellect*, p. 138.
7. Amjad Nasser, 'Darwish wa qasīdat al-nathr', *Al-Karmel* 90 (2009), p. 117. Also see Amjad Nasser, 'Yawmiyyāt Maḥmūd Darwish ka-qinā' li-qaṣīdat al-nathr (Darwish's Diaries, A Mask for the Prose Poem)', *Aljazeera*, 24 March 2014, https://www.aljazeera.net/news/cultureandart/2012/3/24/-يوميات-محمود-درويش-كقناع-لقصيدة-النثر
8. Hussein bin Hamza (Ḥusayn bin Ḥamza), 'Maḥmūd wa qaṣīdat al-nathr: uḥikubi aw lā uḥibuki (Mahmoud and the Prose Poem: I Love You I Love

You Not)', *Al-Akhbār*, 8 August 2009, https://al-akhbar.com/Literature_Arts/128948 (last accessed 20 October 2020).

9. Mahmoud Darwish, *Lā ta'tadhir 'ammā fa'alt* (Beirut: Riad El-Rayyes Books, 2004), p. 73.
10. Ibid. p. 15.
11. Al-Ma'arri's line:

    وإني وإن كنت الأخير زمانه   لآتٍ بما لم تستطعه الأوائل

    > Even though at the end of time, I can still bring forth
    > what those before me couldn't

    Abu al-'Alā' al-Ma'arri, *Saqṭ al-zand* (Beirut: Dār Ṣādir, 1957), p. 193.
12. Darwish, *Lā ta'tadhir*, p. 21.
13. Ibid. p. 22.
14. Ibid. p. 95.
15. Abu Tammam's difficult and instant meanings are the centre of much debate. He defends his 'strange' poetry in many famous accounts and memorable verse. Of the lesser known, however, are these verses which appear in a short invective in which he attacks a poet named Yusuf al-Sarrāj and his dull and easy poetry:

    تزحزح عن بعيد العقل حتى   توّجه أن توجّه في القريب

    > It falls short of the mind's farthest reaches and
    > strives to grasp that which is already within reach

    Abu Tammam, vol. 2, p. 206.
16. Darwish, *La ta'tadhir*, p. 96.
17. Ibid.
18. Mahmoud Darwish, *Ka-zahr al-lawz aw ab'ad* (Beirut: Riad El-Rayyes Books, 2005); al-Tawhidi, vol. 2, p. 145, translation by Hachmeier, p. 381.
19. Darwish, *Ka-zahr al-lawz aw ab'ad*, pp. 18–19.
20. Ibid. pp. 153–54.
21. Ibid. p. 156.
22. Ibid. pp. 158–59.
23. Ibid, p. 168.
24. Ibid. p. 161.
25. Ibid. p. 160.
26. See the following translations of 'Ṭibāq', George El-Hage (trans.),

'Antithesis', *Journal of Arabic Literature* 36 (2005), pp. 50–56, Mona Anis (trans.), 'Edward Said: A Contrapuntal Reading', *Al-Ahram Weekly* 30 September – 6 October 2004; and Elias Sanbar (trans.), 'Contrepoint', *Le monde diplomatique*, 28 January 2005; and Rebecca Dyer, 'Poetry of Politics and Mourning: Mahmoud Darwish's Genre-Transforming Tribute to Edward W. Said', *PMLA* 122.5 (2007), pp. 1447–62.

27. Darwish, *Ka-zahr al-lawz aw ab'ad*, p. 195.
28. Ibid. pp. 196–97.
29. Sinan Antoon and Fady Joudah, both translators of Darwish, have made that connection between Darwish's stance at the intersection of life and death and his more aggressive experimentations in prose. Antoon, 'Preface', p. 8; Fady Joudah, 'Mahmoud Darwish's Lyric Epic', *Human Architecture: Journal of Sociology of Self Knowledge* 7 (2009), pp. 7–8.
30. Sinan Antoon, 'Preface', *In the Presence of Absence*, p. 6.
31. Mahmoud Darwish, *Fī ḥaḍrat al-ghiyāb* (Beirut: Riad El-Rayyes Books, 2006), pp. 9–10.
32. Mahmoud Darwish, *In the Presence of Absence*, trans. Sinan Antoon (Brooklyn: Archipelago Books, 2011), pp. 15–16.
33. Mahmoud Darwish, *Athar al-farāsha* (Beirut: Riad El-Rayyes Books, 2008), pp. 21–22.
34. Ibid. p. 109.
35. Mahmoud Darwish, *Al-A'māl al-jadīda* (Beirut: Riad El-Rayyes Books, 2009), p. 384.
36. لا بد من نثر إذاً،
لا بد من نثر إلهي لينتصر الرسول

    Prose is necessary then,
    A divine prose so that the messenger may triumph.

    Ibid. p. 384.
37. Darwish, *Lā ta'tadhir*, pp. 159–60.
38. Ibid. pp. 161–63.
39. Darwish, *Athar farāsha*, p. 226.
40. Darwish, *Lā ta'tadhir*, p. 164–65.
41. Darwish, *Athar farāsha*, pp. 250–51.
42. Ibid. pp. 251–55.
43. On the modern meta-poetic hunt for the poem, see Stetkevych, *The Hunt in Arabic Poetry*, pp. 225–79.

44. Darwish, *Athar farāsha*, p. 252.
45. Darwish, *Athar farāsha*, p. 226. Of course, this brings to mind al-Jurjani's statement on poetry in *Dalāʾil al-iʿjāz*: 'If recited, you sense in it something and you say: this is it'. Al-Jurjani, *Kitāb dalāʾil al-iʿjāz*, p. 88.

6

Salim Barakat: Poetry as Linguistic Conquest

Salim Barakat is a Kurdish-Syrian poet and novelist who was born in 1951 in Qāmishlī, an ethnically, religiously and linguistically diverse city in Northern Syria. He moved to Damascus in the early 1970s and then to Beirut. In 1982, the escalating political and sectarian tensions in the war-torn city forced him to leave for Cyprus, where he remained for over fifteen years. He currently resides in Sweden. Barakat is often listed among the prominent modern poets in Arabic. He is, however, the most distinct among the writers included under the umbrella of the Arabic prose poem. His language is intimidatingly dense and complex, parading a vast and daunting vocabulary. His texts are the products of an aggressive and intimate excavation of the Arabic language's creative and thinking powers. The bibliography at the end of his most recent poetry collection[1] lists forty-nine works of poetry and prose, including two autobiographies and a collection of critical essays.

Barakat's debut collection, *Kull dākhil sa-yahtif min ajlī wa kull khārij ayḍan* (Every Insider Shall Hail Me and Every Outsider Too), was immediately recognised as worthy of attention. Before the collection's publication in Beirut, Barakat had published individual poems in Syrian and Lebanese literary journals. His very first publication was a piece titled '*Naqābat al-ansāb*' (The Union of Lineages) which appeared in 1971 in the Damascus magazine *Al-Ṭalīʿa*. Subhi Hadidi describes the impact of this first piece as that of 'a heavy lump suddenly thrown into a stagnant pool'.[2] The waves that it created were too high and too loud to be ignored.

In the 1970s, the two major modern Arabic forms, *qaṣīdat al-tafʿīla* (verse poem) and *qaṣīdat al-nathr* (prose poem) had evolved into two competing camps, involving much debate and back and forth in journals and newspapers. However, Barakat appeared on the poetic scene as neither a *tafʿīla* poet nor a prose poet. Side-lining the debate over form that had accompanied the prose poem since the early 1960s, Barakat reveals the potential of the prose poem in re-imagining the notion of the 'poetic' as an aggressive linguistic intervention. He announces:

> My poetry comes from the grammar of language (*qawāʿid al-lugha*), the mastery of words (*darabat al-alfāẓ*) and the ways of rhetoric, which are all scaffolding for the poetic utterance. They are the foundation upon which one can build without emulating anyone else's structure. Once you emulate, you become generic. Once you repeat the given, you cancel yourself and join the common.[3]

In his early work, he experimented with a mixed form of *al-tafʿīla* and *nathr*. In fact, he started out writing *qaṣīdat tafʿīla* but not settling into the form as much as challenging it. Some of his early poems read like broken or distressed *tafʿīla* poems, in which he abides by meter but suddenly and intentionally breaks it or abandons and then picks it up again.[4] Nevertheless, it is in poems or sections of poems where he abandons this squabbling with the *tafʿīla* form that the real potential of Barakat's poetic project begins to materialise more clearly. His real intervention is the turn to the poetic potential of Arabic's grammar and syntax. The opening of his poem '*Dīnūkā brīvā, taʿālay ilā ṭaʿna hādiʾa*' (Dinoka Breva, Come for a Gentle Stab)[5] is an early example of Barakat's individual language:

> عندما تنحدر قطعان الذئاب من الشمال وهي تجرّ مؤخراتها فوق الثلج وتعوي فتشتعل الحظائر المقفلة، وحناجر الكلاب، أسمع حشرجة دينوكا.
> في حقول البطيخ الأحمر، المحيطة بالقرية، كانت السماء تتناثر كاشفة عن فراغ مسقوف بخيوط العناكب وقبعات الدرك، حيث تخرج دينوكا عارية تسوق قطيعاً من بنات آوى إلى جهة أخرى خالية من الشظايا.[6]

> When the packs of wolves descend from the North, dragging their bottoms on the snow, howling and setting the locked barns and the throats of dogs ablaze, I hear Dīnūkā's death rattling.
> In the watermelon fields surrounding the village, the sky was scattering,

> revealing a void roofed by spider-webs and caps of policemen, where Dīnūkā emerges naked leading a herd of jackals in another direction empty of shrapnel.

Most striking about this poem is Barakat's insistent probing of the simple phrase, the seemingly mundane unit of syntax, to create a fascinating and unexpected effect. The two conjunctions in this opening paragraph '*al-ḥadhā'ir al-muqfala wa ḥanājir al-kilāb*' (the locked barns and the throats of dogs) and '*khuyūṭ al-ʿanākib wa qubaʿāt al-darak*' (spider-webs and caps of policemen) reveal a sinister dimension in this ostensibly pastoral scene. From the opening of the poem, the reader's attention is guided in 'another direction', to where Dīnūkā herds her hyenas away from the shrapnel. From here on the reader becomes wary of familiar motifs and prepared for Barakat's upsetting of expectations and disruption of linguistic familiarity.

In reflections on his literary experience published in a volume titled *al-Taʿjīl fī qurūḍ al-nathr* (Expediting the Loans of Prose), Barakat announces his despair with the 'current Arabs'[7] (*al-ʿarab al-rāhinūn*) and clearly states his investment in a conversation with, and an interrogation of, the Arabic literary tradition; an engagement that goes far beyond the superficial modern debate over metrics. He criticises contemporary Arab poets for turning 'modernism' (*al-ḥadātha*) into 'a repetitive generic mode' (*shiʿr mustansakh, mutaṭābiq*) and writing in a language that has 'disowned or forgotten its past imagination' (*lugha hāriba min māḍī khayālihā*), all the while bragging about being influenced and inspired by the wealth of western modernist experiences.[8] The wealth and vibrancy of these experiences, Barakat states, are a result of the efforts that poets exert towards their language, keeping it ever-expanding, evolving and new. Barakat's proclaimed mission then is to unsettle, to stir up the Arabic language and to re-instil it with the 'strange' (*al-gharīb*), 'the abandoned' (*al-muhmal*), and 'the wild' (*al-waḥshī*) from which it has been purged.[9] Adopting prose as a matter for poetry, Barakat demonstrates himself as a poet of linguistic conquest or transgression whose project rests on defamiliarising the Arabic language. This relationship with the language of the Arab other has its motivations in his personality and biography.

Throughout his career, Barakat has rarely conducted himself as other poets of his generation do. Quite the contrary, a very private person who rarely appears in the media, whether intentionally or unintentionally, Barakat has acquired a reputation for being not only a 'difficult' poet but also a 'difficult' man.[10] His isolation and reluctance to engage with literary circles pre-date his move to Sweden. Friends and acquaintances tell stories about his idiosyncratic and often unruly behaviour already while in Beirut. Mahmoud Darwish remembers the following incident in *A Memory for Forgetfulness*:

> He has taken the cultural life of Beirut by storm, overnight. He defends his writing ferociously, with his fists, because he doesn't believe in dialogue among intellectuals, considering it mere babble. Taking his pistol and his showy muscles, he goes into the appropriate coffee shop and lies in wait for lesser critics who write for the cultural pages of daily papers, and he doesn't mince his words about what they'd written against him. One time I said to him, 'Vladimir Mayakovsky used to treat his critics the same way in Gorky Street'. 'This is the only true criticism of criticism', he answered.[11]

Referring to Barakat by only his first initial S., Darwish points to characteristics which apply to both his conduct and his writing. He is 'the neighborhood's eloquent rooster [. . .] Lover of pistols, language, and exposed flesh [. . .] S. the Kurd [. . .] is elated by the war: it has allowed his repressed violence to emerge and ally itself with chaos'.[12] Barakat fought in the Lebanese war alongside the PLO and wrote a memoir of his days as a militia-man, titled *Kanīsat al-muḥārib* (The Warrior's Church, 1976). Needless to say, Barakat does not subscribe to the image of the poet as a cultured and refined person. More interestingly, as portrayed in the incident Darwish narrates above, Barakat deliberately and defiantly performs the stereotype of the Kurd in Arab societies as the disruptive and thuggish other.

Arabic in Another Tongue

Barakat's provocative persona and his confrontational relationship with Arabic are often tied to his preoccupation with what critics have called

'Kurdish themes'. Barakat insists on presenting himself as a Kurd who writes in Arabic. He is blunt in describing his relationship with the Arabic language as both insider and outsider. Arabic is not his first language, but he definitely plunders it and lays claim to it. Other poets and writers have validated this claim. In the blurbs on the back of the second volume of his collected works, *al-Dīwān*, which came out in 2017, the following endorsements by a host of Arab poets and writers describing Barakat appear. Mahmoud Darwish states: 'Since he invaded the Arabic poetic scene, Salim Barakat has heralded a different kind of poetry'. Nizār Qabbānī addresses Barakat in his blurb and pleads: '*Mawlānā*! What have you left for us? Release Arabic poetry from your grip'. Saʿdī Yūsuf does not hold back, proclaiming Barakat to be 'the greatest Kurd since Salāḥ al-Dīn'. It is Adonis, however, who puts it most succinctly when he states: 'The Arabic language is in this Kurdish poet's pocket'.[13]

These endorsements reflect the bold and transgressive ethos of Barakat's work. In his *al-Taʿjīl*, his meditations on poetry and writing, he consistently refers to the Arabs in the third person, deliberately excluding himself from them. He states: 'My Arabic language enlists the Arab as a partner in my Kurdish-ness, a partnership in the heritage of imagination'.[14] Barakat punctuates many of his texts with the Kurdish names of people and places and often builds poems on his own rewriting of Kurdish history and folktales. However, if the Kurdish cause (if we may call it that) is a motivating factor in the background of Barakat's project, it most resonantly manifests itself, not as theme or subject matter, but rather as an invasion of the Arabic language and an 'othering' of it from itself.[15]

All poets see themselves as interventionists or inventors of a new relationship with language. Great poets of the Arabic language are those who have carved within the language languages of their own. However, their relationship with language and their perception of that relationship are starkly different from what we see in Barakat's works. One of the most resonant conventions of *fakhr* (boast) is the Arab poet's assertion about his poetic abilities. A great poet is one whose poetry renders the world comprehensible, audible, visible and knowable, as does al-Mutanabbi when he pronounces:

أنا الذي نظر الأعمى إلى أدبي وأسمعت كلماتي من به صمم[16]

I am he whose poetry the blind can see
and whose words the deaf can hear

Al-Mutanabbi here flaunts his ability to achieve the purposes of language both as art and as means of communication, to the utmost degree. His verses are miraculous in their ability to make the deaf hear and the blind see. In that he resembles Abu Tammam, who boasts about luring his readers/listeners in spite of themselves and brilliantly fulfilling the purpose of *bayān* (clarity of speech, eloquence, rhetoric) by using *badī`* (figurative language). In describing his verses, he says:

بِغُرّ يراها من يراها بسمعه ويدنو إليها ذو الحجا وهو شاسع
يود وداداً أن أعضاء جسمه إذا أنشدت شوقاً إليها مسامع[17]

With virgin lines that are seen with the ears.
To which a man with reason is drawn no matter how far.

Wishing upon hearing them
all parts of his body were but ears.

Unlike the poets above, Salim Barakat's text mystifies the reader and, particularly, his Arab reader. His texts render the familiar unfamiliar and employ the tool of comprehension, language, to dumbfound the reader. He deliberately avoids lucidity. Every word is stripped of its semantic association and becomes an aesthetic value. In that way, Barakat succeeds in turning Arabic and its rhetorical tools against themselves. Instead of revealing, satisfying and confirming, as the poets above tell us great poetry can do, the effect of Barakat's poetry is deafening and disorienting:

فلأنكثنّ بوعدي إذاً،
فالشفاه التي تردد الكمال الصاخب تردد الموت، والموفدون إلى هذا الليل ليبنوا أدراجه
اللولبية يبعثرون الرخام الذي حملوه.
أما المشهد المقام على أنقاض حاله، فهو على حاله،
والحيلة على حالها،
والموت، وحده، الأكثر وحدة بين الأسرى.[18]

Let me break my promise then,
For the lips that reiterate vociferous perfection, reiterate death. And those delegated to building the spiral stairs of this night scatter the marble they have carried.
As for the scene erected upon its own ruins, it remains as it is,
and the ruse, as it is.
Death, alone, is the most lonesome among the captives.

This excerpt from a poem titled '*Asrā yataqāsamūn al-kunūz*' (Captives Divide Treasures) is eerily reflexive. It reads like a comment on Barakat's aesthetic and its impact on the reader. The poet announces that he will break his promise, and what follows here, and probably in every other text by Barakat, might very well be an intentional breaking of a promise. Barakat breaks the contract that guides the relationship among speakers of the same language. In the excerpt above, the attempt to build stairs, a connection or a bridge between two sides or parties, is thwarted by the scattering of 'the marble', the building material. Who are the delegates to the night, and what is this scattering of marble? Are they, too, breaking their promises, are they seeking some loud perfection? If poetry is the reiteration of 'vociferous perfection', as hinted by the lips, is it also a breakdown of common ground or language between poet and reader; is it a frustration of the missions and purposes that we have delegated to language in poetry? Is Barakat on a mission to scatter the marble of language? In order for the scene not to remain as it is, built upon its own ruins, the building blocks ought to be de-familiarised first? The project then is not to rearrange the familiar, in construction or in ruin, but first to estrange it from itself.

Moreover, single words stand out in this excerpt and make its reception more layered and confounding. The word *ḥīla*, which I translated above as 'ruse', is one of several blinding moments in the text. *Ḥīla* as trick or ruse is one possible meaning, but also *ḥīla* as power to act or change, or *ḥīla* as resolution, are shades of meaning that one cannot shake off when reading this sentence. Of course, the echoing auditory connection between *ḥīla* and *ḥalihā* is also difficult to miss. It creates an acoustic logic in the text that bypasses a semantic and syntactical relationship between words and replaces them with a sonically generative relationship where words from the same roots and of the same forms yield each other.

Another similarly charged instance in the excerpt is the resonance and dissonance that he creates between the word 'only' (*waḥdahu*) and the phrase 'most lonesome' (*al-aktharu wiḥdatan*). Death is one among many captives but is 'alone the most lonesome'. An additional layer of tension is added to the phrase 'alone the most lonesome' *(waḥdahu al-aktharu waḥdatan*) when it is followed by the word '*bayna*' (among). Barakat thus disrupts or blurs the dichotomy of alone and together.

'Revenge': Poetry as Avoidance of Meaning

If we describe Barakat's works as 'poetic', we must also redefine what the word means. His is a poetic-ness that rises from a de-familiarisation of language in a manner where the single word is transformed into a non-verbal, non-communicating sign or sound.

'Possessing though he does all the tools of rhetoric and eloquence'[19] in Arabic, Barakat reverses or upsets them, pushing them to their very limits. In a short essay titled '*Madhāhib al-maʿnā*' (The Ways of Meaning), he states:

> Poetry begins with the disparaging of meaning. Poetry is language's perseverance in scandalizing itself to the farthest extent. This is what should motivate us to approach language at its first rhetorical seething, like a fascination. Most 'modern' poetry begins from the modern 'achievements' of language reducing the Arabic lexicon to a limited vocabulary and limited set of rhetorical relationships.[20]

He declares poetry to be the 'impetuosity of language' (*jahālat al-lugha*). The word he uses here is *jahāla*, which is both ignorance, the opposite of knowledge, and impetuosity, the opposite of predictability and methodology; it is the ever-present potential of incomprehension or eruption or disintegration. To Barakat, poetry is a confrontation between 'language' and 'meaning'. Meaning is vision that demands organising language into a coherent finality, but poetry, albeit made of/from language, is a fundamental resistance to precisely that. 'Poetry', he states, is a 'bloody wager which drains language, like blood-letting, so it may either live or die'.[21] It is a violent and deliberate dispelling of the comfort and content we impose upon words.

In a poem aptly titled 'Revenge', from his collection *Bi-sh-shibāk dhātihā, bi-th-tha'ālib allatī taquduhā al-rīḥ* (By the Same Traps, by the Foxes Riding the Winds, 1981) Barakat performs his idea of language as an avoidance of 'meaning'. The title purposefully guides our reading of the subsequent sections and invites us to look for confrontations. The poem opens with the following:

أ.
المعاطف كلها هناك.
الرياح كلها هناك.
الخطى الغائصة في الثلج، والثلج كله هناك.
القناديل، والبيوت، والأشباح الأخيرة، كلها هناك.
فاجمع بين يديك الأليفتين ما تتّسعان من كمالٍ،
واجهد أن لا يكون المشهد صداك الأليف.

a.
The coats are all there,
the winds, all there,
footprints deep in the snow, and the snow, all there,
the lamps, houses, last apparitions, all there.
So gather in your tame hands all the perfection they can hold
and strive, so that the scene may not be your tamed echo.

The word 'scene' (*mashhad*) is a staple word in Barakat's lexicon. It is both expansive and intensive. The 'scene' could be this very poem, this very stanza, all of language, or the entirety of the poetic enterprise. I have translated *alīf* into 'tame' and 'tamed'. The word in Barakat's writing is quite tricky to grasp. Barakat's world exists at the intersection of wild and tamed or domesticated. Is the scene familiar and tame, or is it broken into familiarity and tamed? Regardless, two imperative verbs, gather (*ijma'*) and strive (*ijhad*), anchor possible divergent readings. The poem's other sections are similarly anchored by words that are open unto multiple possibilities.

ب.

بَرَم كطبائع الصباحات يشغل القادمين إلى نهايتي، وأنا، في نزعي تحت الشباك الكبيرة، أعلّق المكان – كسراويل سجين – على الحبل ذاكَ، الرقيق، الممتدّ من أول الملهاة إلى أنينكم.

ج.

وفرة الهباء أنا، المشيئة ظني.

د.

الغضب إشارة الليل، والماء فكرة تتقدّم كمالها.

ه.

كحذاء يلتمع صباغه
كمقبض باب من نيكل:
هكذا صرختك.[22]

b.

An unease, like mornings, preoccupies those approaching my end, and I – In my death throes under the great net – I hang place – like the pants of a prisoner – on the line, that delicate line, running from the origins of comedy to your moaning.

c.

The abundance of naught is I and will is my suspicion.

d.

Rage is the sign of night and water a thought ahead of its own completion.

e.

Like a shoe polished,
like a nickel doorknob,
thus is your scream.

The poem, however, does not end here. Barakat includes a vocabulary list, a list of words and their definitions. The very layout of the list on the page is deceptive. Through its vocabulary list, this text challenges the notion of margin and centre. Driving us to wonder how much of the 'poetic' is reliant on context, on concord and harmony between the text and its surroundings. Furthermore, we are conditioned as readers and language learners to find comfort in vocabulary lists, to trust their ability in alleviating doubt or confusion. Barakat is aware of this association and uses it to expose and mock the deluded claim present in any attempt at containing or 'taming' the impetuosity of words. His vocabulary list is slippery and unsettling and as 'poetic' as, if not more than, the first part of the poem:

مفردات:

النهار: غضب يتخفّى في قناع الهواء.
الريح: خطوة الكلمة في اتجاه سرها.
الصوت: خراب الشكل.
الحنين: ذهب منثور على مخمل النهاية.
الفضاء: مشكل الضوء.
العدم: فكاهة الظلال في مجلسها المضجر.
الكتابة: بطش يمتحن المنسي.
الرقم: حصيلة العبث.
الثمر: برهان الشجرة على ماضٍ يضلل كل البرهان.
القناع: أنين الظاهر.
المسافة: لهاث معاد.
الأكيد: تمتمة في الجهة الأخرى.
القيامة: طفولة تؤكد العقل.
الذهب: عراك في خان.
الحياة: طلقة من ذهب،
أما أنت، أيها المقيم في الخاتمة، فلا تسرحنَّ طويلاً لئلا يبرد العشاء.[23]

Vocabulary:

Day: anger masked in air
Wind: the steps of a word toward its secret
Sound: the ruin of form
Longing: gold scattered on the velvet of the end
Space: shaper of light
Nothingness: the humour of shadows languishing in their seat
Writing: violence testing the forgotten
Number: the yield of futility
Fruit: the tree's proof of a past that eludes all proofs
Mask: the moan of appearance
Distance: repeated panting

Certainty: a murmuring on the other side
Resurrection: a childhood justifying reason
Gold: a fight in a bar
Life: a golden bullet
As for you, dweller in the ending, don't stray too long, lest dinner get cold.

This last sentence, directly addressing the reader, underscores the unsettling experience of reading this poem. Is the reader the 'dweller in the ending'? Is Barakat mocking our dwelling on endings, our need to arrive somewhere, at some meaning or resolution? 'Don't stray too long', he warns us, 'lest dinner get cold?' And straying (*shurūd*) is a wandering off both in distance and in thought. He warns of the risks of dwelling or wandering away from something that is at risk of losing its heat. Am I reading too much? Am I dwelling? Am I straying? It is very tempting to take cues from this vocabulary list for reading the poem, but it seems that that, too, is beside the point. By the end of the text, the poet has had his revenge. The reader is left at a loss in the aftermath of this word play, with nothing, but familiar words discovered for the first time you need to add something here – your meaning is incomplete.

This list of words and definitions is a prime example of Barakat's play with language and his fascination with the format of the dictionary.[24] He often evokes it in order to dispel linguistic complacency. His relentless linguistic excavation opens up limitless horizons of meaning. We are always at the cusp of understanding, exceedingly conscious of ourselves not as readers/speakers of Arabic, but as explorers of what has thus far eluded us. In fact, it seems as if poetry in Barakat's project is a deliberate occlusion of meaning behind the veil of language; language intentionally textured and thickened beyond recognition.

'In an Abridged Context': Journeying in Dictionaries

In what follows I will trace Barakat's linguistic conquest in a poem entitled '*Istiṭrād fī siyāq mukhtazal*' (Digression in an Abridged Context) from his 1996 collection *Ṭaysh al-yāqūt* (The Recklessness of Sapphire). The reader of this poem embarks on a linguistic and metaphorical journey in the landscape, the linguistic body, of the poem. Barakat's employment of diction challenges the dictionary meanings of words and invites words' multiple connotations into the linguistic landscape of the poem. He disrupts the nature of metaphor by making seemingly puzzling connections and erecting precarious bridges. Language in this poem is penetrated, disrupted, occupied and overcome as the poem progresses towards its final Kurdish 'shot', towards the echo within one tongue of another tongue that has been repressed. Thus, Barakat superimposes the linguistic on the ethnic, sublimating the tension of Arab and Kurd into an invasive linguistic intervention. By that, he also disrupts the relationship between language and voice and through his language play urges us to hear, in Arabic, a different voice.

Dictionary work is necessary in reading Barakat, but his Arabic eludes dictionary definitions. He sets the reader up to read the dictionary rhetorically, doubting the seeming certainty of its discourse and looking between the lines for illuminations rather than assurances. Barakat's reader soon learns to resist reading as a process of pinning down and instead to embrace reading as an opening up of the text; a proliferation of words and their indications rather than the tracing of a direct connection, a meaning. This notion of reading does not come easily; rather, Barakat's reader is forcefully initiated into it.

Thus, reading Barakat is a journey of discovery in dictionaries where the dictionary entry is never an arrival but a perpetual launching point. In '*Istiṭrād fī siyāq mukhtazal*', the reader's reimagined relationship with the dictionary becomes crucial to the experience of the poem. The title of the poem hints towards two notions that can guide the reader's experience of the text: 'digression' and 'context'. The reading process, from the first stanza until the end, is repeatedly interrupted, for the text is punctuated with words that elicit digression, words that open on to parallel texts (starting with their entries in the dictionary as text). Thus, the boundaries of this single poem are extended far beyond the words that constitute it.

The poem is divided into twelve numbered sections varying in length and layout on the page. Here is the opening section:

.١
إنها البراهين الحمّى،
وأنت تظللها بالحبر من تهتك اليقين،
وتُوْقع بالكلمات لتغفو البراهين على شجارها.

لا ديكة هنا،
لكنها أعراف النار المتمايلة كأعراف الديكة.
والوجود المارق يروّع السياق المكنون للظهورات.

لا بلاء هنا إلا من ورد،
لا مزراق طائشا إلا مزراق الكون؛
والبرق زراية الليل بالمكان، ثم، المياه هزوٌ،
فمالك تتلقف المشيئات بشعاع منكوب،
وتغدق على الألم إيمان المساء.[25]

1.

Here, the proofs, the fever.
With ink, you shade them from smug certainty
You set trap for words, so proofs may doze upon their quarrels.

No roosters here
but flames prancing like cockscomb
and rebel existence chasing away what hides in the manifestations.

No affliction here but of rose;
no stray javelin but the universe's.
Lightning is the night's disdain of place; and water, a mockery.
So why submit to higher wills your broken ray,
and bestow upon pain the faith of the evening?

The first three lines set up a few guiding juxtapositions. When proofs are fever from the onset of the poem, regardless of what 'proofs' are referring to, we are to anticipate a disruption of our expectations. Taking up this initial juxtaposition of proof and fever, ink in the second line is similarly positioned against or in contrast to 'smug certainty'. In fact, 'smug certainty' in itself is a unit similar to 'the proofs, the fever' which requires unpacking. When certainty is smug or insolent, it loses its trustworthiness, its certainty! 'With ink', the addressed 'you' (which is probably also the 'I' addressing itself) shades proofs, protects them and sets them down to sleep distracted by the 'quarrels of words'. Again, this is a very open, assumptive and perhaps forced reading of the piece; nevertheless, I argue that most other readings would have followed a similar thread, attempting to find relationships, either of contrast or parallelism, between the keywords that stand out in these three lines. This is the process of reading in general, following keywords as stepping-stone; however, in this case, the stepping-stones are unstable and have the ability to proliferate into multiple pathways and side roads.

In the first three lines, the first word that causes pause is *tahattuk*, a verbal noun (*maṣdar*), translated here into the adjective 'smug'. The root *hataka* means, among other things, to tear up, to open, to rip, to unveil, to violate, or to rape. A possible translation of the phrase *tahattuk al-yaqīn* is 'the tattering/ripping of certainty/truth'. However, early on in the *Lisān al-ʿarab* entry, along with tearing up, unveiling and exposing, the connection with scandal is pointed out. Then for the form *tahattaka*, dictionary entries give a definition related to attitude. *Tahattuk* is carelessness, insolence, or lack of fear from exposure or violation. And hence the decision to translate the phrase as 'smug certainty'. The phrase '*tahattuk al-yaqīn*' thus becomes an oxymoron, where the composed and definite certainty (*yaqīn*) is syntactically, grammatically and conceptually linked to the falling apart, the reckless and scandalous. These two words are obviously at odds, involved in a quarrel, yet here they are together; the attempt at making sense of their quarrel is a courting of 'feverish proofs'.

In the image of words quarrelling and feverish proofs, Barakat is perhaps alluding to the very act of composing, of 'trapping words in ink' to defer or delay the search for meaning. Is he commenting in some way on how we read, what we set out to find (meaning, proofs), and what we often end up missing (the quarrel of words)?

The second stanza presents a simile, a familiar rhetorical tool which the reader of this taunting text will probably welcome, in the hope of some clarity. The rooster's comb is likened to the 'prancing flames', and yet the simile is undermined or exposed by the phrase that precedes it: 'no roosters here'. Instead of sustaining the 'suspended disbelief' involved in any subscription to figuration or rhetoric, Barakat qualifies the simile with 'no roosters here' and thereby directs our attention to the process of simile-making and the assumption or exclusion that it entails. Perhaps this is what is referred to afterwards in the phrase 'the concealed context of apparitions'. This phrase clearly connects to the title. A context is abridged, eliminated, concealed, or intentionally chased away.

The play on the notion of exclusion or elimination continues into the third stanza. Barakat repeats the construction of 'no roosters here' but adds an exception to it. 'No affliction here but of rose' and 'no stray javelin but the universe's'. The stanza ends with two striking metaphors: Lightning is the 'night's disdain of place', and 'water is mockery'. The words *zirāya* (disdain) and *huzw* (mockery) both launch us into long digressions in dictionaries. And once we return from these detours, we cannot but wonder about the 'concealed context' that has been chased or frightened away in the process of composing these lines, and all lines of poetry or prose for that matter. For example, consider the line:

والبرق زراية الليل بالمكان، ثم، المياه هزوٌ

lightning the night's disdain of place; and water mockery

With 'lighting', 'night', 'water' and 'place', I find myself thinking of lightning in Imru' al-Qays's *muʿallaqa*: the poet sitting in a high place noticing the bolts of lightning, like hands shining, like a lamp titled.[26] Is 'water' 'mockery' because we know there is a violent flood on its way? Is lightning and the innocuous images used to describe it a diversion then; a distraction from the disdain coming in the form of wrathful water (the flood at the end of the *muʿallaqa*) which leaves 'place' in ruins?[27] There is no proof of this connection in Barakat's text; there are only suspicions that haunt me as a reader.

We cannot engage with this text by Barakat without an acute awareness of what we have been shielded or protected from by our very subscription, as readers, to the linguistically exclusionary practice of writing/composing. After he sends us out to see each word in its full glory of meanings and associations, we return to engage with it trapped in ink. Reading is thus halted, undermined, questioned and governed by digressions and contexts.

The question that ends this first section – 'So why submit to higher wills, your ray broken, why bestow upon pain the faith of the evening?' – whether rhetorical or not, employs keywords which serve to describe our relationship with this text: 'submitting' to higher powers and 'faith' in pain. The fact that the last line is a question posits it also as an incitement. If reading is exclusionary by nature; a subscription to one context among many, this poem here will defy that and open up the text to all its latent possible 'manifestations'.

The subsequent sections of the poem continue, abrupt in their layout and enigmatic in the associations to which they allude:

٢.
مرحى أيها الرهان المغلول:
ها العدم، نازفاً، يتبسَّم لأحفاده.

٣.
أملكَ أملُهُ،
كلاهما نعسان في الدفء الذي يمتدح.
وتُهدران فيجمعكما اليقطين،
كأنّ مجازاتكما غرور الشعاع الأكمل في سفاحه.[28]

2.
Hurrah, you bound wager!
Here, Nothingness, bleeding, smiles at its grandchildren.

3.
Your hope is his hope,
Both, drowsy in the laudable warmth.
You are both spilled and pumpkin will gather you;
as if your metaphors are the vanity of perfect light in fornication.

Al-rihān al-maghlūl (bound wager) alludes to a form of engagement with words, proofs and quarrels which opened the poem. '*Maghlūl*' translated here as 'bound' is obviously much more nuanced and loaded. The most present alternate meaning for the word is 'thirsty'. The root *ghalla* opens on to a wide range of meanings from 'to insert', 'to penetrate', 'to fetter or shackle', 'to be very thirsty', 'to be scornful', 'to be vengeful and angry'. Returning to Barakat's phrase from this digression into definitions, *al-rihān al-maghlūl* (the bound wager) becomes a slippery stepping-stone, leading us towards another similarly loaded word, *ʿadam* (nothingness). In sections two and three, an obvious relationship between the addressed you or I and nothing/nothingness is erected: 'Your hope is his hope' ('his' most probably referring to the masculine *ʿadam* [nothingness]), both are drowsy, spent and joined by pumpkin! Finally, their 'metaphors are the vanity of the light in full fornication'. The mention of 'metaphors' here takes us back to the opening speculation on writing and the quarrel of words. The word *akmal* (full) used to describe light or a ray of light is a digression waiting to happen, and 'fornication' and 'pumpkin' before it as well.

The sections that follow offer much to dwell on: the word *mushāddāt* (quarrels) confronts us again, '*al-ʿadam*' (nothing) and '*mastūr*' (concealed) a synonym of *maknūn* which appears in the first section. There are more couplings like 'you and place, jogging', 'you and the ancient', juxtaposed to or paralleled with the earlier 'you and nothing'. There are also more words that send us off on side expeditions, such as '*qarāʾin*' in the phrase '*qarāʾinaka al-ukhrā*', translated here as 'your other others'. There are many tempting threads to follow here, but I will only point to a couple of them: 'metaphor as vanity' and the developing relationship with 'place'.

Barakat exposes metaphor as processes of digression and manipulation of context. If the sections that preceded focused on destabilised words through play with dictionary meanings and associations, the following sections pick apart metaphor and the process of image-making, as we see in section 4 and section 7.

٤.
الطرُقُ إجاصٌ على شجرات الصباح.
فإنْ هرول المكان، متريّضاً، هرولْ أيضاً:
أمامكما درّاجات الأزل،
وعلى أكتافكما أكياسه الفارغه.[29]

[. . .]
٧.
لا نكران،
والحياة رقمك المستور.[30]

.٨
آفقٌ هذا،
أفقٌ ذاك:
وكلاهما عانة الريح.[31]

4.
The paths are pears on morning trees.
If the place jogs, jog with it:
Ahead of you are eternity's bicycles
and on your shoulders its empty sacks.

[. . .]

7.
No denial,
life is your concealed number.

8.
A horizon here;
A horizon there;
Both are the crotch of the wind.

Section 4 is a flaunting of metaphors, without much context to justify them: paths as pears, jogging place, eternity's bicycles and its empty sacks. The layered metaphors of section 4 stand in stark contrast with the minimalist sketch of section 8. In section 8, Barakat does not show us metaphor, but rather metaphor in the making. 'Here', 'there' and finally 'both' is the formula that leads to 'the crotch of the wind'. We see the shape forming one line at a time. Still, *ʿāna* (the crotch or pubis) of the wind is an unsettling place at which to arrive. However, this breaking down of the metaphor, this exposition of it, will qualify and add a dimension to the metaphors that will follow in the subsequent sections.

The key thread that carries us to the end of the poem is the relationship with place. This poem arrives at place after much allusion to it and to the relationship with it from the opening section. The first intimation of place appears in the second stanza of the first section with the repetition of the word, *hunā* (here).

No roosters here
[. . .]
No affliction here but rose

This negated description of 'here' foreshadows the unsettled, unstable, and developing relationship with place, as we see it 'jogging' in the fourth section. These stabs or hints at the notion of place, disturbed, shaken up and challenged in some way, materialise in the last three sections as a meditation on real places signalled and named: Alexandretta, Wān, Bhutan and Mūzān.

.١٠
عاد الحجّامون.
الإوزّ غاضبٌ، والرياح تتخبّط مسدودة الغلاصم،
فلا تلبثنّ في الفزع الأنيق، هكذا، تدحرج الفراغ، خصيةً خصيةً
على الجسور، وترمي، من صدوع الأبدية خواتيمك
الأبدية.

ولا يكوننّ لك عناد القطيعة،
لا يكوننّ في يديك وبر اليُربوع:
هي ذي السيوف المغسولة بمني الموتى،
والأقحاف التي تتكسّر، في خفّة، تحت نفخ العطارين.

هي ذي الألسن،
الأحاليل،
الكُلى،
الأكباد،
الرضفات القاسية،
في سياق من النور مثل حوافر البغل،
والأمم – محلوجةً – تتناثر فوق العانات الكثيفة للهول.

وقطار واحد
منحدرا من بحيرة «وان» إلى الإسكندرونة،
يحمل في مقطورته الثامنة قلب «شمدين» الضاحك لكوجر الغيم
الذي، مرحاً، يتمرغ فوق أرض «بوطان» والبحار الغريقة.

الجهات تتقوّض، صامتةً، كصناديق البنجر،
والغضب – فتاك الضاحك لا يتعثر قطُّ. رشيقاً ينهب أسواق الأسلاف بكؤوس الشاي، يجرّ
حوانيت الباقلين، كماعز، إلى مسالخ النور.[32]

10.
The cuppers are back.
The geese angry, the wind staggering, stuffy and choked.
Dwell not in this elegant panic; thus you roll space, testicle by testicle,
over the bridge and toss your timeless seals through fissures in eternity.

Don't be stubborn as a schism.
Let there not be in your hands the jerboa's fluff:
Here are swords, washed in the sperm of the dead,
And skulls, which rupture lightly under the apothecaries' breath.

Here are tongues,

orifices,
kidneys,
livers,
and hard kneecaps,

in a course of light like the hooves of a mule,
And nations, scutched, scatter over the densely-haired pubis of Fear.

And a single train,
descending from Lake Wan towards Alexandretta,
bears in its eighth carriage the laughing heart of Shemdin to the Kojars[33] of cloud,
which joyfully rolls over the lands of Bhutan and the drowned seas.
Directions fall apart, silently, like crates of beet.

And rage – your laughing youth, he never stumbles. Gracefully he plunders the ancestors' marketplaces with teacups. He drags grocery shops, like goats, to the slaughterhouses of light.

This is the longest section of the poem. It opens with the 'return of the cuppers' and the description of a mood and setting: 'the geese angry, the wind staggering and choked'. This hints at a build-up of some sort; the sense of something imminent is established. Then a series of imperatives or suggestions follows: 'Do not dwell', 'Do not be' and 'Do not allow/ let'. The imagery here is strikingly disturbing, but we have been prepared in the previous section to receive its blows. The mood of this section is that of disintegration; things are falling apart and scattering. We trace this crumbling with keywords and phrases: *tudaḥrij* (roll), *khiṣyatan khiṣyatan* (testicle by testicle), *ṣudūʿ* (fissures), *tatakassaru* (hatch), leading up to the list of discrete organs: 'tongues, orifices, kidneys, livers and kneecaps', a graphic visualisation of the phrase that follows, 'nations, scutched, scatter over the densely-haired pubis of fear'.[34]

In contrast with the monologue or dialogue of the 'I' and 'you' in the previous sections and their consorting with 'nothingness', 'place' and the 'ancient', the tenth section of the poem introduces a shift in tone. In the middle of the section, the scattered organs, nations and splinters of time and place are seemingly all gathered into, or summoned to, 'one train'. Masterfully, the image of the single train descending through known territory from Lake Wān to Alexandretta not only orchestrates the shards and fragments scattered thus far, but also introduces the necessary element of movement. Now here with the train moving from Wān to Alexandretta, we are travelling in place and time towards myth. The unsettled moving fragments are all carried towards some echoing statement, some resounding truth. All the fragments are abridged into one fragment that can stand for all: the head of Shemdin. Shemdin is a prominent Kurdish tribe with a long history of championing Kurdish nationalism. There are several notable individuals from the Shemdin family going as far back as the times of Ṣalāh al-Dīn and the battle of Hittīn.[35] Barakat mythologises the name and allows it to metonymically stand in for all of Kurdish history.

In mythical time and place, directions collapse, organisation and structures (markets and shops) are set asunder by rage.

.١١

الشفق رغيفك في جهات «موزان»
والغيوم طبول.

11.
Dusk is your loaf of bread in the land of Mūzān
and clouds are drums.

Section 11 further serves to direct us in a specific direction (Mūzān) and prepare us for the final statement towards which the poem has been creeping. In the last section, we find ourselves in confrontation with place, unsettled, fragmented, shaken up, travelling and now reassembling for an anticipated statement which Barakat delivers with the metaphor of 'gunshot':

.١٢

المكان طلقة الخيال التي تُرديك،
لتتعافى حراً، حيث المتاه رجاءٌ،
والكون يغطي بأسماله نوارج اليقين،
حيث الحروب، نقيةً كفراء السناجب، تتماوج في الهبوب
الرحيم للجدل، ويتأهب العدم – ذلك الجناح الأقوى.
الكرد هناك،
في دويّ الطلقة التي ترديك لتتعافى.[36]

12.

Place is the gunshot of imagination that strikes you down,
so that you recover and be free; where the wilderness is hope;
where the universe drapes rags over certainty's threshers;
and where wars, pure as squirrel fur, wave in gusts of merciful
  controversy,
and nothingness – that stronger wing – is on the ready.

The Kurds are there
in the blast of the shot that strikes you down,
so that may you recover.

Place is finally captured and fixed, not in time or place, but in the imagination as a sound or the echo of a sound, a gunshot. Not here, but 'there', the Kurds will always be at a distance. It is not geographical distance, but, more resonantly, a sonic one, in the echo of a sound, in the return of sound. The word Kurds (*Kurd*) itself here becomes a signifier of place, a place that you say and are thereafter transformed by the very power of its resonating echo. After having gone on the journey of this poem with all its linguistic traps and digressions, we arrive at the last stanza, with its blunt statement:

The Kurds are there
in the blast of the shot that strikes you down,
so that you may recover.

One is tempted to reconsider the whole poem in light of this end statement. In the echo of the last resounding shot, the Kurds, the poem acquires an additional subtext and yet another 'context' with its own sets of associations, digressions and assumptions. Thus, the reading process becomes a perpetual re-reading exercise, a never-ending series of digressions and superimposed contexts.

'Dīlānā wa Dirām': Escaping the Trap of Genres

No overview of Barakat's poetic project is complete without considering his works in prose. He is the author of more than twenty novels thus far. He insists that his venturing into the novel form at the age of thirty-two 'was not new experimentation',[37] but rather another manifestation of what he had already been doing in poetry. He stresses the fundamental connection between his processes in poetry and his processes in the novel, to the extent that one might describe his poetry and his novels together as the same quest for the 'poetic'. Barakat does not subscribe to genre limitations and portrays the act of writing poetry or novel as a retrieving of language's initial power to fascinate. Instead of venturing into the labyrinth of Barakat's novelistic oeuvre – a task beyond the scope of this study – I will now turn to his '*Dīlānā wa Dīrām*', a poem from his collection *Al-Karākī* (Pike, 1981). This is a narrative poem in which 'the poetic' is achieved by deliberately disrupting, delaying and challenging the narrative and its modes. In this poem Barakat retells a Kurdish folktale based on the true love story of country youth, Dīrām, and a mature married woman from the city, Dīlānā.[38] The poem opens with a prelude introducing the narrating voice of the 'guide':

تيتل على الهضبة،
وسكون يرفع قرنيه عاليا كالتيتل.
فلا تقتربن أكثر أيها الدليل،
ولا تبتعدن أكثر،
مكانك هو المكان الذي ترى منه الجذور الجذور، والأرض ميراثها

تيتل على الهضبة،
وسكون صلد يرفع قرنيه عاليا كالتيتل.[39]

A mountain goat on a hill
and a stillness that raises its horns high as a mountain goat.
Don't move a step closer, O guide!
Not a step further.
Your place is the place from which roots eye roots
and the earth eyes its inheritance.

A mountain goat on a hill
and a stubborn stillness raising its horns high as the goat.

From the onset, Barakat transports us to a quintessentially Kurdish mountainous landscape. He draws a connection between the guide and the image of the mountain goat, which hints at a difficult and strained relationship between narrator and narrative. The image of a 'stillness raising its horns' is a foreboding opening, haunted by the sense of something reluctantly awakening or opening up. The prelude underscores a rigidity that does not relent, a mountain-like stubbornness, that holds the guide in his place: 'don't move a step closer [. . .] don't move a step further'. But that narrating voice is qualified and restricted. His role is to narrate events he has no power to change. He can only observe (eye) and narrate. It is a voice trapped and helpless in the face of an irrevocable tragedy he is destined to speak.

As the poem unfolds, the narrating voice is further exposed as reluctant, implicated and deeply invested in the story he is telling, further accentuating the sense of foretold doom.

بالله، بالله لا تدعونـي، بعد هذا، أسرد الأرض جهة جهة، والسماء برقا برقا، فأنا استطالة الحكاية، إن رويت رويت قلبي طالعا في العاصفة بقبرات النحاس. لا، لا تدعوني، بعد هذا، أروي الموت بالموت، وأطأ العذوبة بفراغ كحافر البغل، بل انظروا، أنتم الجالسون على سور المغيب، تروا عشرين رجلا يغطون ديرام وديلانا بعباءاتهم، قبل أن يسيل خيط واحد من الدم، متعرجا، بين الحصى والقش، ويغيب في آخر العراء.[40]

By god, by god, do not let me, after this, narrate the earth, direction by direction, and the sky, bolt by bolt. For I am the extension of the story, and if I speak, I speak my heart rising in the storm with the copper larks. No! Do not let me, after this, to narrate death with death, and to tread upon sweetness with a void like a mule's hoof. But look, as you sit there on the fence of sunset, look and you will see twenty men covering Dīrām and Dīlānā with their cloaks, before a single line of blood has trickled, winding its way among pebbles and straw to disappear at the limits of desolation.

The guide/narrator is a structuring element in the poem. His voice is an enveloping web that houses other voices. After the prelude, the guide goes on to address the two lovers for the length of seventeen numbered sections, alternating between addressing him and addressing her. In these seventeen sections, the narrative is delayed and slowed down. The story line is trapped here in a dialectic form, a dialogue both sides of which are narrated by the guide's voice. No longer moving forward towards a possible resolution or a climax, the story line expands in all other directions, widened and deepened. The single thread of the guide's voice frays and unravels into two voices.

١.
انظر إليها، إنها جمع سلال شقراء تحت ومض دمك يا ديرام. انظر إليها كيف تغفو لصق ساعدك، وأنفاسها تتهاوى شهاباً شهاباً في شسع فحولتك النبيلة... أتذكر يا ديرام ساعة جئتها وديعا تتسربل بالسهول، خطاك خطى نهار، وصخبك صخب السنبل؟ أتذكر المساء الذي ترقرق في عينيك، المساء الأول، حيث سطوتما بالقبل على كنوز الكائن، وكشفتما عن مسيل غريب تحت حجر الروح؟ تمهّل ديرام، تمهّل في عبثك الساحر بأعشاش قلبها- قلب ديلانا المعلق كطعنة ملآى بالحياة.
٢.
انظري إليه، إنه سهم أشقر تحت ومض دمك يا ديلانا. انظري إليه يزين المساء بصليل فحولته، ويرقى إلى صليلك سلم اللهاث، كأن كل ترف ترفه، وكأنْ أنتِ كلماته التي ينشد بها نشيد الرجل. فهلا سردت عليه ما يسرد الغمام على بناته، وهلا نزلت إليه من العذوبة العالية، شاهرة مرح الأعالي، لتغمري سهل قلبه بقمح النشيد؟ هيا ديلانا، إنه متكىء قرب يدك ويسرد الفاكهة.[41]

1.
Look at her, a heap of blond baskets under the flashing of your blood, Dīrām. Look, how she sleeps upon your arm, her breaths falling star after star in the vastness of your virility . . . Do you remember, Dīrām,

> the time you came to her, timid, wrapped in plains, your steps the steps of day, and your clamour the clamour of wheat stalks? Do you remember the evening that glittered in your eyes, that first evening when you both plundered with kisses the treasures of the being, and uncovered a strange stream under the bedrock of the soul? Easy, Dīrām! Be gentle in your rummaging in the nests of her heart – Dīlānā's heart, which hangs like a wound, full of life.
>
> 2.
> Look at him, a blond arrow under the flashing of your blood, Dīlānā. See how he decorates the evening with the rattle of his manhood. He climbs to you on a ladder of gasps, as if all luxury is his, as if you are the words by which he chants the song of man. Would you sing to him what the cloud sings to its daughters? Would you come down from your lofty sweetness, revealing the mirth of heights, so you may sweep the field of his heart with the wheat of your song? Come, Dīlānā, he is leaning close to your hand, narrating fruit.

The fact that Dīlānā and Dīrām's voices are communicated through the guide's voice creates a tension of voice that keeps intensifying. Without dialogue, Barakat creates an intense back and forth between the lovers. The successive sections are framed as call and response: 'Look at her [. . .] Look at him', 'Rise Dīrām [. . .] Rise Dīlānā', 'Wake him [. . .] Wake her'. The parallelism between successive sections not only halts the narrative but also imbues it with the tone of feverish escalation, further straining and testing the guide's voice.

After the numbered sections, the narrative disintegrates. The narrating voice fluctuates between different ways, approaches and modes of telling. He narrates in the third person, he addresses the lovers, he turns to himself. He reboots the narrative with three sections near the middle of the poem titled: prelude or opening (*maṭlaʿ*), as if attempting to begin again but failing. Turning to himself and doubting his ability to fulfil the role assigned to him, the guide confesses:

> لم أكن كما ينبغي أن يكون الدليل. كنت سارحا بين أهدابكما، أرى ما تريان وأمتدح، مثلكما، بهاء الملوك الذين أطلقوا المدن ككلاب سلوقية، وخرجوا يبحثون عن شعوبهم.[42]

> I wasn't the guide I should have been. I lost myself between your eyelashes, seeing what you saw, praising, like you did, the glory of kings who released cities like hounds and set out in search of their peoples.

Overwhelmed by his own narrative, the narrating voice and with it the text as a whole, takes an inward turn towards self-questioning – 'Should I say more?'[43] 'Was I hallucinating?'[44] 'Who after me will tell?'[45] – until the narrating voice, distressed and exhausted, arrives at the end of the poem and addresses itself:

فلتنمْ
فلتنمْ أيها الهاذي،
فما قلبك إلا قلب، وما أنتَ إلا دليل عاشقين لم يكملا نهب روحيها.[46]

Sleep then
Sleep, delirious one
You heart is but a heart and you are nothing but a guide for two lovers' who haven't yet finished plundering their souls.

This is the guide's story, too. This poem is the story of voice, striving to be one yet forever torn apart, proliferated and stratified. And is not this attentiveness to voice the proof of poetry? 'Dīlānā and Dīrām' is a narrative resisting itself as narrative through the indulgence, reflexive-ness and non-linearity of poetry. Ultimately one reads not for the slowly unfolding story but for the delaying descriptions and all that which is superfluous to the plot.

The poem is excessive and digressive in all its elements. For instance, the love story is not set against or in the landscape, but rather their love infiltrates and overwhelms the landscape. Barakat does not use images of nature to draw analogies with Dīlānā and Dīrām's relationship. The emotional and sensual bond between them consumes nature and natural scenery and transforms it into a mere manifestation of an overpowering and surging emotional deluge. Thus, 'Dīlānā and Dīrām' is a 'poem of amplitude', as T. S. Eliot puts it; a poem that could have only been written by a poet who is also a 'master of the prosaic'.[47] Barakat himself points to this amplitude, this overflowing abundance as a characteristic of his approach to language, to single words and to meaning, eventually resulting in what he calls a 'magical text':

> My poem is built on the unruly abundance of imagination. In order to find its way to my poem, criticism ought to qualify itself with exegesis; a qualification consonant with readings of a 'magical text'; a text which presents a language of the nebula of meaning. The universe and I are in a confrontation, in a competition to lure the mysterious, the confusing, the problematic, the ferociously contradictory, the serene, the miraculous; all of which are necessities of a different kind. They beget new relationships between words and bestow suspicion onto meaning. There is no certainty. The wonder of being storms the mechanics of the mind, which seeks order and logic.
>
> The poem is there, in its ancientness, and I am the narrator of stray destiny.[48]

The language of 'Dīlānā and Dīrām' is a 'necessity of a different kind'. It is *nathr* (prose) overloaded, exaggerated, allowed to expand and stray endlessly, to the extent that it becomes poetically charged. The language of this text does not narrate or inform or communicate a meaning. In repetition, in exaggeration, in insistent description, meaning is transformed into an effect or impact which the reader senses or feels rather than reasons or puts together. Language here is exploded, and the poem is designed upon the resulting chaos and unruliness.

> ٧.
>
> انظر إليها يا ديرام، انظر كيف تجمع أمام قلبك أسراب الإوز، وتغزل الغيوم. انظر إليها تتهادى قطيعا قطيعاً من آخر السفوح، يدها في يد الأفق الراعي، وثوبها ينحسر- حين تعبر الجداول قفزا- عن جذور لا تلمس الأرض، بل تلمس المديح الذي تتغطى به الجذور كلها. فإذا رأيت أن تأخذ يدها في يديك فخذ الأفق أيضا، وإذا رأيت أن تضمها فلتضمك الجذور ليرشف الثمر بأنفاسك الثمر، أو لتهرع إليك الارض ممتشقة سيلها العرم من اللبن والأشكال.[49]
>
> 7.
>
> Look at her, Dīrām! Look how she gathers flocks of geese in front of your heart and weaves the clouds. Look how she sways towards you, herd by herd from the farthest slope; hand in hand with the shepherding horizon. When she crosses streams leaping, her dress reveals roots that do not touch the earth but touch the praises with which all roots cover themselves. If you decide to take her hand in yours, then take the horizon

> too. If you decide to hold her, then let the roots hold you, so that fruit may sip fruit from your breaths; and the earth rush to you unsheathing her mighty flood of milk and forms.

To borrow from Barakat himself, the poem is a 'storming'. There is no logic or method to the way in which we understand the excerpt above, but we do. We sense a movement, a tension, an escalation. The piece unfolds and opens up with a rising fervour, as if slowly losing restraint, from 'gathers flocks' and 'sways towards you' to 'decide to take her [. . .] and take the horizon too'. Her gradually unfolding presence drives him to action and more action. It is not enough to take her; he takes her and more with her, 'and the horizon too'. The excerpt finally explodes into the 'unsheathing of her storming flood of milk and forms'. Even though meaning of words or phrases is elusive and difficult to pin down, and perhaps nonsensical at times, there is meaning achieved on a different level, through another 'new relationship' between words based on impact, suspicion and music.

In this poem, Barakat succeeds in extracting from *nathr* (prose) a poetic text intense in its interrogation of language and musical despite its lack of obvious sonic pattern. The music here is not of melody or song, but of imagery and sound.[50] It does not exist apart from meaning,[51] but is a product of associations, dissonances and intersections of words.[52]

٩.

> أيقظها يا ديرام، أيقظ فراشة الغيب ويعسوبه الذهبي... أيقظ ديلانا وأيقظ معها البيت حجراً حجراً، ثم أيقظ الساحة المحيطة بالبيت، وأيقظ السياج. وإذ تنتهي من ذلك كله أيقظ الصباح النائم قرب السميات. وقل تعالي ديلانا. تعالي لنشهد السطوع الحيران للأرض وهي تذرف الحديد والبهاء على درعنا الآدمي. ولنكشف، بعد ذلك، ثديينا لنصل الحقول، مرتجفين من عذوبة النصل إذ يغوص إلى حيث يجري السمسم والزعفران، كأنما نحاول، معا، أن نكون الجراح التي لا جراح بعدها...هنا أيقظها يا ديرام.[53]

> Wake her up, Dīrām! Wake the butterfly of the unseen and its golden dragonfly . . . Wake Dīlānā up and with her, wake the house, stone by stone, and then wake the square around the house and wake the fence. And when done with all that, wake the morning which sleeps by the fence. Say: Come Dīlānā, come let us witness the hesitant shining of the earth as it sheds iron and splendour unto our human shield. Come, then, let us reveal our breasts to the blades of the fields, trembling with

> the sweetness of the blade as it sinks deep where the sesame and saffron flow. As if, together, we strive to be the wounds beyond which there are no wounds. Wake her up here, Dīrām.

In the section above, the ninth of the numbered sections, nothing new is disclosed. We are still delving deeper and deeper into that undefeatable pull between the two lovers. And even though the reader might not readily understand what 'the butterfly of the unseen and its golden dragonfly' and 'a blade sunk deep where the sesame and saffron flow' are referring to, in the context of the piece these phrases make sense. They achieve a purpose which, even when blurred and shaky on the hermeneutic level, is clear and effective on the level of music, where music is an effect that arises from a word's relations to words immediately preceding and following it, and indefinitely to the rest of its context and 'from the relationship of its meaning to other meanings which it has had in other contexts, to its greater or lesser wealth of association'.[54]

Barakat's excavations in Arabic conjure up the language's thinking process, its webs of associations and its entire history, sometimes in a single word.[55] He overuses and transforms single words such as praise (*madīḥ*), scene (*mashhad*), nebula (*sadīm*), plunder (*nahb*) into thickened points of intersection and intervention. Each word becomes an entry point that opens up the texts onto endless layers of meanings, sounds, associations and suspicions.

Salim Barakat, in his poetry and his life, has inhabited a space outside binaries and dichotomies. He is not one and not its other. He is neither at home nor in exile. He stands outside categories, as both writer and person. He aptly sums up himself and his experience:

> Splinters of a family. Imprisoned brothers. Sisters scattered all over the world. Lost papers. Unread writings. A policeman who can kick me out of one country to another. A passport with someone else's name on it, and no idea when that too will be taken from me . . . Where is exile then, and where is its other.[56]

The space that Barakat inhabits is also where his writing sits, among genres, generations of writers, languages and critical trends. Moreover, his contribution to the project of the Arabic prose poem is precisely that, a deliberate, exaggerated and defiant commitment to a space beyond the common contending categories of poetry and prose. This is why the label *qaṣīdat al-nathr* (prose poem) falls short and seems quite arbitrary and superfluous when applied to his work. In fact, the label itself stands to gain a lot from its application to Barakat's work. He exposes *qaṣīdat al-nathr* as being one of many sites of experimentation and contemplation in language and sensibilities. He is invested in interrogating and unpacking what he calls the 'imagination of the Arabic language'. His texts, both his poetry and his novels, are an engagement of the language's imagination, its prophecy, its inheritance and its unruliness:

> What is fitting for poetry is fitting for narrative. In composing, I do not categorise language into levels and planes, some of which I degrade and others which I honour . . . It (language) is the endless prophecy of imagination.[57]

To Barakat, the imagination of language, in both poetry and prose, is the 'poetic'. He believes that ultimately there is something magical at the source of language's ability to create, something that he calls the poetic (*al-shiʿrī*). Even when writing novels, he strives to return prose to its poetic origins, to 'liberate the novel from the story' and 'to render it into signals or the temptation of signals'.[58]

Barakat's posture towards language involves processes of uncovering, reclaiming and de-familiarising. He does not deny that it is also a difficult posture, one that does not come easy to either him or his reader. He is nevertheless unfalteringly committed to it, although at times he does not hide his bitterness and frustration at the lack of acknowledgement by others; what he calls the 'unjust silence' (*al-ṣamt al-lā munṣif*)[59] with which his work has been received thus far:

> I don't know why I should go up the wooden stairs to the attic in one country and descend the wooden stairs into the cave of writing in another, seven days a week, in summer, winter, autumn and spring, at the same hour, and submit myself to a perilous terrifying test of the blank page and

> its claws [. . .] But I know I have readers whose abilities texts cannot take lightly. They are demanding and just.[60]

His only consolation is an imagined reader, someone who is willing to follow the signs and cross beyond the easy binaries; a reader demanding, just and as difficult as the text that Barakat presents.

Notes

1. Salim Barakat, *Tanbih al-ḥayawān ilā ansābih* (Beirut: Dār al-Madā, 2018).
2. Hadidi, *Shiʿriyyāt al-taʿāqud al-ʿasīr*, p. 105.
3. Salim Barakat, *Al-Taʿjīl fī qurūḍ al-nathr* (Damascus: Dār Zamān, 2010), p. 112.
4. The poems '*Naqābat al-ansāb*', '*Qunṣul al-aṭfāl*' and '*al-Faṣīla al-maʿdiniyya* are some examples of Barakat's early toying with the metrical prescriptions set down by the pioneers of the free verse movement. See Salim Barakat, *al-Dīwān* (Beirut: Dār al-Tanwīr, 1992).
5. Dinoka is a Kurdish woman's name, and Breva is the name of a Kurdish village in the countryside of Qamishli. Dinoka Breva translates as Dinoka of the village of Breva.
6. Barakat, *al-Dīwān*, p. 7.
7. Barakat, *al-Taʿjīl*, p. 113.
8. Ibid.
9. Ibid.
10. Ibid. p. 115.
11. Mahmoud Darwish, *Memory for Forgetfulness*, trans. Ibrahim Muhawi (Los Angeles: University of California Press, 2013), pp. 78–79.
12. Ibid. p. 83.
13. Salim Barakat, *al-Dīwān 2* (Damascus: Dār al-Madā, 2017). Most of these blurbs are excerpted from a special issue of the journal *Hajalnama* featuring Salim Barakat: *Hajalnama* 11–12 (2007), pp. 181–223. *Hajalnama* is a Kurdish cultural journal published in Sweden.
14. Barakat, *al-Taʿjīl*, p. 102.
15. Barakat is often studied or mentioned in work on identity politics. See, for example, Tetz Rooke, 'Feathers from Heaven: Or What the Paprika Plant Said to the Hero', *Middle Eastern Literatures* 9.2 (2006), pp. 179–88, and Hashem Ahmadzadeh, 'In Search of a Kurdish Novel That Tells Us Who the Kurds Are', *Iranian Studies* 40.5 (2007), pp. 579–92.

16. ʿAbd al-Rahman al-Barquqi (ʿAbd al-Raḥmān al-Barqūqī), *Sharḥ Dīwān al-Mutannabī* (Beirut: Dār al-Kitāb al-ʿArabī, 1986), vol. 4, p. 83.
17. Abu Tammam, vol. 2, p. 485.
18. Barakat, *al-Dīwān*, pp. 285–86.
19. Jayyusi, *Modern Arabic Literature*, p. 43.
20. Barakat, 'Madhāhib al-maʿnā', *al-Karmil* 43 (1992), p. 166.
21. Ibid. pp. 166–67.
22. Barakat, *al-Dīwān*, pp. 281–82.
23. Ibid. p. 282.
24. Salim Barakat, *Al-Muʿjam* (Damascus: Dār al-Madā, 2005), and '*Fihrist al-kā'in*' (The Index of Creatures) in *Al-Dīwan*, pp. 207–18, and '*Mazraʿat Rān*' (Ran's Farm) in *Al-Mujābahāt, al-mawāthīq al-ajrān, al-taṣārīf, wa-ghayruhā* (Beirut: Dār an-Nahār, 1996), pp. 63–70, are three examples of Barakat's subversion of the easily recognisable form of the dictionary or encyclopedia entry.
25. Salim Barakat, *Ṭaysh al-yāqūt (The Recklessness of Sapphire)* (Beirut: Dār al-Nahār, 1996), p. 87.
26. The lighting scene in Imruʾ al-Qays's *muʿallaqā.* See al-Zawzani (Husayn b. Aḥmad al-Zawzanī), *Sharḥ al-muʿallaqāt al-sabʿ* (Beirut: Dār al-Jīl, n.d.), pp. 50–51.
27. The final flood scene in the *muʿallaqā.* Ibid. pp. 52–56.
28. Barakat, *Ṭaysh al-yāqūt*, p. 88.
29. Ibid. p. 89.
30. Ibid. p. 92.
31. Ibid. p. 93.
32. Ibid. p. 98.
33. The name of a Kurdish tribe.
34. We have already encountered the word *ʿāna* (genitals, pubis, crotch) in this poem. This is a recurrent word in Barakat' poetry. Like *mashhad* (scene) and *madāʾiḥ* or *madīḥ* (praises or praise), *yaqīn* (certainty, truth) among many others, it is a word that he claims, distorts and recurrently uses without reservation. He creates a new history for such words and a new field of connections and associations. After encountering them in Barakat's linguistic world, it becomes quite difficult to think about these words in the same manner as before.
35. See Josias Leslie Porter, *A Handbook for Travelers in Syria and Palestine* (London: J. Murray, 1868), p. 355, and Djene Rhys Bajalan and Sara Zandi

Karimi (eds), *Studies in Kurdish History: Empire, Ethnicity and Identity* (New York: Routledge, 2015), p. 162.

36. Barakat, *Ṭaysh al-yāqūt,* p. 100.
37. Ibid. p. 115.
38. Jayyusi, *Modern Arabic Literature*, p. 169.
39. Barakat, *al-Dīwān*, p. 159.
40. Ibid. p. 165.
41. Ibid. p. 159–60.
42. Ibid. p. 169.
43. Ibid. p. 178.
44. Ibid. p. 179.
45. Ibid. p. 189.
46. Ibid. p. 199.
47. Eliot, p. 458.
48. Barakat, *al-Taʿjīl*, p. 111.
49. Barakat, *al-Dīwān*, p. 161.
50. Eliot, p. 463.
51. Ibid. p. 455.
52. Ibid. p. 459.
53. Barakat, *al-Dīwān*, p. 161.
54. Eliot, p. 459.
55. T. S. Eliot states: 'Not all words, obviously, are equally rich and well connected: it is part of the business of the poet to dispose the richer among the poorer, at the right points, and we cannot afford to load a poem too heavily with the former – for it is only at certain moments that a word can be made to insinuate the whole history of a language and a civilization'. Ibid. p. 459.
56. ʿAql al-ʿAwit (ʿAql al-ʿAwīṭ), 'Interview with Salim Barakat', *Hajalnama* 11–12 (2007), p. 12.
57. Barakat, *al-Taʿjīl*, p. 107.
58. Ibid. p. 108.
59. Ibid. p. 118.
60. Ibid.

7

Wadiʿ Saʿadeh and the Third Generation of Prose Poets: An Arabic Poetics of Translation and Exophony

The writers and artists of Beirut's Hamra Street remember one day in 1973 when a young man from the northern village of Shabtin stood handing out his poetry to passers-by. It was Wadiʿ Saʿadeh (b. 1948) with a stack of handwritten copies of his first poetry collection, *Laysa lil-masāʾ ikhwa* (The Evening Has No Brothers).[1] Stepping outside the established avenues for 'making it' in the world of writing and publishing, Saʿadeh placed himself and his writing out in the open, literally on the side of the street. Circumventing the institutions and networks of poets, critics, editors and publishers, he went out to meet the abstract reader, in person. 'I wanted to see, face to face, people's reaction to poetry and the poet'.[2]

Saʿadeh often remembers his unconventional debut in interviews. The amusing and unexpected story tells us much about his spontaneous and daring personality. More importantly, however, is that it reveals penetrating features of his poetic stance, features which shaped his first work and continued to evolve in his twelve subsequent collections. Saʿadeh's poetic experience directs itself to the most open and abstracted concerns of writing, or rather of speech, and its impossibilities. He is unburdened by consideration of status or literary affiliations or influence, or the politics of reception and fame. Similarly, his writing itself, although clearly poetic in its aspirations, is unburdened by formal considerations or genre limitations. He is a poet of texts, not poems; a poet of sayings which have not yet settled into a category. He speaks out into the open without guidelines or expectations. Thus, his experimentations in writing and the experience of reading them both remain without pretences, without goals or models, and open unto limitless possibilities.

Saʿadeh is not quite of the pioneers of the prose poem, joining the *Shiʿr* group relatively late. Moreover, he was neither involved nor interested in the prose poem theorising efforts, as were Adonis and Unsi al-Hajj. He, therefore, stands as an important midpoint in a thread that extends from the first practitioners to the younger generation of prose poets who came to prominence in the mid-1990 and at the turn of the twenty-first century. This chapter addresses Wadiʿ Saʿadeh's contribution to the prose poem project in Arabic as a perpetual threshold. I argue that he represents a stage after which the prose poem becomes less of an oppositional poetic practice and a deliberate theorising effort, but rather an open space for free writing.

A Lebanese émigré residing in Australia since 1988, Saʿadeh turns in his Arabic prose poems away from the diligent interrogation and excavation of language we see with Adonis or Salim Barakat, and away from the subtle formal concerns of Darwish and the other verse poets. Somewhat Maghutian in his position from the prose poem project and from the poetic endeavour in general, Saʿadeh dissociated himself from the critical, linguistic and formal concerns and is preoccupied with the very possibility/impossibility of speech in the first place. However, unlike al-Maghut's, Saʿadeh's oeuvre does not have prevalent political or social impetuses. If he is cynical, Saʿadeh directs his cynicism inward at the very absurdity of attempting to say something in the first place.

Building a poetic world of dust, clouds, smoke and transient ripples which will soon disappear, Saʿadeh presents us with a poetics of disintegration, both on the level of form and ideas. His language is neutral and uncontending. He does not quarrel with language but attempts to use it, with the recognition of its ultimate failure as a means of expression or communication. Thus, his statements and his texts recoil and mournfully turn onto themselves, ultimately shutting down and undoing themselves.

In two seminal articles which introduced Wadiʿ Saʿadeh to the English readership, Clarissa Burt captures the elegiac essence of his poetic voice. Saʿadeh 's writing, she states, 'is writing that mourns itself [. . .] his writing accuses, denigrates, cannibalizes and obliterates itself . . . '[3] Most pressing about this elegiac mood, however, is its self-reflexive-ness, its direction inward. The crisis is not a verbal, structural, or auditory one; the crisis is one of being and un-being. At this murky divide is where Saʿadeh stands composing his texts. He guides us 'into a now post-modern elegy through his fatalistic wordplay and pushes us to pursue the object of loss into the mists of unbeing'.[4] From a devastating reconciliation with defeat, Saʿadeh attempts to connect something with something else; he strives to send out a voice with little hope of it reaching too far.

Saʿadeh does not flaunt any linguistic or formal feats. On the contrary, he prefers to keep his poetic efforts all focused on the threshold of a project, an attempt, a beginning, not a thing as much as a gesture toward a thing as demonstrated in this short piece:

غريق
رفعَ يدَهُ
كأنَّهُ كانَ يريدُ
أنْ يقولَ كلمة.[5]

A Drowning Man
He raised his hand
as if he wanted
to say a word.

This piece draws on movement and on the shape of a movement, comparing the drowning person's raised hand not to words, but to the immanence of words in a gesture. The past tense 'wanted' (*kāna yurīd*) further underscores the hesitation to speak. Although seemingly simple and straightforward, this short piece showcases Saʿadeh's deep suspicion towards language. The impetus of his poetic voice thus is a deeply diffident stance rooted in the belief that, ultimately, silence is more graceful than words. He does not build this piece on a simile or a metaphor, but rather a gesture towards the possibilities of similes and metaphors in the simple observation of a drowning person's raised hand.

The moments of poetry, he seems to tell us, are too fragile to categorise. Nevertheless, when asked to name what he writes, Saʿadeh advances an argument similar to that of the proponents of the prose poem without insisting on the label. He prefers the term 'modern poetic text' to the term poem or prose poem and argues, as do most prose poets, that writing without prescriptions is the more tasking and more delicate endeavour. 'In a *qaṣīda*, meter and rhyme may hide flaws, whereas in a poetic text nothing can be camouflaged or passed, all is exposed'.[6] Thus, the texts he writes are open spaces, multi-generic and multi-medial attempts at capturing moments in an otherwise disintegrating universe. 'What I write is not a poem in the traditional sense', he insists, 'it borders on narrative, on philosophical meditation, on cinema'.[7]

After Saʿadeh, the stakes of the prose poem as a subversive poetic endeavour in Arabic are lowered and the tension which held the prose poem in a confrontational stance is relaxed. His loaded gesturing and this reluctant language, which leaves more unsaid than said, make it more tempting for younger poets to take him up as a launching point for their own attempts at saying, their own attempts at drawing circles in the air. Saʿadeh's openness and abstract engagement with the possibilities of speech make his poetic world unpretentious, inviting and accessible. With Saʿadeh as a running thread, this chapter presents an overview of the present moment in Arabic poetry, bringing into the conversation contemporary Arab prose poets, mainly from the Levant, who, I argue, have adopted Saʿadeh's 'modern poetic text' (*al-naṣṣ*) as opposed to the Arabic poem which, even if nominally or appositionally, remains a *qaṣīda* (*qaṣīdat al-tafʿīla* and *qaṣīdat al-nathr*). Although writing in Arabic, these poets disengage from poetry as a linguistic event in Arabic and engage with poetry as an attitude towards the world.

In the works of these younger prose poets, we see an abstract concern with poetry and a neutral language which toys with ideas. Saʿadeh's contribution to the prose poem repertoire in Arabic has provided younger prose poets with a wide inviting doorway into poetry as a mental/conceptual engagement or exercise. His poetic legacy is unimposing, and his engagement with form is open enough to allow for anything to pass as poetry, as long as it initiates a shift or tilt or an agitation in thought. Thus, the engagement with form and the interrogation of language which motivated some pioneers of the prose poem in Arabic are diluted in the works of younger prose poets in favour of a quest for 'poetic ideas' which do not depend on a formulation of any sort. Poetry becomes a multi-generic practice which subsumes other forms of writing and expression, eventually becoming formless.

A Poetics of Disintegration

From distributing poetry on the street to publishing all of his work online,[8] Saʿadeh is committed to the immediacy of poetic experience and to an unmediated relationship with his reader. He is content to bask in the momentary poetic charge he succeeds in creating in a text, without worrying about sustaining it or attending to the critical reactions or consequences.

In his very first poetic statement, the opening piece of *The Evening Has No Brothers*, Saʿadeh resigns himself to a rupture or a shattering that necessarily results in loss and disintegration:

في هذه القرية
تُنسى أقحواناتُ المساء
مرتجفةً خلف الأبواب.
في هذه القرية التي تستيقظ
لتشرب المطر
انكسرتْ في يدي زجاجةُ العالم.[9]

In this village
the evening chrysanthemums are forgotten
shivering behind the doors,
in this village which awakens
to drink the rain,
the glass of the world broke in my hand.

This opening to Saʿadeh's work sums up his poetry approach and its movement away from prescriptions. The quest for poetry begins with a breaking of some sort, a spilling out. The struggle of the poetic, however, remains to imagine or remember, even if momentarily, the world contained in a bottle. The image of broken glass is one to which Saʿadeh continues to return in his writing, underscoring the tragic fact that what is broken will forever and in vain long to be whole again. He reminds us of al-Maʿarrī's broken glass when he says:

يحطّمنا ريب الزمان كأننا زجاج ولكن لا يعاد له سبك[10]

The ravages of time shatter us like glass
which cannot be moulded back together

Saʿadeh places this tragic awareness of fragility and the potential of shattering in language, which to him is a very flimsy thing. The need for language is in itself the beginning of shattered-ness. Silence is whole, but the need to speak is a lack; the need to speak is the creeping of cracks, an aching. And thus, movement towards any kind of utterance is painful as we see in the following piece titled 'Absence' from his 1992 collection *Bisabab ghayma ʿalā al-arjaḥ* (Because of a Cloud, Most Likely).

ذاكَ النهار
تحتَ سنديانةِ الساحة
ظَلَّ فقط مقعدان حجريّان فارغيْن،
كانا صامِتَيْن
ينظران إلى بعضهما
ويَدْمَعان.[11]

Absence

That day
under the oak in the yard
only two stone benches were left empty.
They were silent,
eyeing each other
and tearing up.

The tension in this short piece extends from 'empty' (*fārighayn*) to 'tearing up' (*yadmaʿān*). Only when we arrive at the last line does that tensions reveal itself, driving home the tragic realisation of loneliness and desolation. The two stone benches are alone, and they know it. Being left alone is not the crisis; it is the realisation of aloneness and the need to connect that drives this piece towards tears (*yadmaʿān*). Similarly, the following piece captures the devastating tragedy of realisation. It is not the state of being that pains, but one's consciousness of it. The following piece titled '*al-Mutʿabūn*' (The Tired) is from his 1987 collection *Maqʿad rākib ghādara al-Bāṣ* (The Seat of a Passenger Who Left the Bus):

المتعبون في الساحة، وجوههم ترقُّ يومًا بعد يوم
وشَعرهم يلين
في هواء الليل والأضواء الخفيفة،
وحين ينظرون إلى بعضهم ترقُّ عيونهم أيضًا
إلى درجة أنهم يظنون أنفسهم زجاجًا
وينكسرون.[12]

The faces of the tired in the square
soften day after day;
Their hair becomes brittle
in the night air and the tender light.
When they look at one another,
their eyes soften too,
until they think themselves glass
and they break.

What primarily motivates Saʿadeh's poetry is an overwhelming consciousness of dispersal, of the inability to build something that lasts. Transience, the transient moment of containment, and disintegration, the inevitable scattering or shattering that follows, are the two forces that shape Saʿadeh's poetic. The texts he writes are built on observations of fleeting instances such as the following:

فراشةُ الحُبّ تطير بعيدًا
وعطلةٌ قصيرة على كفّها
لكنَّ يدي أضاعت مفاتيحَها.
أتدلّى
فوق سور الأسماء
وغيمةٌ تشبه اليد
ترفع لي قميصَ الشتاء[13]

Love's butterfly flies away
with a short repose on its palm,
but my hand has lost its keys.
I hang
over the wall of names
and a cloud like a hand
lifts winter's shirt for me.

The two images in this short piece are intricate and brittle, too fragile to be visualised clearly. They are more like the effect or the trace of images rather than images. We catch the butterfly in movement, 'flying away', with a state of mind, a repose, stillness (*ʿuṭla*) in its 'palm', and we glimpse a formation of cloud also in the subtle movement of 'lifting', revealing a dimension of the winter sky. The two delicate images balance on 'but my hand has lost its keys', yet another statement of surrender and resignation to the ultimate inability to comprehend or decipher (lost its keys); another affirmation of silence. The I 'hangs' over a pile of words, 'wall of names', without keys, without the ability to formulate or to name, surrendering itself to the subtle movements and signals of the world. More eloquent and less effortful than attempting to force a statement is listening to the signals of the world. The 'I' laid upon a pile of words allows the hand of cloud (as opposed to its own hand which had lost its keys) to reveal something, to guide it towards some discovery 'a cloud like a hand/ lifts winter's shirt for me'.

Saʿadeh's poetic 'I' is not only reconciled with disintegration, but also fascinated by it to the extent of distraction. One cannot anticipate anything or contemplate anything beyond the devastating realisation of inevitable dissolution or collapse.

أيُّ زمن سيأتي
بقميص أبيض؟
أيّ درب ستأتي
ونلعب مع الأطفال؟
أيّ خروف
نطعمه أيدينا؟
أيّ حلم
وكلّنا على قارعة الطريق
نلملم انهيار الوجوه.[14]

What time will come
in a white shirt?
What path so we may
frolic with children?
What sheep

will we feed our hands to?
What dream,
when we are all here on the sidewalk
gathering pieces of fallen faces.

The intensity of the transient moment that Saʿadeh captures is only heightened by our anticipation of it and our preparation to lose it. Saʿadeh's poetic voice constantly nudges us to 'move on', lest the ground under our feet gives way.

الذكرى ثلج
لا يُضمن الوقوفُ فوقه طويلاً
إرحلْ.[15]

Memory is ice,
standing upon it for long is not guaranteed,
move on.

Moving on or passing through, 'ʿubūr', is without a doubt the most recurrent word in Saʿadeh's oeuvre. 'The most beautiful is the one passing through', Saʿadeh insists. His texts succeed most when he does not attempt a grand statement but remains intent on catching glimpses of something just as it disappears or begins to negate itself. One of the most powerful expressions of his poetics of disintegration, his transient poetics of passing through, is this piece titled '*Jamāl al-ʿābir*' (The Beauty of the Transient) from his 2000 collection *Ghubār* (Dust):

العابرون سريعًا جميلون. لا يتركون ثقَل ظلّ. ربما غبارًا قليلاً، سرعان ما يختفي.
الأكثر جمالاً بيننا، المتخلّي عن حضوره. التارك فسحةً نظيفة بشغور مقعده. جمالاً في
الهواء بغياب صوته. صفاءً في التراب بمساحته غير المزروعة. الأكثر جمالاً بيننا:
الغائب.
قاطعُ المكان وقاطع الوقت بخفَّةٍ لا تترك للمكان أن يسبيه ولا للوقت ان يذرّيه
...
وبلا صوت، لأن الصوت ثقَل في الهواء.
لأن الصوت قد يرتطم بآخر. قد يسحق صوتًا آخر في الفضاء. قد يزعج النسمات.
وبلا رغبة. لأن الرغبة إقامة، ثبات.
العابرون سريعًا جميلون. لا يقيمون في مكان كي يتركوا فيه بشاعة. لا يبقون وقتًا يكفي

لترك بقعة في ذاكرة المقيمين...
بخفَّةِ خفقة الطير وانفتاح النسمة للجناح. بخفة انفتاح هواء العبور واندمال هواء الانطلاق.
عابرون سريعًا، كلحظة انقصاف

...

ذاكرة تعيق الراغبين في الموت. وتجعل الراغبين في الحياة موتى.
فلندفنها إذن.
لندفن الذاكرة ونحن نغنّي.
إنها حفلة سخيفة في أية حال، ولكن بما أننا وصلنا، فلنغ ّن ونرقص.
ثوانٍ، قد نكون فيها جميلين.
لكن أجملنا سيبقى: الغائب.[16]

The Beauty of the One Passing Through

Beautiful are those who quickly pass through. They don’t leave the heaviness of a shadow, maybe just a little dust, which soon disappears.

The most beautiful among us is he who gives up his presence. He leaves a clean space in his empty seat, a beauty in the air where his voice is not, a serenity in the soil where his lot is left unplanted. The most beautiful among us is the absent one.

Traversing place, traversing time with a lightness which keeps place from capturing him and time from scattering him asunder …

Without a voice, because voice is a heaviness in the air,

because a voice may clash with another, may crush another, may disturb the breeze.

Without desire, because desire is settled and stagnant.

Those passing through quickly are beautiful. The do not reside in a place to leave it ugly. They do not stay long enough to stain the residents’ memory …

Light as the flutter of a bird or the breeze making way for a wing. Lightly as the air opens for passing through and caves in for launching, passing through quickly, like a moment snapping …

A Memory hampering those who wish for death, and making dead those who desire life. Let us bury memory then while singing. It’s a ridiculous celebration in any case, but since we’ve already arrived then let’s sing and dance. For a few seconds, we may be beautiful. But the most beautiful of us will always be: the absent one.[17]

Saʿadeh finds beauty in the lightest and least interfering manners of being. Ultimately, this ends up being absence, not quite non-being, but the trace of being, the reminder of a presence that has now lifted or 'passed through'. Saʿadeh here, and in most of his writing, conflates opposites such as presence and absence dissolving the two poles of a binary by his logic of disintegration. Thus, in the same manner as absence is the best form of presence, Saʿadeh insists that the most eloquent speech, the most beautiful way of using language, is silence. This resignation to silence in his approach to language or speech motivates and shapes his poetic voice and consequently his approach to poetic form.

At the Edge of Silence

From his first collection, Saʿadeh reveals his longing for another means of connecting with the other side. 'There must be another way', he hopes:

يجب أن يكون هناك طريقٌ آخر
إلى الغابة
الوترُ المشدود بين عينيَّ و الأشجار
على وشك الانقصاف.
أيّتها الكلمات يا غابتي
يا شجرتي اليابسة في فمي
على طول الطريق سواقٍ و أزهار
حجارةٌ لمن تعبوا
شمسٌ للنهار قمرٌ للّيل
وليس على حروفك عصفورٌ يسلّي.
يجب أن يكون هناك طريقٌ آخر
الأصواتُ أقفاص.[18]

There must be another way
to the forest.
The cord stretched between my eyes and the trees
is about to snap.
O Words, my forest,
the tree dead in my mouth,
along the way are fountains and flowers,
stones for the tired,

a sun for the day and a moon for the night,
but no consoling bird on your letters.
There must be another way.
Voices are cages.

Unlike other poets who find in their quarrels with language an outlet for expression and a possibility for agency or creation, Sa'adeh finds language suffocating (cages) and intrusive (a heaviness in the air). The very act of formulating ideas into language burdens him. The craft of linguistic composition is superfluous and, as a poet, he can only approach it with a belief in its ultimate futility.

Writing at the edge of silence, Sa'adeh's texts are ephemeral, a sound spoken into the air, soon to cease. In *The Text of Absence* (1999), he addresses 'words' proclaiming: 'You come out of my mouth, you kill me'.[19] One's words are a means of self-negation and betrayal, not affirmation or expression. In this text which he presented as his 'last words', foreshadowing his 2002 decision to stop writing, Sa'adeh portrays writing as death. For life only truly exists outside of the text, outside the pretence of language:

إنها الكلمات الأخيرة... وها أنا أهْجرها

هل أقول الوداع للكتابة؟
أقول الوداع.
حوار الكتابة حوار الصمت. زمن الكتابة زمن الغياب. مكان الكتابة عدم المكان.
لا حياة بالكلمات. الحياة قد تكون هناك، خارجها. هناك قد يكون الآخرون، وأنا أيضًا. في المقلب الآخر من الكلام، خارج النَصِّ.
الكتابة غياب الحياة. الحياة قد نصادفها بالمشي، قد نصادفها بالجلوس، تحت شجرة أو على رصيف. ربما تأتي سهوًا، بقبلةٍ أو برصاصة، لكن ليس بالكتابة.

. . .
لا مكان للكلمات، إنها حالة غياب. حالة استحالة. تأتي كأنما ظِلٌّ أتى وتذهب كأنّما ظِلٌّ ذهب، ولا وجه لها أو قامة أو مكان.
ظلالٌ، ظلال، ولا أثر.
كلماتٌ كثيرة، ولكن يُستحالُ قولُ أيِّ شيء.[20]

These are the last words . . . and here I am, leaving them behind
Do I bid writing farewell?

I say goodbye.
The conversation of writing is a conversation of silence. The time of writing is a time of absence. The place of writing is a negation of place. No life with words. Life is perhaps there, outside words. There the others may be, and I too. On the other side of speech. Outside the text.
Writing is the absence of life. We might fall upon life in walking or sitting under a tree or on the sidewalk. It might come inadvertently in a kiss or a bullet, but not in writing.
[. . .]
There is no place for words. They are a state of absence. A state of impossibility. They come like shadows and leave like shadows. Without face or body, or place.
Shadows, shadows, without a trace.
Words are many, but it is impossible to say anything.

In Saʿadeh's poetry, Clarissa Burt writes, 'the inevitability of dissolution betrays the creative promise of poetry'.[21] Poetry, in his world, is not consoling or redemptive; it does not even offer the illusion of creation. Having announced his cessation from writing once in his career so far, Saʿadeh seems to constantly be weighing the effectiveness of words against the effectiveness of silence. Even when he resorts to words, he reveals their potential to annihilate themselves. This reflects itself in his poems, which often collapse and cave in on themselves.

وجهه
رسمَ وجهَهُ ورآه
يشبهُ وجهًا آخرَ
أضافَ خطوطًا وملامحَ
أضافَ تعرُّجاتٍ
ساحاتٍ
طُرُقاتٍ
مزَّقَ الورقةَ ...
واختفى.[22]

His Face
He drew his face and found

it resembled another's.
He added lines and features.
He added wrinkles,
squares,
roads …
He tore up the paper
and disappeared.

Often, Saʿadeh's texts move towards their own erasure, as is evident in the piece above. In the short and very short poems, which are his signature compositions, he begins with one simple idea, then slightly nudges it in one direction, tilts it in another and eventually lets it crumble unto itself. The movement in these short pieces is devastating. From an initial question, address, or discovery which peaks the reader's interest and draws her in, to a quick circling back to the futility of the initial idea. Despite their brevity, these short pieces have the ability to fully develop an idea and then completely negate it. The following three short poems from his collection *Tell the Passer to Come Back, He Left His Shadow* (2012) demonstrate this cycle of disintegration:[23]

غيوم

في عيونه غيوم
ويحدّق في الأرض
علّها تمطر.

Clouds

In his eyes are clouds
He stares at the ground
Perhaps it would rain.

Dreams, the clouds in the eyes, are ultimately futile. No matter how long you stare at the ground, it will not rain. There is a disconnect between what the eye wants to see and what is in reality. This disconnecting barrier is one that Saʿadeh often contemplates. In the following piece, he similarly juxtaposes the small self-involved human effort with the overwhelming and ultimately victorious reality.

كيف؟

كيف للسابح أن يصل
والبحر يغرق؟

How?
How will the swimmer make it
If the sea is drowning?

Arriving to the other side or 'making it' in any sense is an illusion. The state of being is a state of drowning as the rhetorical question above makes clear. We are not able to see ourselves in the bigger picture of the world around us, and we continue to strive to swim across, to communicate, in vain.

لا

لا تدقّ على الباب
امشِ
مَن في الداخل يدقُّ على الباب أيضاً
ولا أحد يفتح له.

No

Don't knock on the door.
Leave.
The one on the other side of the door is knocking too,
and nobody opens the door.

Ultimately, the severest barrier in Saʿadeh's poetic world is language; it is a closed door. The very attempt at saying consistently fails. Nevertheless, one fatalistically perseveres in this hopeless endeavour. After having given up on poetry for a while, Saʿadeh eventually returned in 2006 with a collection titled *A Restructuring of Wadiʿ Saʿadeh's Life* (*Tarkīb ākhar li-ḥayāt Wadīʿ Saʿāda*). He returned, however, with a harsher self-examining eye and a surrender to the idea of writing as a doomed effort:

اللغة

لا المنادي ينادي ولا المنادَى يصغي إنَّها الريح
تتحدَّث مع عبورها

ويرمي كلاماً في الريح
لا كي يقول شيئاً بل
كي تتفكَّك مفاصلُ الكلمات
وتندثر.

اللغةُ هي نثارها
الكلامُ هو
تبدُّدُ الصوت.

في اندثار الأحرف
في الريح
اللغة.

Language

Neither the speaker speaks nor the listener listens.
It's the wind
talking to itself, passing through.
He tosses words to the wind
not in order to say anything
but so that the joints of words may give way
and disintegrate.

Language is its own chaff
and speech is the
diffusion
of voice.

The fading of letters
in the air
is language.

Wadi' Sa'adeh continued to write poetry/texts motivated by suspicions and hesitations towards writing. This is why his most important perceptions are the ones conceived in a space before language, where the idea is still in the phase of emerging and fading, not yet fully formed. His poetic concerned are formal and sonic in the least. His texts revolve around ideas or half-formed ideas in such a way that each piece is riddle-like, confronting the reader with a mental quandary rather than a linguistic event or auditory formulation. And thus, his language does not actively contribute to or participate in shaping meaning or structuring images. It remains a neutral medium, stripped and simple, as if just spoken and at the risk of being taken back at any moment.

Burt maintains that Saʿadeh's 'poetic texts form a universalist post-modern elegy, an existential assertion of the predations of existence upon itself'.[24] The cyclicality of this statement is significant, and the keyword here is 'predation'. Saʿadeh's notion of poetry exists in a similar space of predation, a moment before 'the putting together or the formulation'. His texts themselves are merely symptoms of the failure to articulate the idea of poetry, to execute it. Poetry is a dream, or an illusion adulterated by the attempts to find materialisation for it in language.

Saʿadeh's work has often been described as 'philosophical', an adjective which is not necessarily always laudatory when referring to poetry. When the poem is burdened by ideas not yet reworked or transformed by language into something different, the poem relaxes its claim as poetry and is content to be a text, an engagement with poetry in the absolute, outside language as a thinking and creative entity. And Saʿadeh does not insist on the claim of poetry or poem-making; he admits that his engagement with the poetic practice draws on other mediums and forms of expression such as the narrative, the philosophical meditation, visual arts and film, as he attempts to say something about poetry and language more so than saying poetry or intervening in language in some dramatically altering way.

Saʿadeh's unassuming approach to poetry-making in Arabic can be generally linked to the Arab modernist's claim of autonomy and the movement's insistence on apolitical cultural engagement, as Robyn Creswell shows in his study of the *Shiʿr* group.[25] *Shiʿr*'s radical internationalism allowed them, as Creswell argues, to advance a theory of personalist lyric poetry, on one hand,[26] and to escape 'the taint of partisan politics',[27] on the other. Nevertheless, the *Shiʿr* project with its ostensibly apolitical internationalism still aimed to intervene in the Arabic tradition and radically alter the definition of Arabic poetry.[28] We see this preoccupation clearly in Adonis's work, and it is just as prevalent, even if negatively, in Unsi al-Hajj's work, as well as many other *Shiʿr* activists.

Conversely, Saʿadeh's expressed lack of interest in intervening or altering the definition of poetry in Arabic has no ulterior motive. His involvement with Arabic and its poetic memory is tangential. His creative obsessions are pre-lingual, at the threshold of the attempt of the poetic in any language. The Arabic language just happens to be the medium here, often featured as if stripped of its poetic, meta-poetic and critical baggage. In that sense, Saʿadeh represents a veering away from the prose poem as a confrontational or reconciliatory intervention in the Arabic poetic tradition. It merely becomes a space where poets/writers strive to translate their observations of the world into language in the abstract sense; any language and not necessarily the private thoughts of one language in particular. The challenge is that of *taʿbir* (expression) and *ʿubūr* (making it across to the other side, in both senses of surviving and getting a message across).

The end, the goal, of poetry is thus to survive the specific instantiation in the language of composition towards a non-linguistic space unfettered by specific signs. That is also the end of poetry, its demise, when it ceases or fulfils its purpose as a passage outside of language into an abstract universal space of poetic ideas or ideas about the poetic. In a poem addressing the American writer Jack Kerouac, Saʿadeh expresses this longing for the end of poetic exercise, this crossing or passing through.

كيرواك
كثير من الأخطاء في الإشارات والأسماء على الطريق يا جاك كيرواك
الأسهم المشيرة إلى أمكنة
توصل إلى أمكنة أخرى
واليافطات المكتوب عليها ينابيع
صحارى.

ماذا جرى يا جاك كي أرى السهل حوتاً يريد أن يبتلعني
والفراشة جداراً؟
وهل السنونوة التي سقطت ميتةً أمامي
كانت تعبر كي ترسم الطريق أم كي
تمحو العبور؟
يا جاك، يا جاك، إنزعِ اليافطات عن الطريق
إلغِ الينابيع والغابات والأمكنة
دلّني فقط إلى الممرّ الذي بلا إشارات ولا أسماء
أريد أن أعبر.[29]

Kerouac
Many mistakes in the signs and the names along the way, Jack
Kerouac.
The arrows pointing to places
lead to other places
and the signs that say 'springs'
lead to deserts.

What happened, Jack, that I see the field as a whale that wants to
swallow me.
and the butterfly a wall?
Was the swallow that fell dead in front of me
passing through, tracing the way
or erasing the passage?

Jack, O Jack, take down the signs on the road.
Cancel the springs, the forests, and the places.
Just point me to the path with no signs and no names:
I want to pass through.

Saʿadeh complains to the author of *On the Road* about the 'mistakes in the signs and the names along the way'. Language in a poetic world is disorienting. It derails rather than guides; thus, he calls upon his addressee to 'take down' and 'cancel' the signs. Addressing the American writer is significant in itself here. It does not necessarily prove an intimate or critical engagement with Kerouac's work or American literature in general, but rather reveals a striving for connection beyond or outside the one language, one closed-off system of signs; a striving which in turn feeds into Saʿadeh's notion of poetry as a primarily conceptual not linguistic event. Poetic texts are, thus, attempts at getting across (*ubūr*) to the other side of the creative process; of surviving it, of escaping the linguistic entanglement to arrive at the conceptual clearing, that poetic idea which has no moorings in one language. And this perhaps is why Saʿadeh's poetic widely appeals to a later generation of Arab writers and poets who relate to the Arabic language, even when it is their mother tongue or the only language they know, from a position of exophony and translation.

The Arabic Poem of the Twenty-first Century

The prose poem, which in the 1960s and 1970s was a blatant announcement of rebellion against the parameters set for poetry in the Arabic tradition, is now the form adopted by most young contemporary poets of Arabic. The debates around form and meter are no longer pressing, as they might have been before, and the poets of this later phase do not necessarily think of themselves as breaking away. Instead, the open space/text of the Arabic prose poem now poses new questions and reveals new imperatives which inform the Arabic poetic endeavour in the twenty-first century as a whole. These new imperatives exhibit themselves most clearly in a new posture and engagement with the Arabic language itself.

Tracing a thread from Muhammad al-Maghut and Wadiʿ Saʿadeh to the third generation of prose poets writing at the turn of the twenty-first century reveals an Arabic poem whose investments increasingly exceed the bounds of the Arabic language. The motivation and the direction of this generation's poetry are outside the exercise of any one language: Arabic is one medium for expressing poetic ideas or ideas about the poetic, it is not where the poetic impetus grounds itself. The disengagement from the Arabic tradition which we see with the Egyptian poets of the nineties develops with the younger generation into a more a deliberate search for other non-Arabic engagements. To understand this phenomenon, I focus here on a generation of poets who were all born in the 1970s and who began publishing at the turn of the twenty-first century. The generation includes names such as Joumana Haddad (b. 1970), Samer Abu Hawwash (b. 1972), Nazem El-Sayed (b. 1975) and Golan Haji (b. 1977), among others.

This is a poetry released from the hold of a single language's poetic memory. It takes on adjectives such as universality, philosophical, transnational and migrant, and it subsumes other languages and various registers of language to communicate a mood or a state of mind that is not a product of language thinking of itself, but rather precedes or bypasses the engagement with language altogether. The poetry of this younger generation is a poetry of ideas that could have been written in any language.

Instead of the stripped, colloquial and neutral Arabic of the Egyptians poets of the nineties, the Arabic of these twenty-first-century poets clearly bears the mark of other languages. Many of the poets discussed in this chapter are bi-lingual and/or dedicated translators of foreign poetry and fiction into Arabic. The prose poem, thus, is an obvious choice of poetic form considering its tenuous place in the Arabic poetic tradition and its strong connections with non-Arabic traditions. All specifically Arabic prescriptions for poetry are superfluous to this new sensibility. These poets are instead attuned to a notion of poetry dissociated from its bearing in the Arabic language. And to many of them, translation is operative at the inception of language. The Arabic poem in the twenty-first century is thus multilingual, exophonic in its motivations and 'born-translated'. I borrow the term 'born-translated' from Rebecca Walkowitz's rich argument in her *Born Translated: The Contemporary Novel in an Age of World Literature*. Walkowitz uses the term to describe contemporary works that 'build translation into their form' and refuse 'to match language to geography'.[30] Such works, Walkowitz claims, participate in world literature, which itself becomes a 'series of emerging works, not a product but a process'.[31] Her argument is far-reaching in its consequences and relevance to this generation of Arabic poets and their engagement with language and translation, as well as their relationship to their national literatures and their larger Arabic tradition.

The producers of the 2009 work *Beirut 39: New Writing from the Arab World*, an anthology of young Arab writers, recognised this feature of contemporary poetry. The result of a 2009 collaboration between the Hay Festival and Beirut World Capital of the Book, it brought together a group of poets and fiction writers under the age of forty and was edited by Samuel Shimon, prefaced by Hanan al-Shaykh and introduced by Abdo Wazen. As al-Shaykh writes, 'These thirty-nine Arab writers have flung open the doors on Arabic culture'.[32] The doors of poetry or its limits are flung wide open in the work of this group as well. All the tensions we could have pointed out in the works of the poets before them are relaxed. This is the poetry of individual isolated present moments, self-absorbed, closed-off and unconcerned with intervening or renovating or reconciling with anything prior to it. Moreover, they are less concerned with rejecting than are the Egyptian poets of the nineties whose stance has been described deliberately anti-Arabic.[33] With the poets of the twenty-first century, even the investment in an 'anti'-stance is abandoned. Their linguistic formations and experiences are not grounded in any one tradition or language, and thus their notion of the poetic passes through language/languages but ultimately materialises outside the exercise of any one language. The motivation of the poem is the delivery of a poetic 'idea' or 'situation' which can migrate among languages.

In a long poem titled 'The Geology of the I' excerpted in the *Beirut 39* anthology, Joumana Haddad displays the poetic of this new era. Opening with an epigraph from Bob Dylan (A Poem is a Naked Person), this poem centres on the 'I' of the poet, which Haddad will continue to excavate. Reminding us of the motivation of Saʿadeh's 'poetic texts', this piece spills out. Expression, finding voice (*taʿbīr*) and getting across (*ʿubūr*) are ultimately its ends.

أنا اليومُ السادسُ من شهر كانون الأول من سنة ألفٍ وتسعمئةٍ وسبعين
أنا الساعةُ الأولى بُعيدَ الظهر
صرخاتُ أمّي تلدني
وصرخاتُها تلدها
رحمُها تقذفني لأخرج منّي
وعَرَقُها يحقّق احتمالي
أنا صفعةُ الطبيب التي أحيتْني
(كلّ صفعةٍ لاحقة حاولتْ إحيائي قد أرْدتني)
أنا عيونُ العائلة عليَّ
أنا حدقاتُ الأب والجدّ والعمّة والخالة.[34]

I am the sixth day of December of the year 1970;
I am the hour just after noon.
I am my mother's screams giving birth to me.
and her screams giving birth to her.
Her womb releasing me to emerge from myself,
her sweat achieving my potentiality.
I am the doctor's slap which revived me.
(Each subsequent slap trying to revive me quite destroyed me.)
I am the eyes of the family upon me,
The gazes of father, grandfather, of aunts.[35]

The self-absorbed voice continues to weave layer upon layer around the 'I' which remains throughout the piece an individual closed ego. The poem meanders, stubbornly insisting on the same sentence structure (I am the . . .). The tension of form, the concern with image-making, the attention to music are all sacrificed in this baring of the self. The poem is Haddad's naked I, expressing itself at length without imposed or self-imposed limits.

Another poet of this generation who similarly builds his texts around the observation of the self and its immediate surrounding is Nazem El-Sayed. However, where Haddad's persona expands and dominates the text, El-Sayed's intensively turns to minute details, relentlessly scrutinising and breaking them down into compact flash-like images, albeit in the same self-indulgent posture as Haddad's. The tone and mood of El-Sayed's work is whimsical, self-deprecating, cynical and ultimately tragic in its capturing of experiences such as coming of age in times of war, family dynamics, dispossession and displacement. In a manner akin to Saʿadeh's, El-Sayed is a fan of capturing dissipating images as we see in this short piece:

كل شيء على حاله

حين عدت
وجدت كل شيء على حاله
بما فيه
الظل الواهن الذي رسمته في الهواء تلويحتي الأخيرة.[36]

Everything as it was

When I returned
I found everything as it was
Including
The frail shadow traced in the air
By my last wave farewell.

In his introduction to the *Beirut 39* anthology, Abdo Wazen celebrates the 'disobedience' of this generation of Arab writers and their 'rebellion against traditional literary culture'. He then touches upon the most central manifestation of their rebellion: their disdain for using proper Arabic language.

> These writers believe that the new era, the information age, the computer and internet age does not leave them with enough time to decipher the mysteries of grammar and rhetoric. They seek the language of life. These writers are not afraid to make grammatical errors. Some purposefully don't finish their sentences, others are fond of slang and street talk and dialect.[37]

With little or no patience for grammar and rhetoric, these young writers, Wazen argues, 'transcend geography and local identity [. . .] aligning themselves with global literary currents and movements'.[38] And a necessary step towards joining the global current, it seems, is taking the Arabic language and 'wringing its neck'.[39] Foreign languages and their poetic traditions have been one of the active stimuli of the Arab modernist movement from its first budding in the 1940s. And foreign poetic sensibilities continued to be an operating element to varying degrees in all the subsequent phases of the movement until today. We often speak of echoes of the international modernist movements, especially the English and French, in the works of the Arab modernist. Even poets who did not master languages other than Arabic were not immune to the infiltrating effect of translated poetry and theory. However, the engagement with non-Arabic poetry was never as thorough and as simultaneous with the Arabic creative act as it is in the works of this group.

Linguistic purity, Margorie Perloff states, 'can hardly be the norm, given the polyglot speech of our tribe of citizens'.[40] By 'tribe', Perloff is not only referring to Anglophone writers but to a global phenomenon that applies to poets of all linguistic traditions in our 'world of relentless global communication',[41] which continues to shrink due to waves of migration, displacement and refugeedom. In fact, she opens her article with the example of poet and fiction writer Yoko Tawada, a native speaker of Japanese who writes in both Japanese and German; Tawada writes 'exophonically', as Perloff argues, in a language other than her mother tongue.[42] While the poets I examine here do not write in English, their creative processes are informed by tensions similar to the one Perloff describes, as they write between English, as a major Western language, and their Arabic which is perceived as minor or peripheral in comparison. And thus I borrow the term 'exophonic' from the works of scholars such as Perloff, Chantal Wright and Mohamed A. H. Ahmed to describe this poetry.[43] However, I use the term metaphorically, in order to describe an attitude and a predisposition towards the Arabic language by poets who still write in Arabic, while at the same time deliberately or inadvertently defamiliarising it and distancing themselves from its literary and poetic memory. They are thus more conscious and more detached from Arabic and its thinking processes than their predecessors were and write in it from the perspective of outsiders. For these poets, the launching point is not Arabic but the point of traffic between languages. Even if some of them only speak and write in their mother tongue, it remains a language infiltrated by other languages at its most basic phases of acquisition. Even though all the poems I am considering here are written in Arabic, the foreign is now embedded in the Arabic,[44] and they are necessarily multilingual.

It has thus become almost impossible to imagine any one language alone in soliloquy. Granted, scholars of Arabic poetry have always been aware of the commerce with other languages, for instance, in the polyglot culture of the Abbasid age. Nevertheless, an ideal of linguistic purity, even if not realistic, still persisted. Even when we study the rise of the Arabic modernist movement in the 1940s, we acknowledge the western non-Arabic influences and contributions, but still imagine Arab poets moving towards other languages and poetries from a grounding in Arabic, as is the case in the works of Nazik al-Malaʾika and Badr Shakir al-Sayyab and even Adonis. We still imagine a space beyond influence, translation and the exchange with other languages, a space where Arabic alone thinks the poem.

Reading twenty-first century poets writing in Arabic, the ideal of purity has become more and more difficult to imagine. It is worth nothing here that important work has been done on the phenomenon of exophonic writing in a global context. Significant work also exists on the exophonic writings by writers of Arab heritage.[45] The study of such writings in English or French is not my purpose here and falls beyond the scope of this monograph. My purpose is to examine the transformation of a new poetic practice among contemporary poets writing in Arabic; a practice informed and shaped by global literary currents and attitudes which displays a relative divestment from the Arabic literary tradition, especially when compared to the more immediate modernist predecessors' engagement or contention with that tradition.

If the Maghutian trend reflected in the works of the Egyptian poets of the 1990s established a detachment from an Arabic model of poetry, this one insists on a linguistic detachment from the processes of the Arabic language. It is a trend which launches itself from an exophonic stance, even when the text is written in Arabic. Unlike proper exophonic writers, who write in languages other than their native tongue, these poets have not yet abandoned Arabic. They write at its interface with other languages, at its points of infiltrations by other languages. And where in exophonic studies we examine the ways in which the new adopted language is moulded and defamiliarised through stylistic innovations,[46] how it echoes the native tongue, and how the native or the first tongue is manipulated and contorted to reveal echoes and imperatives of other languages and poetic traditions,[47] here Arabic itself is amnesiac, deliberately detached from its own poetic memory.

Samer Abu Hawwash and the Pending Poem

Samer Abu Hawwash is a poet of this generation whose engagement with American poetry and literature of the twentieth century has been a pivotal stimulus of his own writing. He is a Palestinian born in Lebanon in 1972. He graduated from the Lebanese University with a degree in journalism in 1996 and has worked for a number of cultural newspapers and platforms in Lebanon and the Arab region. He currently resides in the United Arab Emirates where he is editor-in-chief of *Mawqiʿ 24*, 'Website 24', an online news outlet. He is a prolific writer and translator with two novels and nine poetry collections of his own so far. In 2008, he came out with a fifteen-volume series of translated American poetry published by Kalīma, a translation initiative funded by the Abu Dhabi Authority of Culture and Heritage, and Dar al-Jamal, a publishing house based in Beirut and Berlin. The series includes the works of writers such as William Faulkner, Sylvia Plath, Billy Collins, Charles Simic, Jack Kerouac, Ted Kooser, Charles Bokawski, Ann Saxton and others.[48]

We can easily detect in Abu Hawwash's work nods towards Elizabeth

Bishop's intensive imagery, William Carlos Williams' transcendentalising of the mundane, Billy Collins' wit and humour and even Bob Dylan's risk-taking eclectic eye. Still, Abu Hawwash's translation of these influences into his own writing is primarily concerned with ideas. His language is not only neutral but reads as if it were pending translation. He sometimes distorts constructions as if writing his Arabic sentence with an English ear. He consistently prefers nominal sentences, employing interjections and adverbs in defamiliarising ways. In his long text titled *Selfie akhīra ma' 'ālam yuḥtaḍar* (A Last Selfie with a Dying World, 2015), Abu Hawwash arranges poetic scenes relying on the simple simile, the Maghutian favourite, on repetition and juxtaposition, and on the Sa'adian shift or tilt of an idea which delivers the poetic punchline, all while using an Arabic infiltrated by the tone and the logic of other languages, primarily English.

يمكنك دائما أن تصرخ
وأن تصرخ
وتصرخ
وتصرخ
كمئة ألف امرأة
في مخاض.

ويمكنك أن تصمت
وتصمت
وتصمت
كمئة ألف رجاء
ضلت طريقها
في دهليز الأدعية.

أو يمكنك الاكتفاء بصورة سيلفي أخيرة
مع عالم يحتضر،
مع جميع الموتى الشاحبين
يحتشدون خلفك
كنجوم الأوسكار.[49]

You can always scream
and scream
and scream

and scream
like a hundred thousand women
in labour.

And you can be silent
and silent
and silent
like a hundred thousand hopes
that lost their way
in the tunnels of prayer.

Or you may be content taking
a last selfie
with a dying world,
with all the pale dead
crowding behind you
like stars at the Oscars.

Language is always changing, and it is the poets' job to make the best of these changes – even its deteriorations.[50] Most of the poets of this generation grew up speaking an Arabic dialect permeated by English or French slang and the language of TV, the internet, the languages of the global marketplace. In school they learn formal 'proper' languages, with Arabic most often relegated to a less urgent second language compared to English and French. Thus, when they come to write as poets, their language has no one grounding, no one root; it is an assemblage or orchestration of 'rhizomatic fabrications, alternations of cybernetic communications and languages'.[51] Their language is the Arabic of the information age, of texting and chatting, of emails, of bilingual and multilingual speakers; the Arabic shaped by the experience of the twenty-first century's polyglot tribe.[52]

Poetry in the work of these twenty-first century Arab poets is therefore a product of arranging the disparate elements of the text, of setting up or directing in a manner that produces the effect. Conceptual is perhaps an apt word to describe this poetics, if conceptual poetry is understood as oppositional to established aesthetics, author-centred and constructed out of the materiality of the words and signs. It is writing motivated by an abstract appreciation of poetic quality unmoored from form or language.

Abu Hawwash's most recent collection *Laysa hākadha tuṣnaʿ al-pizza* (This is Not the Way Pizza is Made) is representative not of poetry as much as what can *become* poetry. The found phrases, words, quotations, conversations, passing thoughts become poetry by direction and orchestration. He arranges google search results, recurrent conversations about weather,[53] and imitations of other writers and poets[54] into poems. In a short piece titled 'The Sun is Strong this Morning', we see the poetic created by way of arranging and setting up:

فجأة
أو بغير فجأة
العشب يطلق شظاياه نحو السماء؛
العصافير القليلة المتبقية
تهوي أرضا،
بأجنحة مشتعلة
كطائرات حربية
تعرّضت للقصف.[55]

All of a sudden
Or without sudden
The grass shoots its shrapnel towards the sky
The few remaining birds
Fall to the ground
With burning wings
Like war planes
shot down.

The piece opens with a meditation on the interjection *faj'atan* (all of a sudden) which literally translates as 'with surprise or surprisingly'. The poet goes on to pick apart the common phrase when he retracts it with 'or not suddenly', or literally 'without sudden or surprise'. This defamiliarising of the stale and hardened expression is a mining for the poetic effect in the seemingly unpoetic ordinary. The piece then traces a movement, a rising, then a falling. The simile that ends the poem evokes a clear unmistakable cinematic image any reader can visualise, that of a plane diving nose down with burning wings. This poem is an idea; an idea that *becomes* poetic in its arrangement or its unfolding on the page. This underscores the importance of lineation, layout on the page and the role of visuality in making the claim of poetry here. A poem such as the one above appears to be a poem on the page but does not necessarily have the effect when heard or read out loud.

In another piece from the same collection, Abu Hawwash is further fixated on the materiality of easily recognisable words and signs. His fixation, however, can be easily disembodied from the language in which he is writing. The piece is a reflection on loneliness launched from the connections between the words lonely, alone and only.

الوحيدون

على مقاعد الحدائق
أو مراحيض البيوت
يجلس الوحيدون
وحيدين تماماً
لا أحد يعرفهم
ولا يعرفون بعضهم
ولا أحد يعرف
أنهم وحيدون
لأنهم وحدهم
الوحيدون
دائماً
من كل شيء.[56]

The lonely

on benches in parks
or toilet seats in houses
the lonely sit
entirely alone.
No one knows them
and they don't know each other
and nobody knows

that they are alone
because they alone
are the lonely ones
always
in all things.

In the following piece titled 'After Bob Dylan', Abu Hawwash is not only suggesting to us that imitation, parody and paying homage can pass as poetry in their own right, but also that the reading of others' work carries in itself poetic potential. This here is his reading of or listening to Bob Dylan, framed as a poem:

بعد بوب ديلان

رأيت رجلا يجر منزلا قال إنه يريد أن يضعه على حافة البحر، وامرأة جميلة تعرج جارة وراءها شعباً من الأطفال العرج، ومستويات مختلفة من الصمت، تجرها الخيول. شاهدت أكياس نايلون سوداء تطير في الصحراء، وشقراء بشعر طويل، ترفع نهدها إلى الله، وتبكي. شاهدت الصديق الذي مات في نومه يبتسم خلف المطر. شاهدت المطر أيضاً. شاهدت قطارات تقتحم غرف نوم، ومرايا براقة تحطمها النظرات. نظرات تتحطم وحدها. وكان صبي بالشورت يقفز، ليلمس فراشة يحسبها غيمة. وكان عجائز سود يتدرّبون على «الراب» بالكزّ المستمر على أسنانهم. وكان فلاسفة يحاولون عبثاً تفسير جوز الهند. شاهدت طيناً ينصب خيمة، ووحلاً يحفر سراديب سرية. شاهدت الستينيات تتقدم نحوي مادة ذراعيها، وعلى كتفيها ينعب غرابان أسودان. شاهدت السعادة عارية تقفز الحبل. شاهدت جدتي تسبح في كأس. شاهدت أبي ينمو على جدار. شاهدت التسعينيات طائرة ورقية تذوب في الضباب.[57]

After Bob Dylan

I saw a man pulling a house. He said he wanted to place it at the edge of the sea. I saw a beautiful woman, limping, dragging behind her a population of limping children and different levels of silence, all drawn by horses. I saw black plastic bags flying in the desert and a blond with long hair, raising her breast to God and weeping. I saw a friend who died in his sleep, smiling beyond the rain. I saw the rain too. I saw trains crash into bedrooms and shiny mirrors shattered by glances, and glances shattering by themselves. A boy in shorts was jumping up to touch a butterfly he thought was a cloud. Old black men were rehearsing their 'rap', constantly grinding their teeth. Philosophers were trying, in vain, to explain coconuts. I saw clay erect a tent, and mud dig a secret dun-

> geon. I saw the Sixties run towards me with open arms, on her shoulders two black crows cawing. I saw Happiness naked, jumping rope. I saw my grandmother swimming in a glass. I saw my father grow on a wall. I saw the Nineties, a kite melting in the fog.

One does not feel anxious about translating this poem from Arabic. The setup that makes it a poem carries over. Similarly, the following piece titled '*Tamyīz kalimāt al-baḥth*' (Refining Search Words), is found or further revealed in translation:

> ...وكنت أفكر في قصيدة عن "الأمل". وكتبت في "غوغل": "قصيدة عن الأمل". و"تم
> تمييز كلمات البحث": قصيدة+عن+ الأمل= ١٧٢٠٠٠ نتيجة:
> "قصيدة عن تماسيح اليوم كككك"، "قصيدة عن العراق منتديات ماجدة"، "فضاءات الألم
> والغربة"، "قصيدة عن تعدّد الزوجات"، "قصيدة بين اليأس والأمل"، "رد على قصيدة بين
> اليأس والأمل"، "قصيدة الأسبوع"، وأشياء أخرى عن أشجار أفريقية إكزوتية، وصبي شنق
> نفسه في الصين مقلّداً إعدام صدّام، وصلوات في إندونيسيا بحثاً عن طائرة مفقودة...و"هذه
> ليست إلا غرفة"، رحت أقول في نفسي،
> هذه ليست إلا غرفة، أيها الأحمق.[58]

> . . . and I was thinking of a poem about 'hope'. I googled: 'A poem about hope', 'the search words were refined: poem+about+hope = 172000 results:
> 'A poem about alligators today kkkk', 'a poem about Iraq in Majida forums', 'spaces of pain and alienation', 'a poem about polygamy', 'a poem between despair and hope', 'a response to a poem between and despair and hope', 'poem of the week', and other things about exotic African trees and a boy who hung himself in China in imitation of Saddam's execution, and prayers in Indonesian searching for a missing plane . . . and 'this is only a room', I kept telling myself,
> Only a room, you fool.

Written to be read in a different language or to be received outside language, translating a piece like the above becomes the *sincerest* way of reading it. Besides, the poem in Arabic sometimes possesses a shakiness, a flimsiness that clears up or settles when the piece is translated, as if translation completes the writing process. These texts are in ways 'formed', 'found' or 'unlost' in translation.[59] The assumptions we usually make about the original text and the target text do not hold with regards to the work of this generation of poets. For translation as creative process is present in the make-up of the original, from its earliest stages of inception.

Golan Haji and the Migrant Poem

Golan Haji (b. 1977) is another poet/translator from this generation. He is a Kurdish-Syrian poet, translator and physician, currently based in Paris. He is the author of five books of poetry. His first collection *Nādā fī al-dhulumāt* (He Called in the Dark) was published in 2004. His subsequent works include *Thammata man yarāka waḥshan* (Someone Sees You as a Monster, 2008), *al-Kharīf hunāk sāḥir wa kabīr* (Autumn Here is Magical and Vast, 2013) and *Mīzān al-adhā* (The Balance of Hurt, 2016), in addition to an edited a volume of women's accounts of the Syrian revolution titled *Ilā an qāmat al-ḥarb* (Until the War Erupted, 2016). His translations include: Mark Strand's *A Dark Harbour*, Robert Louis Stevenson's *The Case of Dr Jekyll and Mr Hyde* and three works by Alberto Manguel, the Argentinian-Canadian novelist. With translator Stephen Watts, Haji has co-translated a selection of his own poetry in a volume titled *A Tree Whose Name I Don't Know* (2017).

With the feeling of one writing at the frontier of Arabic poetry and on the edge of the Arabic language at its interface with other languages, Golan Haji declares: 'I feel an end is coming soon'.[60] Both as a Syrian in the aftermath of the Syrian crisis which began in 2011 and before that as a Kurd with the perpetual sense of refugeedom and uprooted-ness, Haji finds in his practice of writing an unending migratory experience, a continuous embarking upon something new. The prose poem, a form on the edge of poetry and held together by the tension of opposites, becomes a manifestation of such an experience and its most apt artistic correlative. Haji states in an interview:

> I am very interested in the prose poem as a form. I think it's very tempting and rewarding. I have been concerned with words, first and foremost. I am responding to another 'new' world I live in, i.e. France, and poetry continues beyond all articulated intentions. The poems I write start, like me, to move away from Syria. I feel an end is soon to come. I live this

ambiguous sense of an ending in what I write. Anyhow, when the poem works and lives, it speaks better for itself.[61]

The poem, for Haji, is written in the moment of 'moving away' from homeland to exile, from known to unknown, from mother to foreign tongue. Making sense of or accounting for this migration can only manifest itself not in poetry as we have known it, but poetry as it becomes or begins to take form in a new world. Haji adds:

> I was very much affected by migration [. . .] In this violent disintegration, I cannot forget the somehow sinister feeling of being frequently uprooted from where I used to live. I have always lived struggling with words. I spent part of my childhood trying to change my Kurdish accent in Arab-speaking institutions. Later, with more consequent forced displacements in various countries, I gave up trying to sound like the dominating other. I preserved my accents & became a foreigner in every language I speak, even in Kurdish, except in the silence of writing.[62]

Thus, moving away from one's home and becoming new or other are at the core of Haji's and his generation's poetically exophonic stance. Their language and their poetic sensibility are products of transformative and transforming literary and linguistic spaces.

Ultimately, exophony, in the context of Haji's experience, is the translation of the self into new spaces, sounds and configurations of thought. Such an experience does not afford one to think *about* the new, for it dictates that one thinks *with* the new. Thus, a poet finds him- or herself outside or in the across between what language is and what it is turning into, what poetry is and what it is becoming. Haji's thoughts about his relationship to the Arabic poetic tradition, both the recent and the distant one, are most telling of this space of 'outsider-ness' which his generation inhabits. Speaking of al-Maghut, Adonis and Nizar Qabbani, Haji states:

> I respect all of the aforementioned names, but rarely read or reread them. They have become canonical (in the sense that we move from them onwards and not toward them). I've almost lost my curiosity about most of them. I might prefer reading the Moroccan poet Abdallah Zrika, the Syrian Nazih abu Afache, the Iraqi Salah Faik or the Egyptian Imad

> Abu Saleh, who live in their own rich lights and shadows. However, I keep reading classical poets such as al-Maʿarri who lived and died in northwest of Syria, and whose work 'The Epistle of Forgiveness' might have influenced Dante's 'Divine Comedy'. Al-Maʿarri and al-Mutanabbi, these two contradictory classical poets, both influenced poets like Khayyam and Rumi.[63]

Again, the urge to 'move away' appears in his attitude towards his recent modernist predecessors. His poetic project has a different orientation. While launching itself from a moment in which he stands as heir to al-Maghut, Adonis and Nizar Qabbani, he does not contend with that heritage but packs it up and moves it into a space where both he and it will be transformed into something different. Even his turn to the Abbasid poets al-Maʿarri and al-Mutanabbi is different from that which Adonis makes. He does not enact an inward engagement with the Arabic tradition as much as he seeks connections leading out of it. Signalling the thread from al-Mutanabbi and al-Maʿarri to Khayyam and Rumi, Haji here writes the non-Arabic into the Arabic poetic tradition, which he re-imagines. However, Haji does this in a manner that deliberately distinguishes itself from Salim Barakat's confrontational and stubbornly difficult poetic language.

Upon the publication of Barakat's 2019 collection *Tanbīh al-Ḥayawān ilā ansābihi* (Alerting the Animal to its Lineages), Golan Haji wrote a piece announcing the end of his 'friendship' with Barakat's work and with what he sees as a stubborn, heavy, dead-end project. Haji states: 'Barakat's writing seems to me like the product of habit that haunts him relentlessly, the way a demon haunts one possessed. He will not quit this habit until his heart stops beating. It is his crisis, his curse and his glory'.[64] Without denying his earlier fascination with Barakat, Haji admits that in recent years has stopped reading Barakat's prolific publications in poetry and in prose. 'Perhaps', he comments, 'because his excessive craft, which was initially astounding, has now lost its wonder [. . .] How similar his poems seem to me now to those of his imitators, as if he and they are copying from the same original'.[65] Haji tell us that he will cherish Barakat's earlier works but cannot continue reading him. By that, he announces a break not only from a major early influence on him, but also from the interrogation of one language, Arabic, towards a more open and less confrontational attitude towards language in general.

The long view that Haji's posture allows us is that of poetry beyond language, poetry as a perpetuation of a shared imagination and heritage. And, thus, translation is a crucial access point. From the vantage point of the exophonic poet, translation is what allows the participation in a bank or store of imagination shared by all languages:

> I have always felt this inclination to what's being written in other languages, not necessarily by the well-known names. Translation is crucial for the shared imagination, for mutual understanding among human beings. What comes from the imagination belongs to everybody.[66]

'Every writing is a translation of some sort', Haji declares; a statement many writers have made, especially regarding poetry. Here, however, with Haji and his generation's stance vis-à-vis Arabic, it gains more urgency and pointedness. When asked about his choice or decision to write in Arabic and not Kurdish or any other language, Haji responded:

> A systematic education in Kurdish, as you well know, is not available . . . Kurdish is a language I speak, but I have minimal command of it in reading and writing. It remains, however, part of me, my first memory . . . I write in Arabic, a language in which I only have a stranger's grounding, and perhaps the stranger to a language is able to enjoy it more than its native speakers. I did not choose Arabic; it was in fact my only option. I fell in love with it . . . Often I feel as if I am moving words from one language to another in my head. Every writing is a translation of some sort.[67]

A stranger in all the languages he speaks, including Kurdish, Haji learned to welcome this stranger status into his writing in Arabic. It is an Arabic accented by all the languages it replaces or erases or pretends to be. It becomes a language of 'never-ending approximation', as Haji puts it:

> I feel as if I write in never-ending approximation, as if I had an accent in all the languages I speak. The only place where these differences are

> embraced, without fears or too much hesitation, is the field of writing where I use more than a language through Arabic.[68]

In the blurb of the back of a volume of Haji's poems *A Tree Whose Name I Don't Know*, co-translated with Stephen Watts, the American poet Marilyn Hacker writes: 'Haji, polyglot and humanist, is a luminous arrival for world poetry'.[69] The 'arrival' which Hacker notes is the result of layer upon layer of translation, now presented in this volume after yet another round of translation in which Haji approximates himself yet again. One cannot approach this volume as one does other works of translated poetry. In this volume the poet who already thinks and writes in translation is imagining his poems in English. The Arabic is not an original; it is only a previous translation of poems originally 'imagined' multilingually.

In their English iterations, the poems are Haji's as much as in the Arabic. For this reason, I did not attempt my own translations of Haji's Arabic poems. A literal translation or one that strives to be closer to the Arabic is beside the point here. The point here is to read Haji's English imagination when available, to listen to these poems in his English accent. And this is what we find in his collaboration with Watts. In the following piece titled 'Blood on the Stairs', Haji imagines writing like bleeding, free of languages and their failings:

دم على الدرج

ما هذه التكشيرة
حين تتوقف القهقهة فجأة؟
نهر الكلمات ضحل؛
كان الموتى يسبحون فيه قبلك.
مدّ شفتك السفلى.
ضع النصل.
دع الكلام ينزف.[70]

Blood on the Stairs

What's this grimace when
the crackling stops all of a sudden?
The river of words is shallow,

the dead were swimming in it before you.
Stretch your lower lip.
Insert the blade.
Let speech bleed.[71]

The agony of making or forming speech materialises in the closing image of the blade planted in the lip. The short piece juxtaposes the shallow 'river of words' with a river of blood that flows at the end. Instead of fishing for overused and exhausted words inherited from the dead, Haji is eager for a language that is unmediated and unburdened. Reminding us of his longing to write poems that tap into the common imagination beyond the barriers of languages and their idiosyncrasies, this poem aims at capturing that which is felt and experienced, but which eludes language. It is this feeling or state of mind which Haji wonders about in the opening of the poem when emotion changes from laughter to grimace. Aiming to capture something in between recognisable emotions, Haji's poem expresses a polyglot's striving to write beyond language.

Whereas the previous piece moves outward with the flowing of blood or the opening up beyond words, the second piece moves inward. The attempt to speak here is a retraction, a shutting in.

القفل

أنساني الضجر مخاوفي
فألفت هذا المنزل:
نادما أغلق فمي؛
وحيدا أفتح قلبي.
أنا سعادتي وخرابي.
أفتح الكتاب وأغلقه وأفتحه،
فاتحا في انتصار صغير
باب قبر
أغلقه على نفسي
كطفل يتخفّى في خزانة.[72]

The Lock

Tedium made me forget my fears
so I got used to this house:

remorsefully, I shut my mouth
alone, I open my heart.
I am my own happiness and my dereliction.
I open the book and close it and open it again,
freeing in a small victory
the door of a grave
I pull it tight on my self
like a child hiding away in a closet.[73]

Whether flowing outward or retracting inward, in the two poems above, Haji expresses the desire to escape language, either by breaking out of all the different languages he juggles, or by withdrawing from them. Surviving the multilingual journey or making it across (*ʿubūr*) is the polyglot poet's driving force. Vying with his many languages, what keeps him afloat is the belief in an imagination all languages share; a belief in the ability of different languages to communicate with each other in a space beyond their distinct formulations; a space without language. And poetry lies there in that shared imagined space where different languages, in their silence, listen to and comprehend each other. Thus, the poetic and the translated become one and the same here. Both, the poetic and the translated, are language stretched to their very limits; they are approximations of that 'great light'[74] that begins once language (or languages) exhaust itself.

Haji portrays himself as one seeking that silence in his relationship with all the language he inhabits or that inhabit him.[75] For, ultimately, silence is the multilingual's relief and refuge. Writing in the silence of language or out of its bounds is a driving urge we see in Saʿadeh's work. Of course, it is complicated and compounded in the works of Haji who is much more implicated in the languages with which he contends.

Haji is haunted by overarching and abstract concerns: death, place, presence, absence, pain and their immanent and pervading manifestations. His most pressing concern, however, is positionality and the possibility of language in its most abstracted form. Striving to escape the cacophony of languages towards its silence, Haji does not mind sharing the journey with others. His collaborations further reveal and intensify his exophonic stance. His work as co-translator and co-author are reflections of his relationship with his writing self as other.

'Moving Out' of Arabic

As a co-translator of his own work, one would imagine Haji looking over Stephen Watts's shoulder, participating hesitantly, since Watts is after all the owner of English and Haji only its guest. Assuming the double role of the author and translator mirrors the initial translation, which is at the core of Haji's creative process when he translates his Arabic text from the multilingual space of his imagination. Haji's writing is further revealed as translation in his collaboration with the Arab-American poet and translator Fady Joudah. In a sequence of poems included in the collection authored by Joudah, *Footnotes in the Order of Disappearance* (2018), Haji and Joudah write poems together. The sequence of poems is titled 'Sagittal Views'. Perhaps inspired by both poets' background in medicine, the evocation of a divided view of the body is very apt. These poems are written on a divided plane, two voices, two languages, two imaginations converging and diverging. They co-think or co-imagine in Arabic, but the poems are ultimately formulated in English by Joudah alone. In a note, Joudah states:

> All the poems are based on our correspondence in Arabic, via email, phone, or in person. While the poems' forms and diction in English are mine, their content is mostly shared with varying degrees of 'ownership'.[76]

Haji co-authors the 'content' of these poems. Assuming that it is possible to separate content from 'forms and diction' in poetry, the claim made here is that the two collaborated on the creation of poetic content in one language or more, in the languages of their thoughts, before Joudah 'translates' that content into his English forms and diction. Haji is thus owner or co-owner of that dimension of the texts which is poetry outside of language, or perhaps poetry in the silence of language.

In this experiment, Haji composes Arabic poetry 'by other means', coming as close as possible to actually writing in the silence of language. He participates in the imagining but relinquishes capturing the imagined in one language to someone else. In his mind the poems are thought in Arabic, his Arabic which is already translated and infiltrated by other tongues. And, to us as readers, aware of the process by which these poems came about, the English these poems are written in necessarily has an Arabic accent, or perhaps is an English perpetually in the presence of a silent Arabic. The first poem in the sequence revolves around the idea of silence beyond language or as the title states: 'After No Language'.

> A silent feeling of an invisible punishment or one seen through cataracts; a sentence that isn't meted out or doesn't end; some cuts run deeper than speech: writing may exit the cage but the cage remains and grows, or am I speaking of the life of footnote; I always hold back from writing in the margins of the clearest sentences: those that lost their status as feeling when they were excised by skillful hands wielding sharp instruments, a manufacture of refraction . . . [77]

Language here is a cage, an invisible punishment, a refraction. Clarity is a violent loss of feeling. It is manufactured skilfully with sharp instruments. The poem, in other words, celebrates the poetic before it enters the cage of language. It imagines poetry before the losses it suffers in writing, in translation.

The last poem in the sequence is titled 'In a Cemetery Under a Solitary Walnut Tree That Crows'. It is reimagined, reread and rewritten by Joudah and Haji. The poem exists in earlier iterations, or rather on earlier planes of imagination in Haji's Arabic in his collection *Mīzān al-adhā* (2016):

بئر في مقبرة بعيدة

تحت شجرة جوز زرعها غراب
بئر حفرها مجنون بإبرة
ففاضت حبراً.

كانت الكلمة.
تتأرجح باتجاه الورقة
مثل فانوس يهبط بئراً مطلية بكلس
حبله في يد طفل.[78]

It also exists in this English version he co-authored with Stephen Watts:

A Well in a Distant Cemetery

Under a walnut tree planted by a raven
there's a well that a madman dug with a needle
so that ink gushed forth.

The word was.
Swaying inward towards the page
like a lantern descending a white-washed well
Its rope in the hand of a child.[79]

This English version remains closely guided by the Arabic to the extent of keeping what might seem initially as a typological error, the full stop after 'The word was'. Perhaps, Haji was aiming to intentionally disrupt the grammar in this sentence and at the same evoke the biblical statement. In any case, the effect is confusing in Arabic, and he insists on it in the co-translation with Watts. The version he re-imagines with Joudah, however, strays. The poem is expanded, literally stretched out so that larger fissures appear in its body, cracks that reveal more than its purported original had initially communicated.

In a Cemetery Under a Solitary Walnut Tree That Crows

had planted and whose seeds are hollow
I found a needle and with it

I dug a well
dug and dug until I struck ink

The needle wove fabric for bodies it had injected with song
I painted the well's walls with quicklime and couldn't climb out

There was sun there was moonlight that came into my sleep
I stored leaves and bark but rain washed away my words

A lantern came down on a rope that a girl held
I sent up the part of me that was light[80]

The two stanzas of the earlier versions are interrogated in this last version; they are revealed, opened up and mined. The act of co-authoring this piece thus becomes a generative process. If the germ of this poem is taken from Haji's Arabic text, it is formally, thematically and now musically cultivated by Haji and Joudah together. This final iteration of Haji's imagination, now shared with another writer's voice and formulated in another language's forms of thought, still reveals a dimension latent in the Arabic poem from which the journey was launched.

This sequence of poems tells much about the role of gaps, silences and loss in the creative process. The poems, of course, warrant a deeper reading. However, what stands out about them for my purposes here is the attitude they exhibit towards language, especially Haji's part. His shared agency in imagining the poetic and his subsequent silence in the final manifestation of the poems is representative of his own writing experience between several languages, with several languages, always beckoned by the lure of silence.

The partnership with Fady Joudah opens up the purview of Arabic poetry beyond the exercise of the language.[81] Joudah is involved in the Arabic poetic endeavour as much as are some of the poet of his generation who write in Arabic. 'Every writing is a translation of some sort', Haji declares; a statement many writers have made, especially regarding poetry. Here, however, in Haji and his generation's stance vis-à-vis Arabic, it gains more urgency and pointedness. The Arabic of their poems is not an original anymore; it is only a previous translation of poems originally 'imagined' multilingually. The poets of this generation are the Arabic language's readers, interlocuters, hunters, salvagers. They are its captives, its survivors, its deserters and its translators. But this generation's writings in Arabic may also at times reflect a loss of footing, a linguistic apathy and maybe sometimes . . . incompetence.

Thus, the tension of the early prose poem is relaxed, if not completely alleviated here. These poets are not pressed to make a case for their texts as poems. Their aspirations towards poetry are launched from an understanding of poetry very different from that of the first generation. Circling back to the beginnings of the prose poem project in Arabic, if Unsi al-Hajj had set out to write 'a poem in Arabic, not an Arabic poem',[82] poets of this generation are setting out to imagine their different *Arabics* in other languages. No matter how well-versed or well-read they are in the Arabic tradition, they write at a distance from it, not invested to implant themselves in it or drag it into their present moment. They might know the Arabic poetic tradition. They think about it or of it, but they do not think *with* it.

Notes

1. The collection was later published in 1981. See Saʿadeh, *Laysa lil-masāʾ ikhwa.*
2. 'Interview with Wadiʿ Saʿadeh', *Akhbār al-Adab*, 28 April 2018. https://adab.akhbarelyom.com/newdetails.aspx?id=446509 (last accessed 4 June 2018).
3. Clarissa Burt, 'Memory and Loss: The Exilic Nihilism of Wadīʿ Saʿādah, Australia's Lebansese Émigré Poet', *Journal of Arabic Literature* 4.1-2 (2010), p. 182.
4. Clarissa Burt, 'Connecting Two Shores with Sound: Saʿādeh's World of Loss', *Edebiyat: Journal of Middle East Literatures* 14.1/2 (2003), p. 133.
5. Wadiʿ Saʿadeh, *al-Aʿmāl al-shiʿriyya* (Beirut: Dar al-Nahda al-ʿArabiyya, 2008), p. 186.
6. 'Interview with Wadiʿ Saʿadeh'.
7. Ibid.
8. Saʿadeh's website which offers open access to all his works. He is also active on Facebook where he has a large following of fans, poets and critics.
9. Saʿadeh, *Laysa lil-masāʾ ikhwa*, p. 5.
10. Al-Maʿarrī, *al-Luzūmiyyāt* (Beirut: Dār al-kutub al-ʿilmiyya, 2001), vol. 2, p. 151.
11. Saʿadeh, *Al-Aʿmāl al-shiʿriyya*, p. 172.
12. Ibid. pp. 143–44.
13. Saʿadeh, *Laysa lil-masāʾ ikhwa,* p. 12.
14. Ibid. p. 13.
15. Saʿadeh, *Laysa lil-masāʾ ikhwa*, p. 40.
16. Saʿadeh, *al-Aʿmāl al-shiʿriyya*, pp. 300–01.
17. Also see Burt's translation in 'Memory and Loss', pp. 189–90.
18. Saʿadeh, *Laysa lil-masāʾ ikhwa*, p. 35.
19. Saʿadeh, *al-Aʿmāl al-shiʿriyya*, p. 265.
20. Ibid. pp. 265–67.
21. Burt, 'Connecting Two Shores with Sound', p. 139.

22. Saʿadeh, *Al-Aʿmāl al-shiʿriyya*, p. 184.
23. Burt, 'Connecting Two Shores with Sound', p. 137.
24. Ibid. p. 137.
25. Creswell, pp. 8–10.
26. Ibid. p. 19.
27. Creswell, p. 43.
28. Ibid. p. 9.
29. Wadiʿ Saʿadeh, *Qul lil-ʿābir an yaʿūd nasiya hunā dhillahu wa yalīhi Man akhadha al-naẓra allatī taraktuhā amām al-bāb (Tell the Passerby to Return, He Forgot his Shadow Here Followed by Who Took the Gaze I Left at the Doorstep)* (Beirut: Dār Nelson, 2012), pp. 71–72.
30. Rebecca Walkowitz, *Born Translated: The Contemporary Novel in an Age of World Literature* (New York: Columbia University Press, 2015), p. 6.
31. Ibid. p. 30.
32. Samuel Shimon (ed.), *Beirut 39: New Writing from the Arab World* (London: Bloomsbury, 2010), p. v.
33. Mohamed Enani, 'Introduction', *Angry Voices: An Anthology of the Off-Beat New Egyptian Poets* (Fayetteville: University of Arkansas Press, 2003), p. xxvii.
34. Joumana Haddad, *Kitāb al-jīm aw Jumāniyyāt* (Beirut: al-Dār al-ʿArabiyya lil-ʿAlūm wa al-Nashr, 2012), p. 11.
35. Shimon (ed.), p. 131. The translation of this piece takes too many liberties, sometimes changing the meaning of the original completely. One example is the line 'I am my mother's screams giving birth to me'. A translation more faithful to the Arabic would be 'My mother's screams give birth to me'.
36. Nazem El-Sayed, *Manzil al-ukht al-ṣughrā*, p. 51.
37. Shimon (ed.), p. xiv.
38. Ibid. p. xiii.
39. This echoes Verlaine's call upon poets to overcome the limits of rhetoric: 'Prends l'éloquence et tords-lui son cou'. See Paul Verlaine, 'Art Poétique', from *Selected Poems*, trans. C. F. MacIntyre (Berkeley: University of California Press, 1948), p. 183.
40. Marjorie Perloff, 'Language in Migration: Multilingualism and Exophonic Writing in the New Poetics', *Textual Practice* 24.4. (2010), p. 746.
41. Ibid. p. 731.
42. Ibid. p. 737.
43. In addition to work by Marjorie Perloff cited above, see Mohamed A.

H. Ahmed, *Arabic in Modern Hebrew Texts: The Stylistics of Exophonic Writing* (Edinburgh: Edinburgh University Press, 2019); Chantal Wright, 'Exophony and Literary Translation: What it Means for the Translator when a Writer Adopts a New Language', *Target: International Journal of Translation Studies*, 22.1 (2010), pp. 22–39; Chantal Wright, 'Writing in the 'Grey Zone': Exophonic Literature in Contemporary Germany', *GFL* 3 (2008), pp. 26–42; Alice Loda, *Exophonic Poetics in Contemporary Italy: Versification and Movement in the Works of Hasan Atiya Al Nassar, Barbara Pumhösel and Gëzim Hajdari* (Doctoral dissertation, University of Sydney, 2017); Patricia Haseltine and Sheng-Mie Ma (eds), *Doing English in Asia: Global Literatures and Culture* (London: Lexington Books, 2016).

44. 'In a world of relentless global communication', Marjorie Perloff tells us, 'poetry has begun to concern itself with the processing and absorption of the "foreign" itself'. Marjorie Perloff, 'Language in Migration'.
45. For example, see Sirene Harb, *Articulations of Resistance: Transformative Practices in Contemporary Arab-American Poetry* (New York: Routledge, 2019), and Michelle Hartman, *Breaking Broken English: Black-Arab Literary Solidarities and the Politics of Language* (Syracuse: Syracuse University Press, 2019).
46. Chantal Wright, 'Exophony and Literary Translation', p. 22.
47. Ibid.
48. See the following interview with Abu Hawwash on translation: ʿAbir Yunus (ʿAbīr Yūnus), 'Samer Abu Hawwash: al-tarjama kitāba thāniya (Translation is Another Form of Writing)', *al-Bayān Newspaper*, 28 February 28 2010, https://www.albayan.ae/paths/books/2010-02-28-1.223729 (last accessed 21 October 2020).
49. Abu Hawwash, *Selfie akhīra maʿ ʿālam yuḥtaḍar (A Last Selfie with a Dying World)* (Beirut: Manshūrāt al-Jamal, 2015), pp. 27–30.
50. Eliot, p. 434.
51. In this review of Marjorie Perloff's *Unoriginal Genius: Poetry by Other Means in the New Century* (Chicago: University of Chicago Press, 2010), Aryal explains that 'the word "unoriginal" here does not mean inauthentic or trite but the lack of origin as an essence. As it lacks origin, it does not have a main root but some surface or "rhizomes" diffused in its surroundings as tangible planes'. Yubraj Aryal, 'Unoriginal Genius/Conceptual Writing: Recovering Avant-garde in the Contemporary Poetics', *Journal of Philosophy: A Cross Disciplinary Inquiry* 7.16 (Fall 2011), p. v.

52. There are many studies on the effects of media on the Arabic language in the digital age. For example, see Reem Bassiouney, *Arabic and the Media: Linguistic Analyses and Applications* (Leiden: Brill, 2010). Also see Chapters 4 and 5 of Tarek El-Ariss, *Leaks, Hacks, and Scandals: Arab Culture in the Digital Age* (Princeton: Princeton University Press, 2019), pp. 127–79.
53. Abu Hawwash, *Laysa hākadha tuṣnaʿ al-pizza (This is Not How Pizza is Made)* (Beirut: Manushūrāt al-Mutawassiṭ, 2017), '*al-Taqs rāʾiʿ fī bayrūt*' (The Weather is Amazing in Beirut), p. 72
54. Ibid. '*Baʿd Ziyād al-Raḥbānī* (After Ziyād al-Raḥbānī)', p. 54.
55. Ibid. p. 90.
56. Ibid. p. 64.
57. Ibid. p. 53.
58. Ibid. p. 42.
59. See Tzveta Sofronieva, 'Un-Lost in Translation', *Studies in Slavic Literature and Poetics* 55 (2010), pp. 27–40.
60. 'Syrian-Kurdish Poet Golan Haji: It's Not Easy to Go For What One Loves', *Arablit.org*, 9 January 2018, https://arablit.org/2018/01/09/syrian-kurdish-poet-golan-haji-its-not-easy-to-go-for-what-one-loves/ (last accessed 21 October 2020).
61. Ibid.
62. Ibid.
63. Ibid.
64. Golan Haji, 'Alladhī aḥbabnāh' (The One We Used to Love), *Majallat al-Doha* 149 (2020), p. 61.
65. Ibid.
66. Ibid.
67. Iskandar Habash (Iskandar Ḥabash), 'Ḥiwār maʿ al-shāʿir al-sūrī Golan Haji' (An Interview with the Syrian Poet Golan Haji), *al-Safīr Newspaper*, 6 September 2014.
68. Ibid.
69. Stephen Watts and Golan Haji (trans.), *A Tree Whose Name I don't Know* (New York: Midsummer Night's Press, 2017), back cover.
70. Golan Haji, *Mīzān al-adhā (The Balance of Hurt)* (Beirut: al-Mutawassiṭ, 2016), p. 12.
71. Watts and Haji, p. 15.
72. Haji, *Mīzān al-adhā,* pp. 9–10.
73. Watts and Haji, p. 11.

74. George Steiner, *Language and Silence: Essays on Language, Literature and the Inhuman* (New York: Atheneum, 1967), p. 30.
75. 'Syrian Kurdish Poet Golan Haji'.
76. Fady Joudah and Golan Haji, 'Two Poems', *World Literature Today*, January 2018, https://www.worldliteraturetoday.org/2018/january/two-poems-fady-joudah-golan-haji (last accessed 21 October 2020).
77. Fady Joudah, *Footnotes in the Order of Disappearance* (Minneapolis: Milkweed Editions, 2018), p. 35.
78. Haji, *Mīzān al-adhā*, p. 10.
79. Watts and Haji, p. 12.
80. Joudah, *Footnotes in the Order of Disappearance*, p. 46.
81. For more on Arabic literature as a multilingual and global phenomenon, see Waïl Hassan, 'Introduction', *The Oxford Handbook of Arabic Novelistic Traditions* (New York: Oxford University Press, 2017), and Syrine Hout, 'Reading Multilingual Arab Literatures Globally in the Twenty-First Century', *World Literature Today* Spring (2019), pp. 13–19.
82. Huda Fakhreddine 'A Poem in Arabic, Not an Arabic Poem', *Jacket 2*, 9 January 2019, https://jacket2.org/commentary/poem-arabic-not-arabic-poem (last accessed 21 October 2020).

Afterword

Studies of Arabic poetry often look back at either the near or the distant past. Few are the academic studies, Arabic or English, which arrive at the present moment of Arabic poetry. This book grounds itself in the present moment and approaches the Arabic poetic practice as it is, in fact, live and urgent, informed and shaped by the experiences and challenges of life in the twenty-first century. Although the focus of the book is the prose poem, the scope it covers necessarily involves other genres of modernist poetry and prose with which this new genre was involved, as well as the long tradition of Arabic poetry and prose against which it both defined and sought to legitimise itself. It traced threads of continuity and convergence, as well as points of disconnect and divergence among the poets writing under the aegis of the prose poem.

In its interrogation of poetry and its limit, the Arabic prose poem allows for a new conception of form that does not exist outside the poem but grows from inside of it. It invites us as critics and readers of Arabic poetry to revisit our understanding of structure in poetry (*binā'*) and use that to arrive at form. This has the potential of redefining poetic forms that have been cast as rigid and fixed.

In this book I have presented an in-depth look at a number of understudied poets, such as Salim Barakat, Unsi al-Hajj and Muhammad al-Maghut, who are essential in their own right and in their influence on poets who succeeded them. My study also presented the works of a later generation of Arab poets whose careers were launched after the beginning of the twenty-first century; poets who are still overlooked or undiscovered by scholarship on Arabic poetry in English. In my engagement with the works of already well-studied poets, namely Adonis and Mahmoud Darwish, I was invested in uncovering previously unexplored dimensions of their poetic careers, through their involvement with and response to the prose poem.

This book is neither a survey nor a literary history of the prose poem. It is a close reading of the work of a select group of prose poets who reflect well the diversity, tensions and potentials/potentialities of the prose poem project in Arabic. But the configuration that has been sketched here is not the only one. Due to nothing but the requirements of space, it necessarily excluded poets and projects which are just as significant and representative as the ones it includes. With the awareness of the dynamic of selection present in this study, my hope is that the poets who were included here will serve as bridges to the study of the poets who were not. Below are possible further channels of inquiry that I hope this book will trigger.

The examination of the prose poem manifestos by Adonis and Unsi al-Hajj in 1960 provides a launching board to a close study of *Bayānāt*,[1] three manifestos by Adonis, Muhammad Bennis (Muḥammad Bannīs, Morocco, b. 1948) and Qasim Haddad (Qāsim Ḥaddād, Bahrain, b. 1948) with his co-writer, the novelist and short story writer Amine Salih (Amīn Ṣāliḥ, b. 1950) published in the early 1990s. This work gives us a longer view of poetic manifesto-writing in Arabic. The three manifestos are written with the benefit of having the prose poem project's failure and successes in hindsight. Moreover, these later manifestos expand on Adonis's notion of *kitāba* which I examined in Chapter 3. The works of Qasim Haddad and Muhammad Bennis provide additional and more varied examples of poetry as *kitāba* across genres and mediums. Haddad's collaborations[2] with visual artists and musicians further open up the quest for poetry beyond the verbal arts.

In the vein of my examination of the prose poet's motivated reading of the Arabic literary tradition, there are many later projects which exhibit internal translations of classical Arabic texts or *writing into* the Arabic poetic tradition. Adonis's monumental *al-Kitāb* and Haddad's poetry collections *Akhbār majnūn laylā* and *Ṭarafa ibn al-warda* are such examples.

Mahmoud Darwish's flirting with the prose poem in his generically evasive texts and diaries can lead to a more complicated examination of form and meter in the works of contemporary *tafʿīla* poets who still insist on meter. Does the prose poem acquire different characteristics in the works of poets who have an intimate understanding of meter and intentionally choose to give it up once and return to it another time, sometimes in the same poetry collection or even in the same text? Here I think of Amjad Nasser's (Amjad Nāṣir, Jordan, 1955–2019) significant poetic career which puts in focus the transition from the *tafʿīla* poem to the prose poem and their ongoing negotiations, as well as the development of the poetic narrative which further blurs genre distinctions and expands the notion of the poetic.

Salim Barakat's insular oppositional poetic project, which manifests itself most dramatically in language work and language play, brings to mind other similarly singular poetic projects such as the prose poets Unsi al-Hajj, Fuʾad Rifqa and the committedly *tafʿīla* poet Khalil Hawi (Khalīl Ḥāwī, Lebanon, 1919–82). Moreover, Barakat's career continually pushes us to wonder how the transgressive interventions in language create a 'place' for the 'other' writing in Arabic. In this vein, the works of the Tunisian Moncef Ouhaibi (Muṣif al-Wahāyibī, b. 1949) offer another instance worth examining further, an instance where the non-Arabic invades the Arabic and the poem blends into the novel.

The lines of poetic lineage I traced here between Muhammad al-Maghut and the Egyptian poets of the nineties on one hand and Wadiʿ Saʿadeh and the poets of the twenty-first century on the other are by no means sharp and defined. They are frayed and proliferating, and many other names could have been added on both sides. Sargon Boulus (Sargūn Būlūṣ, Iraq, 1944–2007) looms large when examining multilingualism, translation and the American and other non-Arabic connections,[3] as well as their consequence in contemporary Arabic poetics. Boulus's work connects to a rich and varied prose poem project in Iraq which includes names like Fadhil al-Azzawi (Fāḍil al-ʿAzzāwī, b. 1940), Salah Faik (Ṣalāḥ Fāyiq, b. 1944) and others.[4]

Moreover, the poetic and translation oeuvres of poet-translators such as Muhammad Bennis, Kadhim Jihad (Kāẓim Jihād, Iraq, b. 1955) and Bassam Hajjar can shed additional light on the prose poem as an exercise in creative generative reading. Hajjar's work itself warrants closer attention. He was an established translator of prose from foreign languages, including English and French, as well as an avid and engaged reader of classical Arabic sources, especially in the tradition of *akhbār* and historical records. The prose poem in his hands becomes a *reader-ly* text, in that it draws its force from a dialogue with other texts and a poetic interpretation of borrowed moments and themes. It becomes an exercise in creative reading.

Prose poets in Arabic are not a homogenous trend or a movement or a school. They oppose, echo, build on and converse with each other in a manner that reveals the prose poem to be an experimental critical space in which Arabic poetry and its possibilities are interrogated.

And, thus, in accounting for the varied and continually expansive prose poem project in Arabic, this book is one configuration among many possible ones.

Notes

1. Adonis, Muhammad Bennis, Qasim Haddad, and Amine Salih, *al-Bayānāt*, 2nd edition (Tunis: Sarās lil-nashr, 1995).
2. Huda Fakhreddine, Roger Allen, and Hatem al-Zahrani, 'Poems by Qāsim Ḥaddād', *Middle Eastern Literature* 21.1 (2018), pp. 100–04.
3. For example, see Sinan Antoon, 'Sargon Boulus and Tu Fu's Ghost(s)', *Journal of World Literature* 2 (2017), pp. 297–319.
4. For more on the Iraqi prose poem, see Suneela Mubayi, *Ṣaʿlaka in Modern Iraqi Poetry* (Doctoral dissertation, New York University, 2017).

Bibliography

Poetry Collections

Abu Hawwash, Samer, *Laysa hākadha tuṣna' al-pizza (This is not How Pizza is Made)* (Beirut: Manushūrāt al-Mutawassiṭ, 2017).

Abu Hawwash, Samer, *Selfie akhīra ma' 'ālam yuḥtaḍar (A Last Selfie with a Dying World)* (Beirut: Manshūrāt al-Jamal, 2015).

Abu Salih, Imad, *Jamāl kāfir (Heretic Beauty)* (private publication, 2005).

Abu Salih, Imad, *Kāna nā'iman hīna qāmat al-thawra (He Was Asleep When the Revolution Came)* (private publication, 2015).

Abu Tammam, Habib b. Aws, *Dīwān Abī Tammām*, edited by Muḥīyī al-dīn Ṣubḥī, 2 vols. (Beirut: Dār Ṣādir, 1997).

Adonis, *A Time Between Ashes and Roses*, trans. Shawkat Toorawa (Syracuse: Syracuse University Press, 2004).

Adonis, *Aghānī Mihyār al-Dimashqī*, 2nd edition (Beirut: Manshūrāt Mawāqif, 1970),

Adonis, *Dīwān al-shi'r al-'arabī*, 3 vols. (Beirut: Dār al-Fikr, 1986.)

Adonis, 'Fī qaṣīdat al-nathr', *Shi'r* 14 (1960), pp. 75-83.

Adonis, *Mufrad bi-ṣīghat al-jam': ṣīyāgha nihā'iyya* (Beirut: Dār al-Ādāb, 1988).

Adonis, *Qaṣā'id 'ūlā* (Beirut: Dār Majjallat Shi'r, 1957).

Barakat, Salim, *al-Dīwān* (Beirut: Dār al-Tanwīr, 1992).

Barakat, Salim, *al-Dīwān 2* (Damascus: Dār al-Madā, 2017).

Barakat, Salim, *al-Mujābahāt, al-mawāthīq al-ajrān, al-taṣārīf, wa-ghayruhā* (Beirut: Dār an-Nahār, 1996).

Barakat, Salim, *al-Mu'jam* (Damascus: Dār al-Madā, 2005).

Barakat, Salim, *Tanbih al-ḥayawān ilā ansābih* (Beirut: Dār al-Madā, 2018).

Barakat, Salim, *Ṭaysh al-yāqūt (The Recklessness of Sapphire)* (Beirut: Dar al-Nahar, 1996).

al-Danasuri, Usama, *al-Aʿmāl al-kāmila (Collected Works)* (Cairo: Dār Mīrīt, 2009).

Darwish, Mahmoud, *al-Aʿmāl al-Jadīda* (Beirut: Riad El-Rayyes Books, 2009).

Darwish, Mahmoud, *Athar al-farāsha* (Beirut: Riad El-Rayyes Books, 2008).

Darwish, Mahmoud, *Fī ḥaḍrat al-ghiyāb* (Beirut: Riad El-Rayyes Books, 2006).

Darwish, Mahmoud, *In the Presence of Absence*, trans. Sinan Antoon (Brooklyn: Archipelago Books, 2011).

Darwish, Mahmoud, *Ka-zahr al-lawz aw abʿad* (Beirut: Riad El-Rayyes Books, 2005).

Darwish, Mahmoud, *Lā taʿtadhir ʿammā faʿalt* (Beirut: Riad El-Rayyes Books, 2004).

Darwish, Mahmoud, *Memory for Forgetfulness*, trans. Ibrahim Muhawi (Los Angeles: University of California Press, 2013).

El-Sayed, Nazem, *Ard maʿzūla bil-nawm (A Land Isolated by Sleep)* (Beirut: Riad El-Rayyes Books, 2007).

El-Sayed, Nazem, *Manzil al-ukht al-ṣughrā (The Youngest Sister's House)* (Beirut: Riad El-Rayyes Books, 2010).

Haddad, Joumana, *Kitāb al-jīm aw Jumāniyyāt* (Beirut, al-Dār al-ʿArabiyya lil-ʿUlūm wa al-Nashr, 2012).

Haji, Golan, *Mīzān al-adhā (The Balance of Hurt)* (Beirut: al-Mutawassiṭ, 2016).

al-Hajj, Unsi, *al-Raʾs al-maqṭūʿ* (Beirut: Dār Majallat Shiʿr, 1960).

al-Hajj, Unsi, *Lan* (Beirut: Dār Majallat Shiʿr, 1960).

al-Hajj, Unsi, *Nashīd al-anāshīd* (Beirut: Dār al-Nahār, 1967).

Hajjar, Bassam, *Sawfa taḥyā min baʿdī (You will Survive Me)* (Beirut: Al-Markaz al-ʿarabī, 2001).

Ibn al-Muʿtazz, ʿAbdallah, *Dīwān* (Beirut: Dār Sādir, 1961).

Ibn al-Rumi, *Dīwān*, edited by Majīd Trād, 2 volumes (Beirut: Dār al-jīl, 1998).

Joudah, Fady, *Footnotes in the Order of Disappearance* (Minneapolis: Milkweed Editions, 2018).

Joudah, Fady, and Golan Haji, 'Two Poems', *World Literature Today*, January 2018, https://www.worldliteraturetoday.org/2018/january/two-poems-fady-joudah-golan-haji (last accessed 23 October 2020).

al-Maghut, Muhammad, *al-Aʿmāl al-shiʿriyya*, 3rd edition (Beirut: Dār al-Madā, 2003).

al-Mala'ika, Nazik, *Qaḍāyā al-shiʿr al-muʿāṣir*, 1st edition (Beirut: Dār al-Ādāb, 1962).

al-Maʿarri, Abū al-ʿAlāʾ, *al-Luzūmiyyāt* (Beirut: Dār al-kutub al-'ilmiyya, 2001).

al-Maʿarri, Abū al-ʿAlāʾ, *Saqṭ al-zand* (Beirut: Dār Ṣādir, 1957).

Mersal, Iman, *Ḥattā atakhallā ʿan fikrat al-buyū*t *(So I May Give Up On the Idea of Houses)* (Cairo: Dār al-Tanwīr, 2013).

Mersal, Iman, *These are not Oranges, my Love*, trans. Khaled Mattawa (New York: The Sheep Meadow Press, 2008).

Perse, Saint-John, *Collected Poems*, trans. W. H. Auden, Hugh Grisholm, et al. (Princeton: Princeton University Press, 1983).

Perse, Saint-John, *Manārāt*, trans. Adonis (Damascus: Dār al-Madā, 1999).

Saʿadeh, Wadiʿ, *al-Aʿmāl al-shiʿriyya* (Beirut: Dar al-Nahda al-ʿArabiyya, 2008).

Saʿadeh, Wadiʿ, *Laysa lil-masāʾ ikhwa* (Beirut: al-Mu'assasa al-Jām'īya lil-Dirāsāt wa-al-Nashr, 1981).

Saʿadeh, Wadiʿ, *Qul lil-ʿābir an yaʿūd nasiya hunā dhillahu wa yalīhi Man akhadha al-naẓra allatī taraktuhā amām al-bāb (Tell the Passer-by to Return, He forgot His Shadow Here, Followed by Who Took the Gaze I Left at the Doorstep)* (Beirut: Dār Nelson, 2012).

Watts, Stephen, and Golan Haji (trans.), *A Tree Whose Name I don't Know* (New York: Midsummer Night's Press, 2017).

al-Zawzani, Husayn b. Ahmad, *Sharḥ al-muʿallaqāt al-sabʿ* (Beirut: Dār al-Jīl, n. d.).

Interviews

al-ʿAwit, ʿAql, 'Interview with Salim Barakat', *Hajalnama* 11–12 (2007).

Habash, Iskandar, 'Ḥiwār ma' al-shā'ir al-sūrī Golan Haji (An Interview with the Syrian Poet Golan Haji)', *al-Safīr Newspaper*, 6 September 2014.

'Interview with Wadiʿ Saʿadeh, *Akhbār al-Adab*, 28 April 2018, https://adab.akhbarelyom.com/newdetails.aspx?id=446509 (last accessed 4 June 2018).

Interview with Adonis, Beirut, 11 July 2019.

'Syrian-Kurdish Poet Golan Haji: It's Not Easy to Go for What One Loves', *Arablit.org*, 9 January 2018, https://arablit.org/2018/01/09/syrian-kurdish-poet-golan-haji-its-not-easy-to-go-for-what-one-loves/ (last accessed 23 October 2020).

Secondary Sources

Abu Deeb, K., 'al-D̲j̲urd̲j̲ānī', *Encyclopaedia of Islam*, Second Edition.

Abu Deeb, K., *al-Jurjānī's Theory of Poetic Imagery* (Warminister: Aris and Phillips, 1979).

Adonis and Yusuf al-Khal (trans.), *al-Arḍ al-kharāb* (Beirut: Dār Majallat Shiʿr, 1958).

Adonis, 'Al-Irtidād', *al-Ḥayāt Newspaper*, 7 April 1994.

Adonis, 'Bayān al-ḥadātha', *al-Bayānāt*, 2nd edition (Tunis: Sarās lil-nashr, 1995).

Adonis, 'Conférence d'Adonis donnée à la Fondation Saint-John Perse le 9 octobre 1993', trans. Anne Wade-Minkowski, *Souffle de Perse* 4 (1993), pp. 4–9.

Adonis, *Dīwān al-nathr al-ʿarabī*, 4 vols (Jablah: Dār Bidāyāt, 2012).

Adonis, 'Fī qaṣīdat al-nathr', *Shiʿr* 14 (1960), pp. 75–83.

Adonis, *Hā anta ayuhā al-waqt:sīra shiʿriyya* (Beirut: Dār al-Ādāb, 1993).

Adonis, *Kalām al-bidāyāt* (Beirut: Dār al-Ādāb, 1989).

Adonis, *Muqaddima lil-shiʿr al-ʿarabī*, 3rd edition (Beirut: Dār ʿAwda, 1979).

Adonis, *al-Naṣṣ al-Qurʾānī wa-āfāq al-kitāba* (Beirut: Dār al-ādāb, 1993).

Adonis, *Siyāsat al-shiʿr: dirāsah fī al-shiʿriyya al-ʿarabiyya al-muʿāṣira* (Beirut: Dār al-Ādāb, 1985).

Adonis, *al-Thābit wa-l-mutaḥawwil: baḥth fī-l-ittibāʿ wa-l-ibdāʿ ʿinda al-ʿArab* (Bayrūt: Dār al-ʿAwda, 1974–78).

Adonis, *Zaman al-Shiʿr* (Beirut: Dār ʿAwda, 1972).

Adonis, Muhammad Bennis, Qasim Haddad, and Amine Salih, *al-Bayānāt*, 2nd edition (Tunis: Sarās lil-nashr, 1995).

Ahmadzadeh, Hashem, 'In Search of a Kurdish Novel that Tells Us Who the Kurds Are', *Iranian Studies* 40.5 (2007), pp. 579–92.

Ahmed, Mohamed A. H., *Arabic in Modern Hebrew Texts: The Stylistics of Exophonic Writing* (Edinburgh: Edinburgh University Press, 2019).

Allen, Roger, *The Arabic Literary Heritage: The Development of its Genre and Criticism* (London: Cambridge University Press, 1998).

Anis, Mona (trans.), 'Edward Said: A Contrapuntal Reading', *Al-Ahram Weekly*, 30 September–6 October 2004.

Antoon, Sinan, 'Preface', *In the Presence of Absence* (New York: Archipelago Books, 2011).

Antoon, Sinan, 'Sargon Boulus and Tu Fu's Ghost(s)', *Journal of World Literature* 2 (2017), pp. 297–319.

Arberry, A. J., 'al-Niffarī', *Encyclopaedia of Islam*, Second Edition.

Aryal, Yubraj, 'Unoriginal Genius/Conceptual Writing: Recovering Avant-Garde in the Contemporary Poetics', *Journal of Philosophy: A Cross Disciplinary Inquiry* 7.16 (Fall 2011), pp. i–x.

ʿAsfur, Jabir, *Rūʾā al-ʿālam: ʿan taʾsīs al-ḥadātha al-ʿarabiya* (Morocco: al-Markaz al-Thaqāfī al-ʿArabī, 2008).

al-ʿAskari, Abu Hilal Hasan, *Kitāb al-ṣināʿatayn*, edited by Muḥammad Abū al-Faḍl Ibrāhīm and ʿAlī Muḥammad al-Bajāwī (Cairo: Al-Ḥalabī, 1971).

ʿAwad, Lewis, *Plutoland wa qaṣāʾid min shiʿr al-khāṣṣa*, 1st edition (Cairo: Maṭbaʿat al-Karnak, 1947).

Bajalan, Djene Rhys, and Sara Zandi Karimi (eds), *Studies in Kurdish History: Empire, Ethnicity and Identity* (New York: Routledge, 2015).

Baker, George, 'The Jubjub Bird or Some Remarks on the Prose Poem', *Listener* 85 (1971), pp. 748–50.

Balso, Judith, *The Affirmation of Poetry*, trans. Drew Burk (Minneapolis: Univocal Press, 2014).

al-Baqillani, Abu Bakr Muhammad, *Iʿjāz al-Qurʾān*, edited by Aḥmad Ṣaqr (Cairo: Dār al-Maʿārif, 1972).

Barakat, Salim, 'Madhāhib al-maʿnā', *al-Karmil* 43 (1992), pp. 166–72.

Barakat, Salim, *al-Taʿjīl fī qurūḍ al-nathr* (Damascus: Dār Zamān, 2010).

Barakat, Salim, *Hajalnama* 11–12 (2007), pp. 181–223.

al-Barquqi, ʿAbd al-Rahman, *Sharḥ dīwān al-Mutannabī* (Beirut: Dār al-Kitāb al-ʿArabī, 1986).

Barut, Muhammad Jamal, *Al-Shiʿr yaktubu ismahu* (Damascus: Manshūrāt Ittiḥad al-Kuttāb al-ʿArab, 1981).

Bassiouney, Reem, *Arabic and the Media: Linguistic Analyses and Applications* (Leiden: Brill, 2010).

Baydoun, ʿAbbas, 'Al-Sulālah al-Maghūṭiyyah: qirāʾa fī shiʿr sūrī ḥadīth', *al-Nāqid* 30 (1990), pp. 30–38.

Bazzun, Ahmad, *Qaṣīdat al-nathr al-ʿarabiyyah: al-iṭār al-naẓarī* (Beirut: Dār al-Fikr al-Jadīd, 1996).

Bencheikh, Jamaleddine, *al-Shiʿriyyah al-ʿarabiyyah*, trans. Mubarak Ḥanūn et al. (Casablanca: Dār Tubqāl, 1996).

Bernard, Suzanne, *Le Poème en Prose de Baudelaire jusqu'à nos jours* (Paris: Librarie Lizette, 1959).

Bin Hamza, Hussein, 'Maḥmūd wa qaṣīdat al-nathr: uḥikubi aw lā uḥibuki', *al-Akhbār*, 8 August 2009, https://al-akhbar.com/Literature_Arts/128948 (last accessed 23 October 2020).

Brockelmann, C. and Pellat, Ch., 'Maḳāma', *Encyclopaedia of Islam, Second Edition.*

Brogan, Jacqueline Vaught, *Stevens and Simile: A Theory of Language* (Princeton: Princeton University Press, 1986).

Burt, Clarissa, 'Connecting Two Shores with Sound: Sa'adeh's World of Loss', *Edebiyat: Journal of Middle Eastern Literatures* 14.1–2 (2003), pp. 133–47.

Burt, Clarissa, 'Memory and Loss: The Exilic Nihilism of Wadīʿ Saʿādah, Australia's Lebanese Émigré Poet', *Journal of Arabic Literature* 4.1–2 (2010), pp. 180–95.

Burt, Clarissa, 'The Good, the Bad and the Ugly: The Canonical Sieve and Poems from an Egyptian Avant Garde', *Journal of Arabic Literature* 28. 2 (1997), pp. 141–62.

Casanova, Pascal, *The World Republic of Letters* (Cambridge, MA: Harvard University Press, 2004).

Caws, M. A., 'Prose Poem', *The Princeton Encyclopedia of Poetry and Poetics*, 4th edition, edited by Roland Greene (Princeton: Princeton University Press, 2012), pp. 1112–13.

Creswell, Robyn, *City of Beginnings: Poetic Modernism in Beirut* (Princeton: Princeton University Press, 2019).

Deeb, M. A., 'The Concept of the poème en prose in Modern Arabic Poetry: Native Tradition and French Influence', *Canadian Review of Comparative Literature* Mars-June (2010), pp. 174–87.

Derrida, Jacques, *Monolingualism of the Other or Prosthesis of Origin* (Palo Alto: Stanford University Press, 1998).

Dyer, Rebecca, 'Poetry of Politics and Mourning: Mahmoud Darwish's Genre-Transforming Tribute to Edward W. Said', *PMLA* 122.5 (2007), pp. 1447–62.

Editors, 'Buhlūl', *Encyclopaedia of Islam*, Second Edition.

El-Ariss, Tarek, *Leaks, Hacks, and Scandals: Arab Culture in the Digital Age* (Princeton: Princeton University Press, 2019).

El-Hage, George (trans.), 'Antithesis', *Journal of Arabic Literature* 36 (2005), pp. 50–56.

Eliot, T. S., 'The Music of Poetry', *The Partisan Review* 9.6 (1942), pp. 450–65.

Elsisi, Sayed, *Mā baʿda qasīdat al-nathr: naḥwa khitāb jadīd lil-shiʿriyya al-ʿarabiyya* (Beirut: al-Muʾassassa al-ʿArabiyya, 2016).

Enani, Mohamed, 'Introduction', *Angry Voices: An Anthology of the Off-Beat New Egyptian Poets* (Fayetteville: University of Arkansas Press, 2003).

Encyclopedia of Islam, Second Edition, edited by P. Bearman, Th. Bianquis, C. E. Bosworth, E. van Donzel and W. P. Heinrichs (Leiden: Brill, 1954–2005); available at referenceworks.brillonline.com (last accessed 27 October 2020).

Fahd, T., W. P. Heinrichs, and A. Ben Abdesselem, 'Sadj‘', *Encyclopaedia of Islam, Second Edition.*

Fakhreddine, Huda, 'A Poem in Arabic, Not an Arabic Poem', *Jacket* 2, 9 January 2019, https://jacket2.org/commentary/poem-arabic-not-arabic-poem (last accessed 23 October 2020).

Fakhreddine, Huda, *Metapoesis in the Arabic Tradition: From Modernists to Muḥdathūn* (Leiden: Brill, 2015).

Fakhreddine, Huda, Roger Allen, and Hatem al-Zahrani, 'Poems by Qāsim Ḥaddād', *Middle Eastern Literature* 21.1 (2018), pp. 100–04.

Faysal, Shukri, 'Introduction', *Abū al-‘Atāhiya: akhbāruhu wa shi‘ruhu* (Damascus: Maṭba‘at Jāmi‘at Dimashq, 1965).

Gottschalk, H. L., G. S. Colin, A. K. S. Lambton, and A. S. Bazmee Ansari, 'Dīwān', *Encyclopaedia of Islam*, Second Edition.

Grunebaum, G. E. 'I‘djāz', *Encyclopaedia of Islam*, Second Edition.

Hachmeier, Klaus, 'Rating Adab: At-Tawhidi on the Merits of Poetry and Prose', *Al-Qantara: Revista de Estudios Arabes*, 25.2 (2004), pp. 357–86.

Hadidi, Subhi, 'Al-Maghut wa al-shi‘r: tawqīr wa-taḥqīr', *al-Quds al-‘Arabī*, 4 April 2016, http://www.alquds.co.uk/?p=510578 (last accessed 26 November 2017).

Hadidi, Subhi, 'Al-Māghūt: waṣīt al-nathr, adā' al-shā‘ir, wa jadal al-qaṣīda', http://www.arabworldbooks.com/Readers2009/articles/maghut_hadidi2.htm (last accessed 26 November 2017).

Hadidi, Subhi, *Shi‘riyyāt al-ta‘āqud al-‘asīr* (Beirut: al-Ahliya lil-nashr, 2017).

Haidar, Otared, *The Prose Poem and the Journal Shi'r: A Comparative Study of Literature, Literary Study, and Journalism* (Reading: Ithaca Press. 2008).

Haji, Golan, 'Alladhī aḥbabnāh', *Majallat al-Doha* 149 (2020), p. 61.a

Harb, Lara, 'Form, Content, and the Inimitability of the Qur'ān in 'Abd Al-Qāhir al-Jurjani's Works', *Middle Eastern Literatures* 18.3 (2016), pp. 310–12.

Harb, Sirene, *Articulations of Resistance: Transformative Practices in Contemporary Arab-American Poetry* (New York: Routledge, 2019).

Hartman, Michelle, *Breaking Broken English: Black-Arab Literary Solidarities and the Politics of Language* (Syracuse: Syracuse University Press, 2019).

Haseltine, Patricia, and Sheng-Mie Ma (eds), *Doing English in Asia: Global Literatures and Culture* (London: Lexington Books, 2016).

Hassan, Waïl (ed.), *The Oxford Handbook of Arabic Novelistic Traditions* (New York: Oxford University Press, 2017).

Hijazi, Ahmad ʿAbd al-Muʿti, *Qaṣīdat al-nathr aw al-qaṣīdah al-kharsāʾ* (Dubay: Majallat Dubay al-Thaqāfiyyah, 2008).

Hout, Syrine, 'Reading Multilingual Arab Literatures Globally in the Twenty-First Century', *World Literature Today* Spring (2019), pp. 13–19.

Ibn Jaʿfar, Qudama, *Naqd al-shiʿr*, edited by Muḥammad ʿAbd al-Munʿim Khafājī (Cairo: Maktabat al-Kulliyāt al-Azhariyya, 1979).

Ibn Rashiq al-Qayrawani, *al-ʿUmda*, edited by Muhammad Muḥyi al-dīn ʿAbd al-Ḥamid, 2 volumes (Beirut: Dār al-Jīl, 1972).

Ibn Tabataba, Muhammad Ahmad, *ʿIyār al-shiʿr*, edited by ʿAbbād ʿAbd al-Sātir (Beirut: Dār al-Kutub al-ʿIlmiyyah, 1982).

Jakobson, Roman, 'The Dominant', *Language in Literature*, trans. Krystyna Pomorska, edited by Krystyna Pomorska and Stephen Rudy (Cambridge, MA: Belknap Press, 1990).

al-Janabi, ʿAbd al-Qadir, *Dīwān ilā-l-abad: qaṣīdat al-nathr/anṭulujyā ʿālamiyyah* (Beirut: Dār al-Tanwīr, 2015).

Jayyusi, May and Naomi Shihab Nye (trans.), *The Fan of Swords*, edited by Salma Khadra al-Jayussi (Washington DC: Three Continents Press, 1991).

Jayyusi, Salma Khadra (ed.), *Modern Arabic Literature: An Anthology* (New York: Columbia University Press, 1987).

Jayyusi, Salma Khadra, *Trends and Movements in Modern Arabic Poetry*, 2 volumes (Leiden: Brill, 1977).

Joudah, Fady, 'Mahmoud Darwish's Lyric Epic', *Human Architecture: Journal of Sociology of Self Knowledge* 7 (2009), pp. 7–8.

al-Jurjani, ʿAbd al-Qāhir, *Asrār al-balāgha*, edited by Maḥmūd Shākir (Cairo: Maktabat Madani, 1991).

al-Jurjani, ʿAbd al-Qāhir, *Kitāb dalāʾil al-iʿjāz*, edited by Maḥmūd Shākir (Cairo: Maktabat al-Khānjī, 1984).

Khouri, Mounah, 'Lewis ʿAwaḍ: A Forgotten Pioneer of Arabic Free Verse', *Journal of Arabic Literature* (1970), pp. 137–44.

Loda, Alice, *Exophonic Poetics in Contemporary Italy: Versification and Movement in the Works of Hasan Atiya Al Nassar, Barbara Pumhösel and Gëzim Hajdari* (Doctoral dissertation, University of Sydney, 2017).

al-Mala'ikah, Nazik, *Qaḍāyā al-shiʿr al-muʿāṣir,* 1st edition (Beirut: Dār al-Ādāb, 1962).

Marzolph, U., 'ʿUkalāʾ al-Madjānīn', *Encyclopaedia of Islam*, Second Edition.

al-Marzuqi, Ahmad ibn al-Hasan, *Sharḥ dīwān al-Ḥamāsah*, edited by Aḥmad Amīn and ʿAbd al-Salām Hārūn, 4 volumes (Cairo: Lajnat al-Taʾlīf wa al-Tarjamah wa al-Nashr, 1968).

Mazloum, Mohamad, 'Baḥthan ʿan ẓilāl Saint-John Perse… al-ʿarabiyya', *al-Ḥayāt Newspaper,* 15 December 2015.

Mitwalli, Muhammad et al. (eds), *Al-Jarād* 3 (1996).

Monte, Steven, *Invisible Fences: Prose Poetry as a Genre in French and American Literature* (Lincoln: Nebraska University Press, 2000).

Moreh, S. 'Five Writers of *Shiʿr Manthūr* in Modern Arabic Literature', *Middle Eastern Literatures* 10.2 (1974), pp. 229–33.

Mubayi, Suneela, *Ṣaʿlaka in Modern Iraqi Poetry* (Doctoral dissertation, New York University, 2017).

Muhawi, Ibrahim, 'Introduction', *Memory of Forgetfulness*, by Mahmoud Darwish (Berkley: University of California Press, 1995).

Nasser, Amjad, 'Darwish wa qaṣīdat al-nathr', *Al-Karmel* 90 (2009), p. 117.

Nasser, Amjad, 'Yawmiyyāt Maḥmūd Darwish ka-qināʿ li-*qaṣīdat al-nathr*', *Aljazeera*, 24 March 2014, https://www.aljazeera.net/news/cultureandart/2012/3/24/يوميات-محمود-درويش-كقناع-لقصيدة-النثر-

Newton, K. M., 'Roman Jakobson: The Dominant', *Twentieth Century Literary Theory: A Reader* (New York: St. Martin's Press, 1997).

al-Niffari, Muhammad b. ʿAbd al-Jabbar, *Kitāb al-Mawāqif wa yalihi Kitāb al-Mukhāṭabāt*, edited by Arthur Arberry (Cairo: Maktabat al-Mutanabbī, 1983).

Ouhaibi, Moncef, 'Adonis fī ḍiyāfat al-Ghazālī wa aflāṭūn', *Al-Awān*, 14 February 2008, https://www.alawan.org/2008/02/14/أدونيس-في-ضيافة-أفلاطون-والغزالي-2/.

Perloff, Marjorie, 'Language in Migration: Multilingualism and Exophonic Writing in the New Poetics', *Textual Practice* 24.4. (2010), pp. 725–48.

Perloff, Marjorie, *The Dance of the Intellect: Studies in the Poetry of the Pound Tradition* (London: Cambridge University Press, 1985).

Perloff, Marjorie, *The Poetics of Indeterminacy: Rimbaud to Cage* (Evanston: North Western University Press, 1983).

Perloff, Marjorie, *Unoriginal Genius: Poetry by Other Means in the New Century* (Chicago: University of Chicago Press, 2010).

Pickard, Zachariah, *Elizabeth Bishop's Poetics of Description* (London: McGill-Queen's University Press, 2009).

Porter, Josias Leslie, *A Handbook for Travelers in Syria and Palestine* (London: J. Murray, 1868).

Rooke, Tetz, 'Feathers from Heaven: Or What the Paprika Plant Said to the Hero', *Middle Eastern Literatures* 9.2 (2006), pp. 179–88.

Saʿid, Khalida, '*Ḥuzn fī ḍawʾ al-qamar* li-Muḥammad al-Māghūt', *Majallat Shiʿr* 11 (1959), pp. 98–99.

Saʿid, Khalida, *Jurḥ al-maʿnā* (Beirut: Dār al-Sāqī, 2018).

Salem, Hilmi, 'Laqatat min lawha', *Nizwa*, 1 June 1996, http://www.nizwa.com/لقطات-من-اللوحة/ (last accessed 23 October 2010).

Salih, Saniya, 'Introduction', *Dīwān Al-Maghut* (Beirut: Dār al-ʿAwda, 1978).

Sanbar, Elias (trans.), 'Contrepoint', *Le monde diplomatique*, 28 January 2005.

Santilli, N., *Such Rare Citings: The Prose Poem in English Literature* (Madison: Fairleigh Dickinson University Press, 2002).

Sells, Michael, 'Guises of the *Ghūl*: Dissembling Simile and Semantic Flow in the Classical Arabic *Nasīb*', *Reorientations: Arabic and Persian Poetry*, edited by Suzanne Stetkevych (Bloomington: Indiana University Press, 1994), pp. 130–64.

Shahn, Ben, *The Shape of Content* (Cambridge, MA: Harvard University Press, 1957).

Shimon, Samuel (ed.), *Beirut 39: New Writing from the Arab World* (London: Bloomsbury, 2010).

Sofronieva, Tzveta, 'Un-Lost in Translation', *Studies in Slavic Literature and Poetics* 55 (2010), pp. 27–40.

Steiner, George, *Language and Silence: Essays on Language, Literature and the Inhuman* (New York: Atheneum, 1967).

Stetkevych, Jaroslav, *The Hunt in Arabic Poetry* (Notre Dame: Notre Dame University Press, 2015).

Stevens, Wallace, *The Necessary Angel: Essays on Reality and the Imagination* (New York: Vintage Books, 1951).

Suwaylih, Khalil, *Ightiṣāb kāna wa-akhwātihā* (Damascus: Dār al-Balad).

Talib, Adam, *How Do You Say 'Epigram' in Arabic? Literary History at the Limits of Comparison* (Leiden: Brill, 2018).

al-Tami, Ahmed, 'Arabic Free Verse: The Problems of Terminology', *Journal of Arabic Literature* 24.2 (1993), pp. 185–98.

al-Tawhidi, Abu Hayyan, *Kitāb al-imtāʿ wa al-muʾānasah*, edited by Aḥmad Amīn and Aḥmad al-Zayn, 3 volumes (Beirut: Dār Maktabat al-Ḥayāt, n. d.).

Todorov, Tzvetan, 'Poetry Without Verse', *The American Poetry Review* 34.6 (2005), pp. 9–13.

Van Gelder, G. J. H., 'Al-Mutanabbī's Encumbering Trifles', *Arabic and Middle Eastern Literatures* 2.1 (1999), pp. 5–19.

Van Gelder, G. J. H., 'Pointed and Well-Rounded: Arabic Encomiastic and Elegiac Epigrams', *Orientalia Lovaniensia Periodica* 26 (1995), pp. 101–40.

Van Gelder, G. J. H., *Beyond the Line: Classical Arabic Literary Critics on the Coherence and Unity of the Poem* (Leiden: Brill, 1982).

Vasalou, Sophia, 'The Miraculous Eloquence of the Qurʾān: General Trajectories and Individual Approaches', *Journal of Qurʾānic Studies* 4.2 (2002), pp. 23–53.

Verlaine, Paul, 'Art Poétique', from *Selected Poems*, trans. C. F. MacIntyre (Berkeley: University of California Press, 1948).

Waldrop, Keith, 'Introduction', to Charles Baudelaire, *Paris Spleen: Little Poems in Prose*, trans. Keith Waldrop (Midtown: Wesleyan University Press, 2009).

Walkowitz, Rebecca, *Born Translated: The Contemporary Novel in an Age of World Literature* (New York: Columbia University Press, 2015).

Wright, Chantal, 'Exophony and Literary Translation: What it Means for the Translator When a Writer Adopts a New Language', *Target: International Journal of Translation Studies*, 22.1 (2010), pp. 22–39.

Wright, Chantal, 'Writing in the 'Grey Zone': Exophonic Literature in Contemporary Germany', *GFL* 3 (2008), pp. 26–42

Yunus, ʿAbir, 'Samer Abu Hawwash: al-tarjama kitāba thāniya', *Al-Bayān Newspaper*, 28 February 2010, https://www.albayan.ae/paths/books/2010-02-28-1.223729 (last accessed 23 October 2020).

Zaher, Maghed, 'Three Egyptian Poets', *Jacket* 36 (2008), http://jacketmagazine.com/36/egyptian-poets.shtml (last accessed 23 October 2020).

Index

Abbasid
  age, 43–4, 230
  muḥdathūn, 39, 59–60
  poets, 14, 48, 59–64, 65n
  short compositions, 49–59
abruptness, 46–9
absence, 47–8, 153–67
Abu al-ʿAtahiya, 37
Abu Deeb, Kamal, 37–8
Abu Hawwash, Samer
  'After Bob Dylan', 236–7
  Laysa hākadha tuṣnaʿ al-pizza (This is Not the Way Pizza is Made), 234–8
  pending poem, 231–8
  Selfie akhīra maʿ ʿālam yuḥtaḍar (A Last Selfie with a Dying World), 232–3
  similes, 232–5
  'The Sun is Strong this Morning', 234–5
  '*Tamyīz kalimāt al-baḥth*' (Refining Search Words), 237
Abu Nuwas, 124–5, 136–7n
Abu Salih, Imad, 128–33, 137n
  He Was Asleep When the Revolution Came, 130–3
  'I Grew Up to Be A Poet', 129–30
  Matters Already Decided, 129
Abu Tammam, Habib b. Aws
  al-Mutanabbi, 176
  Darwish, Mahmoud, 145
  ghazal, 51–2, 60–1
  Ḥamāsa, 69
  'strange' poetry, 168n
  'You are not you', 87
Ādāb group, 111, 113, 122–3
al-Adīb magazine, 69
Adonis
  Aghānī Mihyār al-Dimashqī, 78–85
  al-Mawt al-muʿād (The Repeated Death), 83–4
  al-Naṣṣ al-Qurʾānī wa-āfāq al-kitāba, 65n
  al-Shiʿriyya al-ʿarabiyya, 99
  al-Thābit wa-l-mutaḥawwil (The Fixed and the Dynamic), 72, 84–5, 99, 103n
  '*al-Thāʾir*' (The Revolutionary), 76–7
  '*Aslamtu ayyāmī*' (I've Surrendered my Days), 80–1
  Awrāq fī al-rīḥ, 78
  Barakat, Salim, 175
  'Bayān al-ḥadātha', 100–1n
  body, 85–8
  as curator, 71–5
  Dīwān al-nathr al-ʿarabī, 41–2, 72–4, 76
  Dīwān al-shiʿr al-ʿarabī, 71–5, 84–5
  elegies (*marāthī*), 83–4
  '*Fī qaṣīdat al-nathr*, 13, 23
  foreign languages, 230
  Hā anta ayuhā al-waqt (There you are, O Time!), 68–9, 72
  Jubranic style, 15
  'The Knight of Strange Words', 81–2
  language, 78–84
  'The Magician of Dust', 79–80
  Majallat Shiʿr, 13
  'Marthiyyat al-ayyām al-ḥāḍira' (Elegy for the Present Days), 78, 83–4

Adonis (*cont.*)
'Marthīyyat al-qarn al-awwal' (Elegy for the First Century), 83–4
'Mashrū' li-taghyīr al-ashyā' (A Project for Changing Things), 77–8
meaning, 75–8
modern Arabic poetry, 100–1n, 103n
Mufrad bi-ṣīghat al-jam' (Singular on Plural Form), 73–4, 78, 84–100; 'Alī, 93–4; anchoring the expanse, 93–100; beginning and beginning again, 88–93; 'Body', 90–1; 'body', 85–8, 102n; 'Genesis', 85–6; 'History', 89–90; *ruqa'* (patches, tatters, shreds), 94–100; 'Semiology', 91–4; *ṣīyāgha nihā'iyya* (A Final Formulation), 84; three axes: The Buhlūl's Sun, a Notebook of Account and a Secret History of Death, 94–100
Muqaddima lil-shi'r al-'arabī (Introduction to Arabic Poetry), 100
'*Muqaddima li-tārīkh mulūk al-ṭawā'if* (An Introduction to the History of Petty Kings), 104n
negation, 85–100
'New Testament', 82–3
'Nuḥ al-jadīd', 83
'other prose', 39
prose poem manifesto, 1–2
psalms, 78–82
Qaṣā'id 'ūlā, 76–8
Shi'r group, 107–9, 222
Siyāsat al-shi'r (The Politics of Poetry), 38
as translator, 69–71
'*Waḥdahu al-ya's*' (Despair Alone), 76, 78
writing where the world begins and begins again, 68–106
Akhmatova, Anna, 'Requiem', 54–5
anti-symbolism, 30
Antoon, Sinan, 153, 169n
Arabic literature, prose poem in, 39–42
Arabic modernist movement, 3–5, 68, 75–8, 124, 173, 229
Arabic tradition, 34–67
El-Ariss, Tarek, 252n
Aryal, Yubraj, 251n
al-'Askari, Abu Hilal Hasan, 36
'Awad, Lewis, *Plutoland and Other Poems for the Elite*, 5
al-Azzawi, Faddil, 256
al-Bahili, Muhammad b. Hazim, 50
Baker, George, 'The Jubjub Bird or Some Remarks on the Prose Poem', 16
Balso, Judith, 22, 38
Barakat, Salim
al-Dīwān, 175
al-Karākī, 194–203
al-Ta'jīl fī qurūḍ al-nathr (Expediting the Loans of Prose), 173, 175
Arabic in another tongue, 174–8
'*Asrā yataqāsamūn al-kunūz*' (Captives Divide Treasures), 176–8
Bi-sh-Shibāk dhātihā, bi-th-tha'ālib allatī taquduhā al-rīḥ (By the Same Traps, By the Foxes Riding the Winds), 179–82
Darwish, Mahmoud, 158–67
and dictionaries, 182–94
'*Dīlānā wa Dīrām*, 194–203
'*Dīnūkā brīvā ta'ālay ilā ṭa'na hādi'a*' (Dinoka Breva, Come for a Gentle Stab), 172–3
escaping the trap of genres, 194–203
'*Istiṭrād fī siyāq mukhtazal*' (Digression in an Abridged Context), 182–94, 204n
Kanīsat al-muḥārib (The Warrior's Church), 174
Kull dākhil sa-yahtif min ajlī wa kull khārij ayḍan (Every Insider Shall Hail Me and Every Outsider Too), 171
'Kurdish themes', 175–8
'*Madhāhib al-ma'nā*' (The Ways of Meaning), 178–9
metaphors, 182–94
meter, 203n
'*Naqābat al-ansāb*' (The Union of Lineages), 171
poetic (*al-shi'rī*), 202
poetry as avoidance of meaning, 178–82
poetry as linguistic conquest, 171–205
'Revenge', 179–82
scene (*mashhad*), 165–6, 179–82
Tanbīh al-ḥayawān ilā ansābihi (Altering the Animal to its Lineages), 240–1
Ṭaysh al-yāqūt (The Recklessness of Sapphire), 47–8, 182–94
'unjust silence' (*al-ṣamt al-lā munṣif*), 202–3
Baudelaire, Charles, 30
poème-en-prose, 14, 17

Beirut
  al-Maghut, Muhammad, 107–9, 110
  Barakat, Salim, 171, 174
  Darwish, Mahmoud, 140
  Saʿadeh, Wadiʿ, 206
Beirut 39: New Writing from the Arab World, 226–7, 228–9
Beirut World Capital of the Book, 226
Bennis, Muhammad, 255, 256–7
Berger, John, 140
Bernard, Suzanne, 11–12n, 22, 27, 70
  Le Poème en Prose de Baudelaire jusquà nos jours (The Prose Poems from Baudelaire until the Present), 13, 31n
Bishop, Elizabeth, 231–2
'born translated', 226
Boulus, Sargon, 256
Buhlūl, 94–100, 105n
Burt, Clarissa, 207–8, 218
  'The Good, the Bad, and the Ugly', 124

Caws, M. A., 46–7, 49, 53
  'frame of privileged space', 7
Collins, Billy, 232
conceptual poetry, 233–8
Creswell, Robyn, 70–1, 72, 79, 83, 222
'current Arabs' (*al-ʿarab al-rāhinūn*), 173
'cynicism', 116, 119, 121, 127, 137n, 207

Damascus, al-Maghut, Muhammad, 108–9, 113–15
al-Danasuri, Usama
  'Aṣdiqāī' (My Friends), 125–7
  ʿAyn sāriḥa ʿayn mundahisha (A Wandering Eye, A Perplexed Eye), 125–7
Darwish, Mahmoud
  audience, 138–41
  Barakat, Salim, 158–67, 174, 175
  The Butterfly Effect, 153, 155–8, 163–7
  'On the Desire for Rhythm' (*Fī shahwat al-īqāʿ*), 142–4
  'Exile', 148–52
  'Ḥāṣir ḥiṣarak lā mafar' (Tighten your siege. There is no escape), 138
  'The Horse Has Fallen Off the Poem', 157
  '*Ka-washm yadd fī muʿallaqat shāʿir jāhilī*' (Like a Hand Tattoo in a Pre-Islamic Poet's Ode), 149–51
  Ka-zahr al-lawz aw abʿad, 141
  'The Kurd Has Nothing But the Wind', 158–63
  Lā taʿtadhir ʿammā faʿalt (Don't Apologise for What You Have Done), 138–9, 141, 142–4, 158–63
  'Like a Prosaic Poem', 156–7
  Like Almond Blossom or Beyond, 147–52
  A Memory for Forgetfulness, 140, 174
  meter, 143–4
  as middleman, 138–70
  Mural, 153
  'Now in Exile', 148
  In the Presence of Absence, 153, 153–5
  poetry as effect, 153–8
  '*Qul mā tashāʾ*' (Say What You Want), 144–7
  'A Rhyme for the Muʿallaqāt', 157–8
  rhythm, 142–5
  'The Critics Assassinate Me Sometimes', 157
  'Skogas', 163–7
  '*Ṭibāq*' (Antithesis or Counterpoint), 151–2
  '*Tunsā kaʾanaka lam takun*' (Forgotten As If You Never Were), 141–2
  Why Did You Leave the Horse Alone, 157–8
al-Daylami, Mihyar, 103n
deliberateness, 2, 43, 46, 59–64
'dissembling' structure, 94–100
'dominant', 8, 12n, 59–64
Dylan, Bob, 232
  A Poem is a Naked Person, 227–8

Egyptian poets of the nineties, 123–34, 225–6, 231
elegies (*marāthī*), 83–4
Eliot, T. S., 16, 30, 198, 205n
El-Sayed, Nazem, 53–4, 228
  Ard maʿzūla bil-nawm (A Land Isolated by Sleep), 62
Elsisi, Sayed, 134–5n, 137n
exophony, 224, 226, 229–31, 239–45

Faik, Salah, 239–40, 256
foreign languages, 69–70, 111, 226, 229–30, 239–45, 257
form and meaning, 35–7, 76
fragments (*maqṭūʿāt*), 43, 48, 192

'free verse' (*al-shiʿr al-ḥurr*), terminology, 2–3, 4, 10–11n, 17–22
French literature, 68–71

ghazal, 5, 44, 51, 60
gratuity (*majjāniyya*), 26–7, 59

Hacker, Marilyn, 242
Haddad, Joumana, 'The Geology of the I', 227–8
Haddad, Qasim, 255
Hadidi, Subhi, 134
Hajalnama journal, 203n
Haji, Golan
  Adonis, 239–40
  'After No Language', 246
  al-Maghut, 239–40
  Barakat, Salim, 240–1
  'Blood on the Stairs', 242–3
  'In a Cemetery Under a Solitary Walnut Tree That Crows', 246–8
  Footnotes in the Order of Disappearance, 245–9
  'The Lock', 243–4
  migrant poem, 238–45
  Mīzān al-adhā, 246–8
  'moving out' of Arabic, 245–9
  Qabbani, Nizar, 239–40
  'Sagittal Views', 245
  silence, 246
  translations, 238
  A Tree Whose Name I Don't Know, 242
al-Hajj, Unsi
  'al-Qafaṣ' (The Cage), 21–2
  al-Raʾs al-Maqṭūʿ (The Severed Head), 5–6, 47–8
  Arabic, 248–9
  'Black Bird', 58–9
  choatic distruction, 25–30
  clear-headed theorist, 22–30
  flowing formless prose, 7, 11n
  'Identity', 28–30
  Lan (Won't), 1–2, 13, 22–30
  'Memory', 47–8
  qaṣīda, 16–17
  Shiʿr group, 222
  translation of *The Song of Solomon*, 65n
Hajjar, Bassam
  Mihan al-qaswa (The Vocations of Cruelty), 54–8
  'Pain' (*alam*), 54–8
  'Wall', 54

Hamra Street, Beirut, 206
Hawi, Khalil, 116, 256
Hay Festival, 226
Hijazi, Ahmad ʿAbd al-Muʿti, 18
hunt poem (*ṭardiyya*), 5, 44, 45

Ibn al-Muʿtazz, ʿAbdallah, 48–9, 50, 52–3, 65n
Ibn al-Rumi, 48–9
Ibn al-Zuʿburi, 50
Ibn Jaʿfar, Qudama, *Naqd al-shiʿr*, 35–6
Ibn Rashiq al-Qayrawani, 46
  al-ʿUmda, 46
Ibn Tabataba, Muhammad Ahmad, 35–6, 50–1
  'the churning or meaning', 49–59
iʿjāz (Qurʾanic inimitability), 38–9
īqāʿ (cadence or rhythm), 36

Jabra, Jabra Ibrahim, 112
Jakobson, Roman, 8, 12n
al-Jammaz, 46, 50
al-Jarād (The Locusts), 124–34
Jarash Festival, 138–9
Joudah, Fady
  'In a Cemetery Under a Solitary Walnut Tree That Crows', 246–8
  Darwish, Mahmoud, 169n
  Footnotes in the Order of Disappearance, 245–9
  Haji, Golan, 245
  'Sagittal Views', 245
al-Jurjani, ʿAbd al-Qahir
  Dalāʾil al-iʿjāz fī al-Qurʾān (The Signs of the Inimitability or the Qurʾan), 37, 76, 170
  language, 42
  naẓm (formulation or sentence construction), 37–8
  ṣurat al-maʿnā (the image of meaning), 38

Kalīma, 231
Kerouac, Jack, 223–4
al-Khal, Yusuf, 109
al-Khalil, 5, 18
Kurds, 158–67, 171, 175–8, 192–4, 203n, 238–9

lafẓ, 35–7, 76
Lebanese University, 231
Lebanese war, 174

Lebanon, 1, 20–1, 119, 121–3, 207, 231
love poetry, 51–3, 115, 150

al-Ma'arri, Abu al-'Ala', 143, 168n, 210–11
al-Maghut, Muhammad
  al-Badawī al-aḥmar, 112
  al-Faraḥ laysa mihnatī, 112
  'The Burning of Words', 121–3
  commitment (*iltizām*), 113
  'cynicism', 121–3
  Ghurfa bi malāyīn al-judrān, 112
  Ḥuzn fī ḍaw' al-qamar (Sorrow in the Moonlight), 111–16
  '*Janāzat al-nisr*' (The Eagle's Funeral), 116–19
  and poetic detachment, 107–37
  poetics of nonchalance, 109–11
  poetics of 'the ugly' (*al-qabīḥ*), 134
  'posture', 116
  Sa'adeh, Wadi', 207
  wielding the sword of simile, 116–20
  'The Wing of Misery', 119–20
al-Mala'ika, Nazik
  'al-Kūlirā' (Cholera), 11n
  Arabic, 230
  free verse, 4–5, 18–19
  modernism, 122–3
ma'nā, 35–7, 37, 76
manifestos, 13–33
al-Marzuqi, Ahmad ibn al-Hasan, 36
Mattawa, Khaled, 127
Mawqi' 24, 'Website 24', 231
Mazlum, Muhammad, 70
al-Mazza prison, Damascus, 108–9
meaning and form, 35–6, 76
Mersal, Iman, 127–8
  'CV', 127–8
meter
  Adonis, 38, 75–76
  al-Jurjani, 'Abd al-Qahir, 37, 42
  al-kāmil, 80–81
  al-Maghut, Muhammad, 112
  al-Mala'ika, Nazik, 18–19
  al-Rayhani, Amin, 31–2n
  al-Tawhidi, Abu Hayyan, 36–7
  Barakat, Salim, 172
  Darwish, Mahmoud, 141–3, 153, 156, 256
  Ibn Tabataba, Muhammad Ahmad, 50
  qaṣīdat al-taf'īla (free verse poem), 4–5, 19
  Sa'adeh, Wadi', 209
  saj' (rhymed prose), 14, 17
  short compositions, 44
Mitwalli, Muhammad, 124
modernism, 3–5, 68, 75–8, 124, 173, 229
Monte, Steven, 13, 63
Moreh, S., 15
al-Mutanabbi, 65n, 175–6, 240

Nasser, Amjad, 256
naẓm (verse or versification), 4, 17, 37–8
al-Niffari, Muhammad b. 'Abd al-Jabbar, *Al-Mawāqif wa l-mukhāṭabāt*, 40
Nizwa magazine, 124–5

'other', 10, 30, 256
'other prose' (*nathr ākhar*), 16–17, 19–20, 30, 39, 74, 79
'other tradition', 8, 113
'othering', 175
Ouhaibi, Moncef, 105–6n
'outsider-ness', 230, 239–45
  Abu Salih, Imad, 129
  al-Maghut, Muhammad, 107–9, 113
  Barakat, Salim, 160, 175
  Mersal, Iman, 127

Perloff, Marjorie, 229–30, 251n
  'indeterminacy', 30
Perse, Saint-John
  Amers, 69–71
  'Étroits sont les vaisseaux', 76
  the foreign intercedes on behalf of the self, 69–71
Poe, Edgar Allen, 26
'The Poets of the Nineties', 123–34, 225–6, 231
prosody (*'arūḍ*), 5, 36–7, 74, 100–1n, 156
psalms, 78–82

Qabbani, Nizar, 175
qaṣīda (poem), 1, 3–4, 18–19, 34, 43–6, 65n, 74–5
  al-Hajj, Unsi, 23–5
  Darwish, Mahmoud, 146, 157
  meter, 209
  Sa'adeh, Wadi', 209
qaṣīdat al-nathr (prose poem), terminology and origins, 1–2, 4–5, 10–11n, 15–16

qaṣīdat al-taf'īla (free verse poem), terminology and origins, 4–5, 10–11n, 15–16
al-Qays, Imru, *mu'allaqa*, 186
qiṭ'a, 43–6, 48–9, 59–64
Qur'an
  Adonis, 65n
  al-Jurjani, 'Abd al-Qahir, 37
  inimitability of, 38–9
  and 'other prose', 39
  saj' (rhymed prose), 14
  sui generis, 38–9

al-Rayhani, Amin
  al-shi'r al-manthūr, 15
  Hutāf al-awdiya (The Calling of the Valleys), 31–2n
Rimbaud, Arthur, 30

Sa'adeh, Wadi'
  'Absence', 211
  '*al-Mut'abūn*' (The Tired), 211–14
  Bi-sabab ghayma 'alā al-arjaḥ (Because of a Cloud, Most Likely), 211
  Ghubār (Dust), 214–16
  '*Jamāl al-'ābir*' (The Beauty of the Transient), 214–16
  Laysa lil-masā' ikhwa (The Evening Has No Brothers), 20–1, 206, 210–11, 216–17
  Maq'ad rākib ghādara al-bāṣ (The Seat of a Passenger Who Left the Bus), 211–14
  'modern poetic text' (*al-naṣṣ*), 209
  poetics of disintegration, 210–16, 218–20
  A Restructuring of Wadi' Sa'adeh's Life (*Tarkīb ākhar li-ḥayāt Wadī' Sa'āda*), 220–1
  self-reflexiveness, 207–10
  silence, 216–24, 244
  Tell the Passer to Come Back, He Left His Shadow, 219–20
  The Text of Absence, 217–18
  and the third generation of prose poets, 206–53
  transience, 212–16
  untitled poem, 61
Sabri, Khuzama, 111–12
Said, Edward, 148–52, 167
Sa'id, Khalida, 111–12, 116
  'poetic prose', 112
saj' (rhymed prose), 14, 17
Salem, Hilimi, 124–5
Santilli, N., 45, 47
al-Sarraj, Yusuf, 168n
al-Sayyab, Badr Shakir
  foreign languages, 230
  'Hal Kāna Ḥubban? (Was it Love?), 11n
  qaṣīdat al-taf'īla (free verse poem), 4
  '*Unshūdat al-maṭar*' (The Song of Rain), 135–6n
Shabtin, Beirut, 206
Shahn, Ben, 21, 38
al-Shaykh, Hanan, 226
Shimon, Samuel, 226, 250n
shi'r (poetry), 17, 23–5
al-shi'r al-manthūr, 14–15
Shi'r group
  al-Maghut, Muhammad, 107–13, 123
  poetic modernism, 70–1
  qaṣīdat al-nathr (prose poem), 4
  radical internationalism, 222
  Sa'adeh, Wadi', 20–1
Shi'r Magazine
  Adonis, 76, 78, 103n
  al-Maghut, Muhammad, 107–8, 111
  Bernard, Suzanne, 31n
  Lan (Won't), 28
  Perse, Saint-John, 70
  qaṣīdat al-nathr (prose poem), 16
short compositions, 43–51, 59, 60, 65n
silence, 47–8, 89, 153, 208, 211–13, 216–24, 244–8
Stetkevych, Jaroslav
  hunt poem (*ṭardiyya*), 45
  'ultimate poetry', 19
Stevens, Wallace, *The Necessary Angel*, 2
structure (*binā'*), 44, 63
Ṣūfī prose, 39, 40, 73–4

Taha, Ahmad, 124
al-Ṭalī'a magazine, 171
Tawada, Yoko, 229
al-Tawhidi, Abu Hayyan
  al-Imtā' wa al-muānasa, 36–7, 147
  Al-Ishārāt al-ilāhiyya, 41–2
  Darwish, Mahmoud, 152
Todorov, Tzvetan
  'moving process', 11–12n
  'the poetic', 19
translation, 3, 9, 17, 206–53, 250n, 255–7
  Adonis, 69–78

Van Gelder, G. J. H., 'Pointed and Well-Rounded', 49–50

Walkowitz, Rebecca, *Born Translated: The Contemporary Novel in an Age of World Literature*, 226
Watts, Stephen, 242, 245, 247
Wazen, Abdo, 226, 228–9
Williams, William Carlos, 232
wine poem (*khamriyya*), 5, 44
Wittgenstein, Ludwig, 1

Yusuf, Sa'di, 175

EU representative:
Easy Access System Europe
Mustamäe tee 50, 10621 Tallinn, Estonia
Gpsr.requests@easproject.com

www.ingramcontent.com/pod-product-compliance
Lightning Source LLC
Chambersburg PA
CBHW050211240426
43671CB00013B/2297
* 9 7 8 1 4 7 4 4 7 4 9 7 9 *